Standing with the Public

ok is to

Standing with the Public
The Humanities
and Democratic Practice

Edited by
James F. Veninga and Noëlle McAfee

Kettering Foundation Press

© 1997 by the Charles F. Kettering Foundation

For information about permission to reproduce selections
from this book, write to:
> Permissions
> Kettering Foundation Press
> 200 Commons Road
> Dayton, Ohio 45459

This book is printed on acid-free paper
First edition, 1997
Manufactured in the United States of America
Library of Congress Cataloging-in-Publication Data

Noëlle McAfee, 1960-
James F. Veninga, 1944-
> Standing with the Public: The Humanities and Democratic Practice
> p. cm.
> ISBN 0-923993-05-3

Library of Congress Catalog Card Number: 97-69891
                                                            CIP

CONTENTS

Introduction

With the founding, 30 years ago, of the National Endowment for the Humanities, the nation institutionalized its vision that the humanities are vitally important to democratic practice. Yet to many, this connection is still tenuous. What can humanities scholars contribute to public life and how can the imperatives of democratic practice inform the humanities?

At a 1979 conference on federal support for the humanities sponsored by the Lyndon B. Johnson School of Public Affairs at the University of Texas at Austin, philosopher and former State Department official Charles Frankel observed: "Nothing has happened of greater importance in the history of American humanistic scholarship than the invitation of the government to scholars to think in a more public fashion, and to think and teach with the presence of their fellow citizens in mind." Frankel, reflecting on the establishment of the National Endowment for the Humanities (NEH) 14 years earlier, knew well the connection that the Congress had made between vitality in the humanities and the well-being of American democracy. For Frankel, the key ingredient in this correlation is that of ensuring that the humanistic enterprise be citizen-centered, for scholars to "think and teach with the presence of their fellow citizens in mind." The importance of federal support for the humanities for Frankel was found in the invitation rather than in the funds provided. NEH was significant because it offered a reminder to scholars that the humanities are powerful resources for the maintenance and furtherance of American democracy.

Some might find irony in this invitation, for it seems strange that a nation that owes its very existence to the power of humanistic ideas — to the study of philosophy, history, literature, and politics — found it necessary to remind scholars of the importance of their work to the well-being of the nation. Were the humanities headed in the wrong direction when this invitation was issued? Were scholars forgetting the connections between humanistic learning and democratic practice? Was the lure of specialization and expertise diminishing the capacity of scholars to "think and teach" with their fellow citizens in mind? Were we forgetting the connections between the humanities and the preservation of democratic institutions? Or, was the nation simply being farsighted in seeking to protect and nourish the humanities in an age increasingly dominated by science and technology, an age shaped by a relentless Cold War, the outcome of which would, in the end, depend as much on our ability to be a leader "in the realm of ideas and of the spirit," as noted in

1

the legislation, as on our "superior power, wealth, and technology"? From this perspective, the invitation of which Frankel speaks can be seen as a modest but bold effort to help make sure that the humanities not lose their connection to the democratic process. Perhaps there is truth in both perspectives: through its Congress, the nation sought to strengthen the humanities because the future of democracy was at stake, and the humanities needed help.

How far have we come — and what more should we do? The purpose of this book is to deepen understanding of the humanities in a democratic culture and to explore ways whereby scholars and their fellow citizens might work together — side by side — to revitalize the practice of democracy. Our supposition is that the relationship between the humanities and the public is mutually beneficial and their respective tasks are complementary.

This volume is a product of an ongoing conversation among representatives of the Kettering Foundation, the National Endowment for the Humanities, the Federation of State Humanities Councils, and various state councils — a conversation that took on a name: The Humanities and Public Engagement Project. Over the course of three years, at meetings held at the Kettering Foundation in Dayton, Ohio, and at annual conferences of the state humanities councils, these representatives explored contemporary challenges to American democracy and discussed ways whereby the humanities community might interact more fruitfully with the public to expand civic participation and to enhance public deliberation on important issues — as well as to inform and sustain the humanities themselves.

Many observers of American society have noted with increasing alarm the growing gap between millions of ordinary citizens and those traditional institutions of society that once were held in high confidence by the public. Mainline churches, media, government at all levels, universities, and large corporate entities are all too often looked on with skepticism and distrust. Such skepticism and distrust have further weakened civil society and diminished our capacity as citizens to "talk through" tough public issues, to weigh seriously the pros and cons of proposals to address these issues, to come together as local and national communities in common cause.

Participants in the humanities project meetings recognized early on that the humanities provide important resources for understanding these and other contemporary challenges to American democracy. Formal education in the humanities in elementary, secondary, and postsecondary settings encourages the citizen to become an interpreter of his or her life, society, and culture. As such, the humanities help empower citizens. Further, the humanities, with their traditions of inquiry, analysis, reflection, conversation, and action, are indispensable to social and cultural renewal. Thus the humanities as researched, taught, and experienced continue to provide important and vital resources that enhance the capacity of citizens to deal with contemporary public issues. And where the humanities have been in recent decades extraordinarily creative and original, in, for example, the documentation of local and minority cultures, many citizens have gained a public voice.

Yet these participants recognized that not all is well in the world of the humanities, and that many recent criticisms raised against humanities scholars and the colleges and universities with which they are affiliated need to be taken seriously. But focusing on such problems as the primacy given to research and specialization, to graduate over undergraduate teaching, and to promotion and tenure policies that give scant recognition to real public service, may very well obfuscate far more fundamental issues, including the most fundamental issue of all, that of the relationship of the scholar to society, of the multiple ways in which the scholar ought to stand within, not outside of, the body politic.

These participants were deeply concerned that the idea of the scholar as citizen had grown increasingly nebulous and that there seemed to be growing confusion in public as well as academic circles about the public dimension of the humanities. What place do the humanities have in public life and how is their work a public matter? Indeed, these participants noted that even in the realm of the public humanities, in programs and projects involving interaction between scholars and citizens, the predominant model has been that of placing scholars before public audiences, with scholars sharing their learning with the interested public. The dissemination of the humanities as researched and taught has been a driving force behind most public humanities activities. While this is surely a public good, and while such work needs to be appreciated and supported, this model of the public humanities, of the relationship between the scholar and society, does too little to strengthen the connections between the humanities and democratic practice and to our ability to meet contemporary challenges. To put it bluntly, if the academic community succumbs to a truncated vision of the relationship of scholar and society, the nation as a whole, as well as the scholarly community, will be diminished.

Fortunately, other models of the public humanities, some of them promoted by various state humanities councils, have sought a more expansive and more fundamentally important understanding of the relationship between scholars and society, models that see the locus of the humanities as being in the community as well as in the academy. These models place emphasis on interaction between scholars and their fellow citizens, on reciprocity, on the intellectual resources and indigenous insights that diverse communities provide to public problems and proposed solutions. They point to the development of sustained relationships between scholars and communities, rather than to onetime public lectures or one-day conferences with back-to-back panels where there is little time for dialogue and no time for common work — humanities events that seem to have more in common with fast-food restaurants than with extended family meals where selves as well as food are shared.

Participants in these meetings came to a recognition that more needs to be done to promote alternative models of the public humanities, models that would emphasize scholars standing alongside their fellow citizens in doing the kind of public work that makes democracy possible: documenting and interpreting human experience, exploring cultures past and present, giving voice to our fears and dreams, defining and understanding our public problems, exploring our diverse values, deliberating tough public issues, finding ways to act on those issues. Every citizen brings resources to these tasks, the scholar included. To understand the nature of these resources — from the telling of important stories to historical clarification to comparing values and assumptions of cultures near and far, to name a few — is to understand the many gifts of the humanities to democratic practice.

This book is designed to further alternative models for the public humanities. Most of the essays, a few of which were originally given as addresses, grew out of or were connected to the Humanities and Public Engagement Project. Several other essays, not related to the engagement project, were published previously and are included here because of their contribution to the subject.

Part One explores problems related to the humanities and contemporary democracy and offers ideas on how these problems might be countered. Part Two explores from diverse perspectives the public work of the humanities and offers examples of scholars engaged with concerns, interests, and issues of the public. Kettering Foundation President David Mathews offers poignant insight into the relationship of the scholar to society in an afterword. An Appendix contains brief essays by three scholars who have been engaged in experimental work in Milwaukee, Wisconsin's Sherman Park; Walthill, Nebraska; and San Marcos, Wimberley, and Lockhart, Texas — activities undertaken in conjunction with the Humanities and Public Engagement Project.

Perhaps readers of these essays will arrive at a conclusion drawn by the editors of this volume: Charles Frankel got it only half right. To be sure, it is a good and necessary thing for the scholar when engaged in the high tasks of humanities research, writing, and teaching to have the *presence* of their fellow citizens in mind. But much more is asked of scholars, much more needs to be given by scholars, if the fragile connections between scholars and society are to grow stronger. For the humanities to assume their necessary place as protectors and nourishers of democratic culture, scholars must also be *present with* their fellow citizens when the public's work is (or should be) done.

This book would not have materialized without the ideas of the many participants in the meetings noted above. We are deeply indebted to all of them. We are grateful to Sheldon Hackney, chairman of the NEH, who believed in this project and whose initiative, "A National Conversation on American Pluralism and Identity," reminded all of us of the significance of scholars working with citizens in addressing key public issues. We are also grateful to Carole Watson, special assistant to the chairman, and Nancy Rogers, director of Public Programs, who participated in and supported our discussions. Jamil Zainaldin and Esther Mackintosh, president and vice president of the Federation of State Humanities Councils, respectively, made invaluable contributions to this effort during the past three years. David Mathews' commitment to the project was evidenced all along the way, most importantly in launching this effort, in making available the facilities and resources of the foundation, and in exploring with us the lively issues that we were addressing. Special thanks goes to Estus Smith, vice president of the Kettering Foundation, who has been a champion of the state humanities councils for more than 25 years. Estus, a founding board director of the Mississippi Humanities Councils, has worked closely with many councils over the years and, more recently, with the Federation of State Humanities Council, in this process of rethinking the work in which we are engaged. Finally, we thank Melissa Capers, a recent arrival in Austin, Texas, for her invaluable assistance in preparing this manuscript for publication.

— The Editors

PART ONE

THE HUMANITIES AND DEMOCRATIC CULTURE

William M. Sullivan

The Public Intellectual as Transgressor? Addressing the Disconnection Between Expert and Civil Culture

The oddity of this topic lies not so much in what is stated as in the context, a social as well as intellectual context, which gives it intelligibility. The question I wish to address is why the notion of the "public intellectual," a theme that Russell Jacoby and, most recently, Robert Boynton, have brought to our attention, seems nearly oxymoronic to many, why it seems to go against expectations, to transgress the usual use of language in the late twentieth-century American culture.[1]

"Public intellectual," as both Jacoby and Boynton argue, is in one sense redundant. The very idea of an intellectual once connoted, from its origins in the Enlightenment, a learned concern for the "republic of letters" as a major part of a public dialogue concerned with the shaping of public opinion. It is only relatively recently that "intellectual" has come to be applied to activities focused on the more restricted circles of technically, usually academically, proficient experts.

Perhaps the best place to begin is by following Kenneth Burke in trying to gain "perspective by incongruity." Consider this judgment by Cicero, a source that also serves as a needed reminder that the so-called

---

[1] Russell Jacoby, *The Last Intellectuals* (New York: Simon and Schuster, 1987). Robert S. Boynton, "The New Intellectuals," *The Atlantic Monthly*, March 1995.

"Western tradition" does not speak in a simplistic, monotonic voice. We should, writes Cicero, beware of taking the conception of the philosopher put forward by Plato in his *Republic* as a sufficient characterization of the social responsibilities which learning imposes. "For he [Plato] said that they [philosophers] are immersed in the investigation of the truth and that, disdaining the very things for which most people vigorously strive and even fight one another to the death, they count them as nothing. Because of this he calls them just." However, Cicero, argues: "They observe one type of justice, indeed, that they should harm no one else by inflicting injury, *but they fall into another;* for hindered by their devotion to learning, they abandon those whom they should protect."[2]

Developing and generalizing the point, Cicero continues with the observation that "there are also some who … claim to be attending to their own business, and appear to do no one any justice." But, again, in parallel to his criticism of the apparently blameless "ivory tower" of Plato's philosophers, Cicero asserts that, "though they are free from one type of injustice, they run into another: such people abandon the fellowship of life, because they contribute to it nothing of their devotion, nothing of their effort, nothing of their means."[3]

Cicero was speaking for a conception of civic humanism. According to this view, cities exist to realize the good life. An important way in which cities realize this aim is by providing their citizens with opportunities to develop their abilities and be recognized and rewarded for this. But the civic vision goes on to insist that this individual opportunity, the dignity of the individual that would in later development become the idea of individual human rights, can exist only as it is supported by the cooperation of others. This *interdependence*, the life of the whole civic community, which Cicero calls the "fellowship of life," is the soil, we might say the "ecology," in which individuals can flourish. Recognition of the reality of this interdependence and of the claims this common life must make on the individuals was called by the ancients "civic virtue." It is what we might term responsibility.

There is an eerie timeliness to Cicero's critique of the idea that pursuit of knowledge absolves individuals or institutions from wrestling with the public obligations that pursuit places upon them. Consider Daniel Yanklelovich's recent analysis of public opinion data that shows a dis-

---

[2] Cicero, *On Duties*. M. T. Griffin and E. M. Atkins, eds. (London and New York: Cambridge University Press, 1991) bk. I, (28), p. 12.

[3] Ibid., p. 12.

turbingly wide "disconnect" between the views of American knowledge "elites" and experts, on the one hand, and the larger public, on the other.[4] As Yanklelovich reports it, expert opinion tends to regard social problems as technical matters to be addressed largely by technical means, and the elites of government, business, communications, education, the arts, and sciences only reluctantly engage in the kind of public discussion that matters most to Americans, discussion that considers the moral as well as the informational aspects of social issues.

For this reason, Yankelovich finds, experts tend to think the public ignorant, seeking always to provide more facts, while the public generally thinks of the experts as morally insensitive and arrogant for apparently refusing to engage the concerns that the public holds most dear. This lack of common understanding fuels the widespread conception of experts, including university faculty, as mere technicians of knowledge, and self-interested ones at that, who lack moral bearings. The effect is to contribute to a spreading skepticism about the claims of experts to speak for or about the public interest, and even to delegitimate the claims of expert knowledge and its supporting institutions, especially the university.

What is the source of this unfortunate "disconnect" between our most advanced institutions for generating knowledge and the democratic public? The expert culture Yankleovich describes has been formed by a number of sources, but its most important institutional source has been the modern university centered on scientific research. The university is the one institution shared by all of the nation's elites, indeed by all members of the professions. It is literally that *alma mater* of modern expertise. Especially since World War II, the greatest expansion of the university's influence on American life has reinforced the idea that expertise means the ability to apply scientific knowledge to the tasks and problems of life.

The great historic achievement of the natural sciences has been to separate, in the business of investigation, considerations of fact from hopes and wishes, concentrating on the tracing lines of cause and effect. The result has been the enormous expansion of human knowledge of nature through ever-greater specialization of method, with a consequently increased ability to direct natural processes from human aims. As scientific approaches to phenomena have increased the range of technical effectiveness, the prestige of those approaches has encouraged the spread of idealized models of natural scientific research into the tradi-

---

[4]   Daniel Yankelovich, *Coming to Public Judgment: Making Democracy Work in a Complex World* (Syracuse University Press, 1991).

tional fields of the humanities as well as social investigation.

Among the results have been the well-known conflicts over the "two cultures" delineated by C. P. Snow. Technical knowledge has come to dominate the culture of the university, as well as that of most professions. Something of the broader concerns about education suited to provide an orientation to life as a citizen has persisted in the liberal arts colleges. The idea that research and scholarship could and ought to find part of their meaning in the concerns of the public world has also remained alive in certain places. However, the idea that research, learning, and scholarship carry responsibilities toward the larger world, the "fellowship of life" invoked by Cicero, has been eclipsed within university culture by the insularity of the culture of specialized expertise.

A significant cause of this narrowing has been the very success of the university during the post-World War II era, especially in two roles. The university served as an engine of technological advance, which sped spectacular economic growth, while it also trained a national meritocratic elite, significantly contributing to upward social mobility. Both roles were heavily supported by government and big business. It was during this period that universities and, for the first time in American life, significant numbers of their faculties became important sources of expert counsel at many levels of American society. Experts, in this model, "solved problems" by bringing the latest technical knowledge to bear on matters which, it has been widely presumed, the public as a whole was too limited to understand, much less address. This was, then, also the era of public relations, advertising, and the national security state.

The kind of elite developed through the university system during those decades was significantly different from the old elites of inherited wealth and social influence. These men and, increasingly, women, learned through their education that what counted was the acquisition of personal skills, above all cognitive capacities, and knowledge. In their own eyes self-made, the new elites felt little sense of *noblesse oblige* and thought of their responsibilities to American society in terms of deploying their skills rather than seeking to shape opinion toward the public interest.

This was a system well suited to an era of dynamic social stability in which the major institutions worked well and seemed to complement rather than undercut each other, the time of American "consensus" in which large-scale public debate over fundamentals was regarded as unseemly or a sign of political weakness in the face of enemies abroad. The current situation could hardly be more different. Since the late-1960s, American society has undergone a succession of wrenching changes that have challenged almost every part of that once-confident postwar order. The United States is caught up in technological and economic changes, global in scale, which have left the American social fabric significantly weakened. Many, if not most, of the nation's key institutions no longer seem to function well.

This is the context that gives urgency to the reinvention of a "public" orientation to intellectual life within higher education. The great pressing problems that are beginning to define the new century are not matters to be handled by applying a "technical fix" here and another there. They require a more direct engagement with moral and social dimensions of nearly all aspects of national life. For this situation, which demands new definition, analysis, and evaluation of issues and problems, our meritocratic elites are poorly prepared. Little wonder that they, and increasingly the institutions from which they have sprung, find themselves in something of a crisis of legitimacy.

The kind of expertise which is now most needed is civic rather than technical in orientation. This sort of expert contributes to the civic purpose not by circumventing the public through the imposition of technical devices, but by engaging with broader publics, attempting to make sense of what is happening, analyzing the working of our complex systems with reference to values and principles, listening, arguing, persuading, and being persuaded.

If the model for the technocratic university was that of "applied research," the present calls for something more like active partnership and shared responsibility in addressing problems whose moral and public dimensions are openly acknowledged. In order to provide this kind of expertise, and to exert the appropriate kind of leadership, the unquestioned dominance of the applied research model within the university must be opened to question and reform. Reshaping institutional structures so long in place, and so relatively successful, will require sustained effort and great resourcefulness. The final form of its shape has perhaps begun to emerge from the various efforts at civic engagement already under way.

Is there much likelihood that such an enterprise can succeed? Fortunately, there are suggestions that Americans are modestly hopeful about addressing the major problems that confront us. Daniel Yankelovich reports that public opinion continues to show a widespread desire to "reconcile new social mores with America's core values," especially "a sense of community, neighborliness, hope, optimism, and individual responsibility."[5] The question for the higher education world is whether it has the ability and the will to respond through leadership, institutional design, teaching, and research, in creating a new form of intellectual life for the public good.

[5]   Daniel Yankelovich, "Three Destructive Trends: Can They Be Reversed?" Speech to National Civic League's 100th National Conference, Philadelphia, PA, November 11, 1994, p. 15.

Thomas Bender

Academic Knowledge and Political Democracy in the Age of the University

In "Truth and Politics" Hannah Arendt neatly distinguished academic from political truth. The distinction that she drew in that notable essay had implications that she pursued with her usual insight; it implied a tension between the academy, the custodian of truth that would pass the Kantian test, and the polity, the generator of a vitally important but distinctly lesser order of truth.[1]

Most of us, I think, hold to much the same distinction, whether or not we can or wish to articulate it with the precision and eloquence that characterized Arendt's essay. Why is such a dichotomy so easily accepted, essentially without much thought on our part? Considering the difficulty of distinguishing the university from other modern, bureaucratic service institutions, public and private, an assumption that there is a profound difference in the university's culture, its type and standard of truth, is curious. The issue of institutional convergence in the modern era could be pursued, I suppose, as a problem in historical sociology. But I propose in this essay to proceed in a different fashion, relying more on intellectual than on social history, looking as much to epistemology as to sociology. My aim, to be clear at the outset, is to question the usefulness of the

---

[1]   Hannah Arendt, "Truth and Politics," in Peter Laslett and W. C. Runciman, eds., *Philosophy, Politics, and Society*, 3d series (Oxford, 1967), pp. 104-33.

conventional distinction between academic truth and political knowledge. Conceiving the relation of culture and politics in this habitual way could isolate academic intellect. That tendency or result could, in turn, pose an unnecessarily formidable difficulty for any vision of academic intellect's involvement in a democratic culture and polity.

Our unreflective acceptance of this distinction hampers our ability to rethink the dilemma of the relation of expertise and democracy, a theme that runs through most studies of academic intellect. What I believe is a misconception of the relation of academic truth and political knowledge derives from our blindness to the contexts, contexts deeply embedded in history, that frame our consideration of the place of higher learning in our culture and polity. I hope to raise these assumptions that have surrounded academic intellect and our study of academic intellect to a greater level of critical self-awareness. The deeper contextualization I here propose forces some changes, at least in my view, in the way we value modern academic intellectual modes and in our vision of the civic ideal.

The interpretive point that I want to make here is American, but it is only by reaching back to one of the threads of America's European history that one can undertake the sort of contextualization that I am urging. I must begin, therefore, with a European prologue. Our discussions about the civic responsibility of the learned and of higher education are imperfectly embedded in the remnants of a very old set of assumptions. Often we are not aware of them, but it is important to raise these historically rooted assumptions to consciousness before we address the intellectual or public consequences of the historical rise of the modern American research university and the disciplinary professions in the past century.

Although Renaissance Florence never had a distinguished university, that is where our effort of contextualization begins.[2] It is to the Florentine Renaissance, with its ideal of civic humanism, that we must look for the originating ideal of the Anglo-American learned man. (And it was *man*, not person.[3]) The notion that humanistic classical learning and rhetoric best prepared a man for public life was nourished in Florence;

---

[2]   On Florence and its university, see Gene Brucker, "Renaissance Florence: Who Needs a University?" in Bender, ed. *University and the City: From Medieval Origins to the Present* (New York, 1988), pp. 47-58.

[3]   The gender issues were noted by J. G. A. Pocock in the book that did so much to make American historians aware of the whole civic world. See his *The Machiavellian Moment: Florentine Political Thought and the Atlantic Republican Tradition* (Princeton, 1975), 37. Hannah Pitkin addressed the issue directly in her *Fortune Is a Woman: Gender and Politics in the Thought of Niccolo Machiavelli* (Berkeley, 1984).

over the centuries it was incorporated into the ideal of the university, especially the Anglo-American collegiate ideal.[4] The idea was, as Quentin Skinner observed, "embarrassingly long-lived," continuing until the triumph of expertise and specialization in the modern university.[5]

This Anglo–American collegiate tradition and what has been designated in recent American historiography the "Republican tradition" had the same birthplace at more or less the same moment.[6] The civic tradition of intellectual engagement and the republican tradition were not quite the same things, but they are entangled with each other. It is not their political qualities (so often discussed) that are of concern here. Rather it is the psychology and sociology that they share. Both embrace and proceed from the ideal of the undivided personality and an undifferentiated society. Jean-Jacques Rousseau was perhaps at once the most extreme and the most brutally honest advocate of this vision. Few thinkers have been so alert to the divisions that the project of modernity would entail, and no major thinker so seriously proposed forsaking such modernity in favor of the realization of a sense of oneness.[7]

Time does not permit adequate explication of Rousseau, let alone the whole tradition. Let me then assert my primary point about this tradition, even in the absence of the documentation that would be required by argument. The civic tradition is hostile to the premises and conditions of modern, interest-driven, differentiated democracy. We who worry about the condition of public life and the present chasm between academic and civic culture must be aware of how much this tradition infuses our thinking. We must be careful about nostalgic embrace of a tradition of civic engagement possessed of severe limits.[8] We especially must not

---

[4]   See Quentin Skinner, *The Foundations of Modern Political Thought*, 2 vols. (Cambridge University Press, 1978), vol. 1. See also Jerrold Seigel, *Rhetoric and Philosophy in Renaissance Humanism* (Princeton, 1968). The ideal of the educated man tracks the line of political thought, moving north from Italy to the Anglo-American world, that is delineated by Pocock in *The Machiavellian Moment*.

[5]   Skinner, *Foundations of Modern Political Thought*, I:88. (Cambridge University Press, 1978). See also Daniel Walker Howe, "Classical Education and Political Culture in Nineteenth Century America," Intellectual History Group, Newsletter, no. 5 (1983): 9-14.

[6]   On the historiographical career of Republicanism, see Daniel Rodgers, "Republicanism: The Career of a Concept," *Journal of American History*, forthcoming.

[7]   Carol Blum spoke to this issue in her *Rousseau and the Republic of Virtue* (Ithaca, N.Y., 1986). The most penetrating account of Rousseau's thought is that of Judith Shklar. She showed that there was great complexity to this thought, but she too seemed to argue that his point was to urge upon incipient moderns an impossible choice, one he knew was impossible even as he urged it. But such was his courage and insight. By doing what he did, he penetrated the heart of the problem of modern identity, morality, and politics. See Shklar, *Men and Citizens: A Study of Rousseau's Social Theory* (Cambridge University Press, 1969).

[8]   See the enormously illuminating work by Kenneth Cmiel, *Democratic Eloquence: The Fight over Popular Speech in Nineteenth-Century America* (New York, 1990).

allow an anachronistic set of premises to define a vision that cannot be realized, that can only present us with disappointment.

We too often overlook this European prologue when thinking about either intellect or public life. Even as historians we tend to take much too short a view of our own history. As modern academic specialists, we tend to trace our institutional lineage to the founding of the first American graduate schools (at Johns Hopkins in 1876, at Columbia in 1881, at New York University in 1886, and in a few other places before 1890). We tend to be oblivious, however, to the degree that these institutions were founded within the civic tradition. We telescope too much history and we lose too much of the texture of difference when we think of these institutions as our own writ small. And if we do recognize the difference, we are too often inclined to be nostalgic.

The first graduate schools, at least at Columbia, Johns Hopkins, and NYU, were established within a distinctive context of cultural assumptions about the aims and structure of higher learning and its relation to public life, especially in cities. Our experience of the research university is quite different from what the founding generation envisioned, especially in our understanding of the relation of intellect to civic life. When the graduate school at Columbia, the Faculty of Political Science, was established in 1881, it was intended, as the name suggests, to reform our public life, our civic life, our politics. It was committed to train men in the "mental culture" that would prepare them for careers in the "civil service," for the "duties of public life" generally, or as "public journalists."[9] The curriculum was postclassical (the social sciences), but the context was classical, civic humanist.

Such expectations for the educated, the educated with advanced degrees, in public life were not realized in Gilded Age America. The Boss Tweeds and Boss Platts retained considerable power. Yet there was some success. And both the language and the expectations of the founders mark the distance of these early graduate schools from the experience of the twentieth-century research university. In the twentieth century, graduate programs have not sought to train professional gentlemen. Rather, graduate training has been focused on special fields, characterized best as presumptively autonomous disciplines organized as an academic profession.

The fullest realization of the early ambitions of the Johns Hopkins University is to be found not only in the career of a scholar (Frederick

---

[9]   Columbia College, *Outline of a Plan for the Instruction of Graduate Classes ... and for the Creation of a School of Preparation for the Civil Service* (New York, 1880), pp. 4, 11.

Jackson Turner, for example), but as well in the careers of Woodrow Wilson (like Turner, a product of Herbert Baxter Adams' historical seminar at Johns Hopkins) or Theodore Roosevelt (one of John W. Burgess' first students in the Columbia program in public law). Recall too Richard Ely's activism, and it is too easily forgotten that Herbert Baxter Adams was deeply involved with urban social reforms in Baltimore. This social engagement of Adams' was not simply another side of the man, what he did after hours. He understood such work to be an extension of his scholarly self. A very large number of men who became notable Progressive journalists, social workers and reformers, and political figures had passed through his historical seminar in the 1880s.[10] The institutional innovation that produced the modern structure of higher learning in the United States was born within the context of an older notion of civic culture. It anticipated neither "expertise" nor the modern pattern of academic training within disciplines that are also professions and careers.

Only in the 1890s, when higher education generally began to expand *and* the classical curriculum was displaced, did a market for academics in the social sciences emerge. At Columbia, Burgess and E. R. A. Seligman gradually noticed in the 1890s that their students were becoming academics rather than civic leaders, and they adjusted the program accordingly. The work of the graduate school faculty shifted from that of preparing men for public life toward that of reproducing their own academic selves.[11]

This conjuncture of curricular and demographic change is important in two ways. First, the decline of the classical curriculum signaled the exhaustion of the humanist ideal of a common civic culture. Difference, diversity, and expertise became acceptable in public life. Second, the social sciences were welcomed into the American college and university. With enrollments growing and with the classical curriculum in decline, new subjects had to be taught. The growth of faculties was, therefore, in the natural sciences and the new social sciences. Here, not in the founding moment, is the origin of our academic life. With the replacement of

---

[10] See John Higham, "Herbert Baxter Adams and the Study of Local History," *American Historical Review 89* (1984): 1, 225-39. For something of the public service, even "social work" ethos at Johns Hopkins in the 1880s, see Marvin Gettleman, *An Elusive Presence: John H. Finley and His America* (Chicago, 1979), bk. 2. The University of Chicago, which was founded in 1891 (a bit later), may have been modern from the beginning—hence its early distinctiveness in training women as social activists in its graduate social science program. Ellen Fitzpatrick gave a good account of the Chicago women but without inquiring into this question of the possibly modern institutional values at the university. See her *Endless Crusade: Women Social Scientists and Progressive Reform* (New York, 1990).

[11] Bender, *New York Intellect: A History of Intellectual Life in New York City, from 1750 to the Beginnings of Our Own Time* (New York, 1987), pp. 277-8.

the civic humanist ideal of public life by professionalized disciplinary communities and the academic expert, we can more properly recognize our own lineage.

Twenty-five or thirty years ago, this "revolution" in higher education, as Richard Hofstadter denoted it, was understood to usher in our own modernity and was represented in historical narrative without ambiguity as a triumph.[12] More recently, however, historians have been more critical. Or they have been, as I take the title of Bruce Kuklick's *The Rise of American Philosophy* to be, ironic.[13] My own writings belong to this revisionist mode. They have assumed my generation's anti-Whig, critical stance toward professionalization. At times, my rhetoric may even have suggested both a professional self-hatred (generational rather than personal, I think) and a view of professionalization as the decline of the domain of intellect. Of course, I always gave credit to what I called the technical achievement of professionalism, but the sense of decline was associated with the negative influence that professionalization seemed to have put on public life, on the possibility of comfortable relations between intellect and democracy, the highest form of public life. My concern for public life is unabated, but I suspect now that the interpretive frame out of which my judgments flowed may have been faulty.

Like many others, I may have held to an anachronistic sense of both the self and the public, of knowledge and democracy. We need to escape this anachronistic vocabulary (if that is what it is) if we are going to think clearly, critically, and constructively about the relation of academic intellect to public life to democracy.

My recent studies of the history and philosophy of the concept of the public have urged upon me a revision of the revisionist line of my writing on academic intellectuals.[14] In rethinking my position, I would not revise my account of many particulars — or even the general outline of the story of intellect's academicization in the United States. But the emergence of specialized, academic intellect in a specifically modern context changes its meaning for the human being who is an academic and for the public.[15] The legitimation of specialized intellect looks different in the

---

[12] See Richard Hofstadter, "The Revolution in Higher Education," in Arthur M. Schlesinger, Jr. and Morton White, eds., *Paths of American Thought* (Boston, 1963), pp. 269-90.

[13] Bruce Kuklick, *The Rise of American Philosophy: Cambridge, MA, 1860-1930* (New Haven, 1977).

[14] Thomas Bender, *History and Public Culture* (Baltimore, forthcoming). Some of this understanding of the danger of nostalgia is reflected in chapter 6 of *Intellect and Public Life*, the most recently written of the essays.

[15] What I am saying here bears a superficial resemblance to Michel Foucault's idea of a "specific" intellectual. I think what follows will reveal that his and my concepts are quite different. On Foucault's statement on this matter, see Colin Gordon ed., *Power/Knowledge: Selected Interviews and Other Writings of Michel Foucault* (New York, 1980), chapter 6.

context of a postrepublican (or postcivic humanist) understanding of self and the public.[16] And these two shifts bear an interesting relation to the shift in contemporary understanding of knowledge of the sort publicized (that is, I think, the right word) by the philosopher Richard Rorty.[17] Rorty's insistence that philosophical truth is to be found in history, not epistemology, has important implications for the problem of academic intellect's relation to public life, for the relation of academic and political knowledge.

The legitimation of expertise was part of a larger pattern of recognition of the complexity of modern society and the multiple identities of individuals. One need not be absolutely at one with oneself nor with others in the modern notion of the public. The implication of this shift is the opening of the public sphere to a wider range of speakers. Putting the matter rather sharply in a single illustration, let me observe that while no woman could be a civic humanist, women trained in the social sciences at the turn of the century could be and were very prominent in public life.[18] For all its limits, it is important to recognize that the rise of expertise was embedded in a transformation of the public sphere that, however imperfectly conceptualized and realized, might well be characterized as democratic in its tendencies and potential.

That new possibilities have been opened up historically does not mean, of course, that they will be realized. There have been two kinds of restraints on the academic mind in the public. One is broadly social. It could be phrased as the problem of defining the social location, even the class affiliation, of intellect. The other is intellectual, concerning the nature of truth and authority — formally, no less than epistemology. This second point will bring us back to Arendt, and I will conclude with it —

---

[16] Lest I be misunderstood, let me say directly that the shift I am here outlining is not a move from critical distance to accepting embrace. Rather it is a change in the terms of judgment, adopting a more modern sense of self and public, and this implies a change in the angle of critical judgment. And this makes the framing of the problem of academic intellect in a democratic America different but still a problem.

[17] See Richard Rorty, *Philosophy and the Mirror of Nature* (Princeton, 1979); more recently, Rorty, *The Consequences of Pragmatism* (Minneapolis, 1982); and Rorty, "The Priority of Democracy to Philosophy," in Merrill D. Peterson and Robert C. Vaughn, eds. *The Virginia Statute for Religious Freedom* (New York, 1988), 257-82. Others who have explored this same issue from related positions (though resisting some of Rorty's extremes) are James T. Kloppenberg, *Uncertain Victory: Social Democracy and Progressivism in European and American Thought,* 1870-1920 (New York: 1965), and Robert Westbrook, *John Dewey and Democracy* (Ithaca, NY, 1991). For my own caveat regarding Rorty's *Dewey,* in which I follow Westbrook, see my "Social Science, Objectivity, and Pragmatism," *Annals of Scholarship,* special issue on "Reconstructing Objectivity" (forthcoming).

[18] I owe my understanding of this point to Louise Stevenson's essay, "Preparing for Public Life," in Bender, *University and the City,* pp. 150-77. My sense of the issue has been reinforced by Fitzpatrick, *Endless Crusade,* though she does not raise this order of question.

for symmetry's sake. But let me first make a few comments about the social history of academic intellect.

The social history I have in mind is developed in chapter 3 of *Intellect and Public Life: Essays in the Social History of Academic Intellectuals in the United States*, but let me make my point here by drawing on that account for a few paragraphs, taking for my focus a key academic, E. R. A. Seligman. He was a Columbia professor, a founder of the American Economic Association, and the author of the AAUP's founding "Statement of Principles" (1915). Scion of a prominent German-Jewish banking family in the city and one of Burgess' early students in the Faculty of Political Science, he was a major figure in the city as well as a prominent member of the Columbia faculty, a noted economist, and a leader in the social sciences generally. It was this broad prominence in the social sciences that was acknowledged in his last major project in a career that extended from the 1880s to the 1930s: his editorship of the *Encyclopedia of the Social Sciences* (15 volumes, 1930-35). He was also deeply involved in public affairs, serving as an academic expert, for example, to the congressional committee that drafted the Income Tax Law.

After studying with Burgess at Columbia, Seligman went to Germany, where he was introduced to historical economics. This discipline became his vehicle for participation in public life. Academic historical economists, especially at Johns Hopkins, Wisconsin, Columbia, and the early Wharton School at Pennsylvania, rejected the formalism and absolutism that characterized the political economy of Gilded Age journalists, like E. L. Godkin, or of early academic economists, like William Graham Sumner. Against these laissez faire economists, the historical economists established the principle of intervention in the economy on the basis of observed fact. If Godkin and Sumner had addressed the "public" in the language of moral absolutes, the new economists offered a more practical language. Empirical investigation of actual conditions would justify intervention not as a general principle but on a case-by-case basis. Under the cloak of what they called the historical method, Seligman and his generation engineered an ideological victory within the profession and in public life.[19] It was also a victory for the profession. It assumed (and assured) a permanent and continuing role for expertise.

How would that expertise be defined and bounded? Several incidents in Seligman's career illuminate the shaping of academic expertise. One's proper audience was the political and economic elite. One should

---

[19] Others who participated in this movement were more radical than Seligman. One thinks in this regard, most obviously, of Richard Ely at Johns Hopkins, who collaborated with Seligman in founding the AEA. The point holds for the whole spectrum of historical economists.

not speak directly to the masses. Expertise established authority. These propositions emerged over the years, in different incidents.

Let us begin in 1886. In that year, there were two promising young prize lecturers on the Graduate Faculty of Political Science at Columbia. One was Seligman, and the other was Daniel DeLeon. The year 1886 was also the year of Henry George's campaign for mayor of New York. It was a campaign that stirred working-class hopes and provoked bourgeois terror. DeLeon supported George, actively and publicly. When DeLeon invited George to speak on campus, the president of Columbia, fearing for the future of Western civilization, demanded that Burgess fire DeLeon. Burgess, so unappealing in so many ways, believed deeply in academic freedom, and he refused. But, of course, the story does not end there. When DeLeon's three-year term expired, he was not reappointed. Seligman, who had opposed George's candidacy, was promoted into professional ranks.

DeLeon was not sorry to leave the academy. He dreamed of an alliance of intellect and working classes in the Socialist Labor party, of which he became a spokesman. He preferred direct engagement in popular political controversy. Such was not to be the model of academic intellect. Academics looked toward the institutionalization of the authority of experts. Such expertise was understood to be self-contained, monitored only by peers, by the American Economic Association (AEA). Expertise was not thought to be political. Moreover, ideas formed outside the guild of professional economists could be dismissed without argument, simply on the basis of professional authority.

An example is provided by the semipublic debate between Seligman and Henry George, held at the 1890 annual meeting of the American Social Science Association, an old-fashioned, essentially civic organization soon to be superseded by specialized disciplinary associations.

Seligman asserted that no one "with a thorough training in the history of economics" (meaning a Ph.D.) could support such radical theories (as George proposed). In biology, metaphysics, and astronomy, Seligman insisted, "we bow down before the specialist." With the expertise of the seminar room available, why, he asked, should we take seriously the ideas on economics expressed in popular books, in newspapers, and on public lecture platforms?

Henry George angrily rejected Seligman's assertion of academic authority's superiority to political debate. "Political economy," he countered, "is not at all like astronomy or chemistry. It concerns phenomena [that] lie about us in our daily lives, and enter into our most important relations, and whose laws lie at bottom of questions we are called on to settle with our votes." If we cannot properly debate and understand them, "then democratic government is doomed to failure; and, the quicker we surrender ourselves to the government of the rich and learned, the better."[20]

In the decade of the 1890s, the bounds of professional discourse and activity were largely defined in a series of academic freedom cases. In each case, Seligman played a key role in determining the AEA response. Who should be protected? Seligman and the AEA went to the defense of academics who addressed economic issues reasonably within the purview of their supposed technical competence, even if their views on these matters were unorthodox. The custodians of the profession were also anxious to speak out against excessive and especially arbitrary trustee power over academics, arguing always that academic performance could be judged only by peers. Those academics who spoke directly to the public, as opposed to addressing peers or established political or economic elites, and who spoke for a wider range of radical proposals, were not defended.

By 1900, the result of the academic freedom cases was a stronger profession and one that favored the center.[21] Academic economists were both less conservative and less radical. They were also less likely to make direct public appeals or frankly ideological statements. Investigation and objective data became more important than general ideas. The academic ideal of the unremitting search for knowledge, whether trivial or not, was born. Such was the academic envisioned and protected in the AAUP's founding "Statement of Principles."

The position taken by Seligman and his colleagues in the academic freedom cases was embedded in a larger debate within the AEA. Were social scientific experts spokesmen for the dominant classes? Or the subordinate ones? Or were they above, even beyond, the class system?

This issue was pressed forcefully by John R. Commons at the 1898 and 1899 meetings. He insisted that, like Adam Smith and Karl Marx, economists could affect society only by associating themselves with a rising class. Most economists denied the existence of classes in the United States. Seligman, however, accepted the existence of classes and even conflict of interests and classes. He offered an answer that was largely accepted by academic social science. The expert, he argued, would reconcile conflicts of class interest. Taking issue with Commons' claims that

---

[20] "The Single Tax Debate," *Journal of Social Science*, 27 (1890): 44, 85.

[21] This point was made effectively by Mary O. Furner, *Advocacy and Objectivity: A Crisis in the Professionalization of American Social Science* (Lexington, KY, 1975), and more comprehensively by Dorothy Ross, *Origins of American Social Science* (New York, 1991).

the "economists can serve the public only through the classes," Seligman argued that the economist must reject any class association. "The economist," he insisted, "tries to represent the common interest of society." Note well that for Seligman expertise, not politics, was the means of reconciling the conflicts of modern society.[22]

Not everyone was persuaded by Seligman's argument. Several of his Columbia colleagues — John Dewey, Charles Beard, and James Harvey Robinson, for example — worried that social science was tainted by class affiliation, an affiliation with the dominant classes. At least it seemed that way in Nicholas Murray Butler's Columbia University. One of their purposes in founding the New School for Social Research in 1919, after Beard had resigned from Columbia, was to free academic social science from its class affiliation.[23]

The New School experiment failed to sustain this vision of free or independent social science. But the ideal did not die with the resignations of Beard, Dewey, and Robinson from the New School. It remained at the core of Dewey's philosophy of the social sciences. His theory of social inquiry was driven by his commitment to democracy. The pragmatic, public, and democratic process of inquiry proposed by Dewey would, he thought, reduce subjectivities, including those deriving from inequalities in society.[24]

In Dewey's work, then, one finds a resistance to the social constraints that had accompanied the professionalization of social science. Moreover, in his commitment to the public realm, one finds a democratic definition of the truth that dissolves, at least in part, the distinction assumed by academics and theorized by Hannah Arendt. Let me conclude, therefore, by exploring for a moment the understanding of the relation of academic intellect and democracy in Dewey's too much neglected book, *The Public and Its Problems*, published in 1927.

Dewey devoted his long career to bringing philosophy into the world, yet he did not propose thereby to devalue the specialized and technical tasks inherent in the academic discipline of philosophy. Dewey was always anxious that public expression be well grounded in a technically viable philosophical position. In the 1920s, when he was writing

---

[22] See John R. Commons et al., "Discussion of the President's Address," *Publications of the American Economic Association*, 3d series, 1 (1900): 62-88, quotation on 83; E. R. A. Seligman et al., "Discussion of the President's Address," *Economic Studies* 4 (1899): 110-12.

[23] See Croly, "A School of Social Research," *New Republic* 15 (8 June 1918), 167; Mitchell, *Two Lives: The Story of Wesley Clair Mitchell and Myself* (New York, 1953), 340. See also Bender, *New York Intellect*, pp. 300-02.

[24] See Bender, *New York Intellect*, pp. 312-13.

The Public and Its Problems, he was writing some of his most important technical philosophy, including *Experience and Nature.* He regularly published in the *Journal of Philosophy* as well as the *New Republic.* The academic and the civic were for him distinct yet continuous. He did not privilege "expert" truth and devalue the truths of citizenship. He framed intellect within a conception of the public.

He sought to free values from established interests and customs. The aim was not to deny such social facts but rather to open up the truth-making process, to admit into the process of making public truths a variety of interests and emotional commitments. Dewey never fully resolved the problem of how values are created. No one, in fact, who both resists relativism and eschews appeal to some transcendent and absolute source of values can avoid some difficulty on this point. Yet the solution he proposed did have the very important effect of bringing the intellectual into the world in a way that enriched public culture. For Dewey, politics in public constituted a proper source of values, purposes, and social knowledge in a democracy. From this perspective, as James T. Kloppenberg explained, Dewey's "politics is an endless search for better truths."[25]

Such a perspective undermines the ideal of the expert envisioned by Seligman and, even more directly, that offered by Walter Lippmann. During the war, Lippmann had been excited by the possibilities of expertise and disappointed in the capacity of the public, disturbed by how easily the masses could be manipulated. *Public Opinion* (1922) and *The Phantom Public* (1925) were his responses; they proposed a passive public and a government managed by "insiders" and experts. Dewey inverted Lippmann's formulation; he called for an active public and a responsive government. Most important for my argument here, however, he redefined the place of academic expertise in a democratic society.[26] It must be tested in the public world as well as in disciplinary communities; disciplinary truths must be entered into the conversation of the public.

Dewey called for social research, but he denied to social researchers the authority to prescribe solutions. Instead, they must bring their intelligence and their findings into the public realm. He did not fully develop a notion, nor have we, of a place off campus, so to speak, that might serve

---

[25] James T. Kloppenberg, "Independent Intellectuals and Democratic Theory in America, 1880-1920," paper presented to the Hungarian-American Historians Conference, Princeton, NJ, April 1985.

[26] Recent accounts of the Dewey-Lippmann debate include Bender, *New York Intellect,* pp. 245, 312-16; Westbrook, *John Dewey and Democracy,* chap. 9; and Christopher Lasch, *The True and Only Heaven* (New York, 1991), pp. 363-8. See also James W. Carey, *Communication as Culture: Essays on Media and Society* (Boston, 1988), esp. chapters 1-3.

as the forum for the process of discussion and persuasion that would produce Deweyan truths and public policy. But it was to be a place, a local place — a city, even a quarter of a city. The voice, more than print, and the conversation, more than the media message, were the foundation of political discourse for Dewey.[27]

Neither of the two tendencies characteristic of academic social science were, according to Dewey, adequate to the democratic challenge. The academy could not be justified as a "refuge" for "specialism" and "scholasticism." Nor should social science be assimilated into administration. Democracy needed something else. If democracy "had its seer in Walt Whitman," then, Dewey passionately believed, "it will have its consummation when free social inquiry is indissolubly wedded to the art of full and moving communication" in public.[28]

In one respect what Dewey proposed had already been envisioned by Immanuel Kant, one of the first academic philosophers and one intensely aware of the doubleness of being a philosopher and a citizen. In his famous essay, "What Is Enlightenment?" Kant proposed that human progress would come from truth telling in public. Only in that way would humans mature.[29] Kant had anticipated the construction of truth from philosophically justified and transcendent categories. Such rational truth, being superior to other forms of understanding and knowledge, would establish political obligation. One finds this conception of the relation of truth and politics residual in Hannah Arendt's essay with which we began, "Truth and Politics." Residues of this philosophical tradition are apparent as well even in Jürgen Habermas' rather different theorization of the "public sphere."[30] Such a truth — at least as viewed from the perspective I am developing here — diminishes political truths, relegating them to an inferior order of reason. The implications for democratic theory are significant; for John Dewey this mode of understanding drove a wedge between philosophy as truth seeking and democracy as the collective search for better truths.[31]

---

[27] See the rather curious statement in Lasch, *The True and Only Heaven*, p. 556.

[28] John Dewey, *The Public and Its Problems*, (Athens, OH, 1954); orig. ed. 1927, pp. 168, 184.

[29] Immanuel Kant, "What Is Enlightenment?" in Hans Reiss, ed., *Kant's Political Writings* (Cambridge, 1970), pp. 54-60.

[30] See Jürgen Habermas, *The Structural Transformation of the Public Sphere*, trans. Thomas Burger (Cambridge, MA, 1989); idem, *The Philosophical Discourse of Modernity*, trans. Frederick Laurence (Cambridge, MA, 1982). See also Martin Jay's recent review of the latter book, a review that takes the occasion to speak more generally about current issues in Habermas' work, in *History and Theory* 28 (1989): 94-113.

[31] John Dewey, "Philosophy and Democracy," in JoAnn Boydston, ed., *The Middle Works, 1899-1924*, 14 vols. (Carbondale, IL, 1982), 11:41-53. More generally, see Kloppenberg's interpretation of Dewey in his *Uncertain Victory*.

For Dewey and (in our time) Richard Rorty, philosophies that focus on certitude, that give priority to the epistemological project of Kant, were associated in Dewey's phrase with a "metaphysics of feudalism." This program for philosophy, Dewey felt, put "democratic practice" at an "immense intellectual disadvantage." Such philosophies "have failed to furnish it [democracy] with articulation, with reasonableness, for they have at bottom been committed to the principle of a single, final and unalterable authority, from which all lesser authorities are derived."[32]

Dewey had a very different conception of philosophy — and of truth. As Rorty and others recently emphasized, Dewey rejected the epistemological project of Kant. He urged instead the grounding of truth in experience and history, emphasizing contingency and uncertainty over the quest for certainty as the foundation of democratic practice. A philosophy animated by a commitment to democracy, Dewey wrote, will propose a "universe in which there is real uncertainty and contingency, a world which is not all in, and never will be, a world which in some respect is incomplete and in the making, and which in these respects may be made this way or that according as men judge, prize, love, and labor." He deeply believed that, for such a democratic philosophy, "any notion of a perfect or complete reality, finished, existing always the same without regard to the vicissitudes of time, will be abhorrent."[33]

One must be cautious in interpreting Dewey here. There is a danger that Dewey may be understood to be more radical (philosophically) than he, in fact, was. Richard Rorty, who has done so much to recover Dewey for our time, makes precisely this error. He misstates or overstates Dewey's position, making Dewey into a justification for his own antifoundationalism. While it is true that Dewey exchanged epistemology for history, it does not necessarily follow that he rejected metaphysics as well — a point tellingly made in Robert Westbrook's critique of Rorty. Dewey's *Experience and Nature* is effectively a metaphysics that — in Westbrook's phrasing — makes believing in democracy possible.[34] Dewey did not expect to arrive at universal reason, at absolute truth. His truths would be contextual, specific to time and place, always experimental, rooted in history but continually refined, reduced of their subjectivities through the process of public discussion.

---

[32]   Dewey, "Philosophy and Democracy," p. 52.

[33]   Ibid., p. 50.

[34]   See Rorty, *Philosophy and the Mirror of Nature*; Rorty, *The Consequences of Pragmatism;* Rorty, "The Priority of Democracy to Philosophy"; and Westbrook, *John Dewey and Democracy*, pp. 362, 539-42.

If Dewey developed a philosophical anthropology that accepted historical contingency and uncertainty, he did not thereby embrace subjectivity. He acknowledged the difference that social position produced in politics and philosophical outlook. He granted a role to interest and difference. But if he never denied the inevitability of subjectivity, his aim was always the reduction of subjectivity in the forming of public truths.[35] What Dewey wrote in *Experience and Nature* helps clarify both the process of truth making and its connection to social justice in a modern, differentiated society.

The ultimate contradiction in the classic and genteel tradition is that while it made thought universal and necessary and the culminating good of nature, it was content to leave its distribution among men a thing of accident, dependent upon birth, economic, and civil status. Consistent as well as humane thought will be aware of the hateful irony of a philosophy which is indifferent to the conditions that determine the occurrence of reason while it asserts the ultimacy and universality of reason.[36]

Dewey did not offer the prospect of permanent truth, nor even rational certitude. What his participatory community of truth makers may achieve is a reasoned truth. Such truth will not be objective in any absolute sense, although the contest it implies will at once accommodate interest and reduce subjectivity. What he proposed for us is the possibility of ever more secure, but never completely secure, truths.

Such truth, it seems to me, is what the turn from epistemology to history is all about, and it nicely undermines the division proposed by Arendt in "Truth and Politics." Academic truth and political truth turn out not to be fundamentally different. Politics and inquiry converge in the quest for better truths. Such a notion of truth may make us uneasy — both as academics and as citizens — but it may also make it easier for us to be at once academics and citizens in a democracy.

---

[35] From a rather different philosophical perspective, this sense of objectivity is proposed by Thomas Nagel in *A View from Nowhere* (New York, 1986).

[36] John Dewey, *Experience and Nature* (1925), in JoAnn Boydston, ed., *The Later Works* (Carbondale, IL, 1981), 1:99.

Noëlle McAfee

Ways of Knowing:
The Humanities and the Public Sphere

In the most general sense, politics is the art of deciding what ought to be done about matters of common concern. When we engage in politics, no matter how partisan, the ultimate question is always, "What should we do?" It's a prescriptive question, asking what a future course of action should be.

How do we know how to answer that question? Or to put it another way, what kind of knowledge do we need in order to decide what course of action is best? If we don't get that question right, we're bound for trouble, for there are very different ways of knowing and some are not at all suited for deciding what to do. Let me be blunt: we're already in trouble, because our political community seems to be going about it all wrong. Yet we can change course, first by understanding the problem and then by calling on those who can help.

It is tempting to call this area of inquiry *political epistemology*, because epistemology is the study of knowledge. But the term comes from the Greek word *episteme*, which means understanding or measuring something that is. In politics, however, what has to be known is *what should be* or *what we should do*, not what is. In this essay, I want to investigate the ways of knowing needed for politics, how this knowledge is best developed, and what it encompasses. Borrowing from Richard

Rorty, I'll say that there have been two approaches to political ways of knowing: objectivity and solidarity.

Objectivity is the view that the best course of action is decided by stepping outside our context and culture so that we can dispassionately decide what course of action to take. The idea here is that we cannot grasp "the truth" so long as our particular situation colors our thinking. We should think clearly, without bias, in order for our knowledge to be valid. To do so, we must imagine ourselves divested of our actual circumstances, culture, history, and material concerns. Usually those who are taken by the ideal of objectivity hold a companion ideal: that the standards we are looking for are universal. That is, they are unchanging and good for everyone in all contexts.[1] The desire for objectivity doesn't necessitate a notion of universal truths. But the two only make sense together. The only reason someone would need to try to know free from any particular interests would be if the truth were the truth no matter what your particular concerns were. In other words, only in a universe that has universal truths would particular concerns be irrelevant. In such a universe, particular concerns just get in the way of knowledge.

Alternatively, there is the view that we are able to know *because* of our experience; we know what course of action is best through our active involvement in the world, from our "situatedness," our context and history. In this view, we know the world as we help make it. We know it by virtue of our *relationship* to it. This view often gets called, disparagingly, *relativism*, because in it truth (whatever that might mean) is relative to a particular point of view. A more charitable, even accurate, term is the one that Richard Rorty uses: *solidarity*. It describes the view that "there is nothing to be said about either truth or rationality apart from descriptions of the familiar procedures of justification which a given society — *ours* — uses in one or another area of inquiry."[2] In other words, matters are judged according to criteria held by the group, not according to any external, supposedly universal criteria. Truth is right here, in our midst.

When it comes to political matters, according to solidarity, choice and purpose are internally derived. That is, the community decides what is

---

[1] One such standard often appealed to is that of equality, that all persons are equally deserving of respect and dignity. By appealing to this standard, many groups of people have been able to fight for better living standards and for the ability to take part in political decision making. I don't want to lose sight of the issue, though. The question is not whether standards like equality are worthwhile; the question is whether those standards are universal and best found objectively.

[2] Richard Rorty, "Solidarity or Objectivity?" in *Objectivity, Relativism, and Truth* (Cambridge University Press, 1991), p. 23.

best according to its own history, customs, and values. From the stand-point of solidarity, there are no external standards to appeal to in making choices about purpose and direction. Rather than try to "measure up" to some external standard, the community creates its own standards which it may well refine over time.

Of the two points of view about political knowledge, the objectivist one has reigned for well over 2,000 years. Its first ardent spokesman was Plato, and its most recent eloquent defender is Walter Lippmann. Both argue directly against "solidarity" or the contextualist point of view. In this essay, I'll come to solidarity's defense. I'll argue that the bias toward objectivity is a bias against knowledge that the public holds, and thus a bias against democracy. To mount a strong defense, I will look at knowl-edge in its many forms, from the objective approach of the natural sci-ences to the contextual approach of the humanities and of the public. I'll argue that the latter is superior for politics.

In the Ancient World

The lines of the objectivist-solidarity debate were first fully drawn in the ancient world, namely in Athens during the fifth century B.C. The philosophers took the objectivist position and the Sophists worked out of solidarity. The Sophists were, on the whole, itinerant teachers who earned their living by educating.[3] They taught by rhetoric: telling stories, questioning old myths (like the Eleatic myth of another reality greater than the phenomenal one), unraveling inconsistencies, and looking for explanations. Their mission was to prepare men for success in the city, since the Athenian conception of a realized human being was that of a citizen — just as Aristotle (very much an anti-Sophist) claimed that man was a political being. The Sophists believed that young men could learn the virtues or excellences (*arete*) needed for citizenship by learning how to persuade and speak publicly, by learning as much as possible about their own culture and history — by learning the literature and grammar of Greece past and present. In many respects, the Sophists broke with the old traditions and saw religion as a human invention. They examined the difference between nature and convention, arguing that it was impor-tant to know how to use the conventions of whatever city one visited. They argued that there was no truth apart from what was true in a given city, which helps explain Protagoras' dictum: "Man is the measure of all things; of the things which are, that they are, and of the things which are not, that they are not." Many of their critics (at the time and through the

---

[3] My description is an amalgam—very much a generalization of the Sophists' various views and methods.

ages) blamed them for corrupting young men, for teaching someone how to make something bad appear good and something false appear true.

In the midst of this way of knowing and educating came Socrates and Plato, who asked whether virtue could really be taught (no, they said) and even if it could whether the Sophists' way of teaching would provide an answer (no, again). Both Plato and after him Aristotle argued against the Sophists' contextualist approach to knowledge, saying that rational inquiry was superior to contextual accounts.

Plato indicted the Sophists most vigorously. He did so by arguing for an objectivist view of truth. In his view, there were two worlds: the everyday, visible world of material objects, which are apprehended through the senses, and the invisible world of the Forms (the immaterial models for all the particular things in the visible world), which is only known through pure reason. For Plato, this second world of the Forms was the real world — because in it were the unchanging, eternal universal Forms. This world *caused* the everyday, visible world. The visible world just reflected the unchanging world of the Forms. One couldn't really know anything about the visible world, because this world is always in flux. True knowledge is of the invisible world. True knowledge requires the intelligent grasp of the universal Forms.

According to Plato, everyone already has knowledge of this world of Forms. The knowledge is innate, but unfortunately forgotten. Most people live their lives thinking that the everyday world of material objects is all there is, but they are mistaken, Plato argues. The everyday world is a mere reflection of the real, and so these unfortunate people only see mere images, images always liable to change. Instead of knowledge, these people have only opinions. Instead of knowing what's best and true, they only know what *seems* to be best and true. They are caught up in the world of seeming and becoming, and have no clue about the real world of being.

To awaken the knowledge we were born with requires having the right nature (that of a philosopher) and decades of education. In Plato's ideal state, those with the philosopher's nature would be trained to recognize the Forms, namely the most supreme one: the Form of the Good. Once able to know the Form of the Good, the philosopher would be a just ruler, able to make just political decisions because he or she is properly enlightened.

The Good is known objectively, by those who have risen above the flux and fray of the everyday world. It is outside of human experience, so knowing it requires looking beyond the phenomenal world of appearances. Those who have this knowledge are able to decide what courses of action are in the true interests of the *polis*. Others are not. Therefore only these philosopher-rulers, possessing objective knowledge of the Good, can and should make political decisions.

Plato argues for this view because he thinks there must be — and is — a standard by which to know which actions are just. The Form of the Good is this standard. Only with this standard could a philosopher-ruler make sound decisions. Without a standard, a ruler would decide arbitrarily and irrationally. All sorts of injustices would prevail: some might rule out of a lust for power, others for vanity, others by whim.

For such reasons, Plato criticizes democracy. The democratic man, Plato claims, is always at the mercy of his desires. He thinks that whatever he desires at the moment is the highest good and lets these desires rule him.

> And so he lives on, yielding day by day to the desire at hand. Sometimes he drinks heavily while listening to the flute; at other times, he drinks only water and is on a diet; sometimes he goes in for physical training; at other times, he's idle and neglects everything; and sometimes he even occupies himself with what he takes to be philosophy. He often engages in politics, leaping up from his seat and saying and doing whatever comes into his mind. If he happens to admire soldiers, he's carried in that direction, if money-makers, in that one. There's neither order nor necessity in his life, but he calls it pleasant, free, and blessedly happy, and he follows it for as long as he lives.[4]

The democratic man, as Plato calls him, values the freedom to do whatever he feels like doing at any given time. In this, he values freedom above all else, namely the freedom to change his mind about what is good. But for Plato, this is folly. There is only one Form of the Good. While many actual things might partake of this Form, they don't do so willy-nilly. Whether something is good or not is an objective fact. When the mass of people rule, as in a democracy, they are usually mistaken about what's good, including what's good for them. The only way to ascertain what is good is to step outside human experience and desire and to look instead to what is unchanging.

With these epistemological views, Plato naturally took issue with the Sophists, who used human experience in the phenomenal world as their guide. Like the democrats, the Sophists favored experience over philosophic abstraction; they relied on history, literature, and culture for their

[4] Plato, *The Republic*, 561 c-e.

accounts, not on external notions of the Good. For the Sophists, it did not make sense to look outside a culture to educate those within it. A culture already had a repository of educative material.

Plato worried that this sort of training would leave people vulnerable to manipulation and demagoguery. These orators and itinerant teachers gave the public mere images and spurious narratives. Instead of such teachers, the public should be guided by a specially trained class of experts. At bottom, Plato's theory of knowledge underlay his criticism of democracy. For their own good, the people should not rule. This view did not die with the ancient world. It is as alive today as ever.

Seduced by the Sciences

There is a curious similarity between Plato's era and ours. Just as Plato thought that guardians rather than the people should rule, a movement of "Progressives" around the turn of this century argued that a select group of trained professionals should help run the country, whether by advising leaders or by helping lead and manage directly. We could call these eras "postdemocratic" because both were backlashes against democracy.[5] "Who knows what's good for the public?" The postdemocratic answer to this question is "the disinterested judge." Someone who stands outside particularities and contexts and is able to judge dispassionately.

In the modern era, the model for this approach is the natural sciences, which seem to epitomize the value of objective research, with the scientist-subject looking dispassionately at the objective world. Some argue that research in the natural sciences is not really so objective (e.g., Thomas Kuhn and Paul Feyerabend), but for the sake of argument let's grant that the natural sciences may call for objectivity. The important question for us is this: Should the supposedly objective standpoint of the natural sciences be the model for political knowledge? For better or worse, many in the century have answered affirmatively.

In the name of science, progress, and professionalism, the Progressive movement in the early part of this century called for careful managing of society. As Oscar Handlin writes, "From the Progressives of the first two decades of the century Americans had learned that government was a science and, like any other, was best left in the hands of trained experts."[6]

---

[5]   Plato was reacting to democracy associated both with Pericles and to the regime that followed "the thirty." The Progressives were responding to supposedly scientific studies that showed that 60-70 percent of enlisted men were "mentally deficient." If so many average Americans were incapable of reasoning, then how could they be able to govern themselves? For a summary of this history, see Robert Westbrook, *John Dewey and American Democracy* (Ithaca: Cornell University Press, 1991), pp. 182-90.

[6]   Oscar Handlin, *America: A History* (Chicago: Holt, Rinehart, and Winston, 1968), p. 834.

Just as with Plato's model, the modern notion of leadership was tied to education and expertise: "Only men educated to understand the intricate machinery could administer either industry or government."[7]

Moreover, the expert needed to be able to rise above the partisan interests that tended to drag down government. "The expert had the additional virtue of disinterestedness," Handlin writes. Ideally, the expert would excel in nonpartisan efficiency.[8]

This movement became entrenched in America's understanding of ideal governance. As Robert Westbrook writes, the neoprogressives of the 1930s

> argued for the identification of the good society with the rationalized society, which to them meant a society managed by an elite of far-sighted planners. They called for the creation of a new social order guided by "experts who are not representatives of the capitalists but of the public interest."[9]

The ideals of expertise, disinterestedness, objectivity, and efficiency pervaded other areas as well: engineering, the clergy, social work, and the other emerging professions. With the rise of professionalism came a growing gap between the people and its leaders.

Influenced by the Progressive movement — though departing from it considerably — came one of the most influential critics of participatory democracy, Walter Lippmann. During the First World War he helped develop propaganda for the army, and afterwards he became a journalist and a lay political theorist. Lippmann is famous (or infamous, depending on your point of view) for his book on the supposedly phantom public: "The accepted theory of popular government," he wrote, "rests upon the belief that there is a public which directs the course of events. I hold that this public is a mere phantom. It is an abstraction."[10] In part he meant that there is no fixed public; it shifts all the time, depending on what issue is on the table. In a later book, *The Public Philosophy*, he gave another reason to be wary of phrases like "The People." Such phrases are ambivalent: On the one hand they connote a unitary, historic community that encompasses the living, as well as their predecessors and successors. On

---

[7]   Ibid.

[8]   Ibid., pp. 834-5.

[9]   Robert Westbrook, *John Dewey and American Democracy* (Ithaca: Cornell University Press, 1991), p. 455. In this passage Westbrook is quoting from "What We Hope for," *New Republic*, 10 February 1932: 337.

[10] From Walter Lippmann's *The Phantom Public* (1925). This and all other Lippmann quotations I cite are from *The Essential Lippmann*, eds. Clinton Rossiter & James Lare (New York: Vintage Books, 1965).

the other hand, "The People" is also equated with the actual living numerous members of a society, its voters.

> It is often assumed, but without warrant, that the opinions of *The People* as voters can be treated as the expression of the interests of *The People* as an historic community. The crucial problem of modern democracy arises from the fact that this assumption is false. The voters cannot be relied upon to represent *The People*. The opinions of voters in elections are not to be accepted unquestioningly as true judgments of the vital interests of the community.[11]

The People as voters, as those actual citizens of a political community, are incapable of knowing what is in their own interests as a political community. They might individually know what seems to be good for themselves or their neighborhood, but they cannot know what is in the greater good. They are unable to look beyond their self-interests to the public interest. After all, the two interests may clash. Moreover, most people are too busy, Lippmann argues, and the environment is too vast for people to make sound judgments. When their imperfect, self-interested views are aggregated, as they are in an election or in a public opinion poll, the result is no better. And it's certainly not, according to Lippmann, the same thing as the true public interest.

The true public interest is what is good for everyone, despite what everyone thinks. Citizens are often mistaken about their true interests, especially given that their knowledge about the environment is imperfect and that they may desire harmful things. Various individuals will hold different notions about what would be in the public interest, but the true public interest is the same for everyone: "Living adults share, we must believe, the same public interest." And this interest "is often at odds with, their private and special interests."

> Put this way, we can say, I suggest, that the public interest may be presumed to be what men would choose if they saw clearly, thought rationally, acted disinterestedly and benevolently.[12]

Here we have one statement of Lippmann's epistemological criteria for how to ascertain what is in the public interest. As he makes plain, the people lack these criteria: they are irrational; they have entirely too many interests at stake; and they are too concerned for their own well-being to look after someone else's. Rather than rely on the people, who are too much in the thick of things, we should rely on those who have risen

---

[11] From chapter 3 of *The Public Philosophy*, reprinted on p. 86 of *The Essential Lippmann*.

[12] This quotation and the ones in the paragraph preceding it are all from chapter 4 of *The Public Philosophy*, reprinted on pp. 88-9 of *The Essential Lippmann*.

above the fray. These are the statesmen of the world — not mere politicians who are still beholden to particular interests but those men whose
minds are "elevated sufficiently above the conflict of contending parties"
that they are able to "adopt a course of action which takes into account
a greater number of interests in the perspective of a longer period of
time."[13]

The true statesman, according to Lippmann, is able to do single-hand-
edly what a whole public is unable to do — objectively discern what is
in the public interest. To do this, Lippmann advises that the statesman
make a point of *not* consulting the public. He makes this astounding
point so bluntly that I must quote at length:

> It is not deference to democracy for public men to evade their
> responsibilities and ask the mass of the people to do the work that
> public men are supposed to do. Once they refuse to lead opinion
> and prefer to be led by public opinion, they make impossible the
> formation of a sound public opinion. For obviously the President
> and the Administration officials and the congressmen in touch
> with them have the means for informing themselves on the reali-
> ties of the labor situation and of the defense program and of the
> war that no one else, not even the most conscientious newspaper
> reporters, can possess. If with their responsibilities and their
> means of knowing what is what, they sit around waiting for the
> Gallup poll and the fan mail, they will get a Gallup poll and a fan
> mail from a people that have not been able to know what men
> must know in order to judge wisely.[14]

So what should a statesman know, according to Lippmann, in order to
judge wisely? He needs to know the "hidden interests" of the public
"which are permanent because they fit the facts and can be harmonized
with the interests of their neighbors."[15] To be able to have this amazing
knowledge without ever consulting the public, the statesman should
have "the insight which comes only from an objective and discerning
knowledge of the facts, and a high and imperturbable disinterestedness."[16]

There we have it: the paradigmatic case for objectivity. In case the
reader is not as appalled by this as I am, let me make a few comments.
Note that the model of objectivity calls for the virtue of disinterestedness.

---

[13] From chapter 13 of *A Preface to Morals* (1929) reprinted in *The Essential Lippmann*, p. 455.

[14] From chapter 2 of *The Public Philosophy* (1955) reprinted in *The Essential Lippmann*, p. 99.

[15] Ibid., p. 456.

[16] Ibid., p. 457.

This is an interesting word, *disinterested*. As my friend Ernesto Cortés says, *interested* comes from *inter-esse*, to be between. So to be disinterested is to have nothing at stake, to be completely uninvolved, to be elsewhere. The twentieth-century ideal of disinterestedness really means being removed from society. Those we look to for guidance in this century, then, have — or at least pretend to have — nothing at stake here. Why should the disinterested statesman bother at all with the good of the public? It seems all too likely that those who claim to have nothing at stake in public matters may well believe that the public does not matter much after all.

Apart from being offended by Lippmann's sentiments, I also think that he is simply wrong. As I'll argue in due course, the model of objective knowledge that he holds so dear doesn't work in politics. No one but an omniscient god could know without consulting the public what the public will value over the long run, how citizens' different interests can be harmonized, and what is really "good" for them. These "public facts," if you will, do not reside in some platonic heaven; they are contingent, provisional facts, produced by the public.

Ten years ago, I attended graduate school in public policy and quickly learned that *public policy* did not refer to policy made by the public but rather policy made for the public by an elite cadre of experts.

While policy schools have only been around for 30 years, they draw from a long history. For centuries there have been those trained and destined to serve in some public capacity. These intellectuals tended to see themselves as easily transplantable, that is, rootless — able to move from one country to the next, serving one leader or another. Before this century, they were trained in the humanities, though they were prototypes of "disinterested" experts for they lacked any sustained relationship to the communities that they served.

They were what we might call "traditional" intellectuals, to follow the phrasing of the Italian communist leader Antonio Gramsci.[17] The term *traditional intellectual* refers to certain intellectual workers who came to see themselves as independent of any particular groupings or strata, as free inquirers into truth. Gramsci noted that, though these intellectuals claim to be independent, they in fact act to preserve the status quo, wittingly or not. A traditional intellectual is bent on preserving the norms, even as he or she dabbles in a particular area of scholarship. Nothing will

---

[17] Imprisoned by Mussolini during the Second World War, Gramsci spent his days writing his notebooks, now widely read commentaries on the prospects of transforming Western capitalist societies. To avoid the prison censors, Gramsci steered clear of the jargon of communism, and in the process he developed a set of terms and concepts that have remarkable applications.

really change. This intellectual's masquerade as independent is dependent on there being a certain organization of society — one that remains untouched. So in the long run, he or she is completely indebted to this social order.

Today's traditional intellectuals, let me venture, are equally indebted to society being constructed in a particular form. (So we might wonder just how objective they truly are.) For one, they need a society in which expert knowledge is valued and lay knowledge is disdained. In other words, for the expert's knowledge to have any value, we must ensure that the everyday knowledge of regular people — call it common sense — is disparaged. What this means is that practical knowledge always trails far behind scientific knowledge, that expert knowledge is always the ideal. Moreover, we come to equate knowledge with expertise and public opinion with error.

Marginalization of the Humanities

In our modern romance with the natural sciences and objectivity, the fields of inquiry that use other forms of knowledge have been seriously disparaged. I'm referring to the humanities: literature, rhetoric, ancient and modern languages, speculative philosophy, narrative history, art history, women's and ethnic studies, as well as certain approaches to the social sciences. While the "hard sciences" deal with facts, the humanities, it seems, deal with subjective impressions and opinions.

Of the branches of knowledge, those engaged in research in the natural sciences as well as technological research (from engineering departments to business schools) get the most respect and support. Throughout the Cold War, these branches, which produced immediate, instrumentally useful knowledge for the nation, found their coffers overflowing with research grants and contracts. Disciplines that tried to mimic the natural sciences, namely the social sciences, benefited from the overflow of these funds. Meanwhile, the humanities got by on relatively less and less. Now that the Cold War is over, there is far less public money available to higher education, with even less going to the humanities.

The humanities have been devalued because the knowledge they produce seems inferior to the knowledge that the natural sciences produce. The knowledge of the humanities doesn't seem to be *worth* very much anymore, not when worth is measured by economic value or objective standards. In the humanities, there are no external measures for deciding the truth or worth of some text. On the whole, the humanities engage in interpretation, whether interpreting the meaning of texts or the effects of one's words. Without external criteria, it seems that the humanities do not measure up to the rigorous standards of other branches of knowledge.

Yet there is another reason that the humanities have been marginalized. It is not just a matter of the rest of society disparaging the humanities' mode of inquiry. Many humanities scholars have bought into the cult of expertise, marginalizing themselves in the process. In trying to mimic expertise and objectivity, these scholars have sought to become experts on narrower and narrower areas of scholarship. As their focus narrows, their connection to the public world disintegrates. The humanities scholar today tends to aspire to knowing more than anyone else — and on having the definitive judgment — in a particular field. But when the humanities scholar becomes the specialist, then the old aims of the humanities become irrelevant.

Think of the old aims. In the ancient world, the humanities were the centerpiece of education. In ancient Greece, the goal of education was to make students better citizens, because the most realized human being was one who was thoroughly engaged in the life of the city — a political being. To become a better citizen — and thus a better human being — meant learning about history, rhetoric, literature, culture, and language. While many universities have in their charters this same mission — educating citizens for public life — their practice is quite different. And many humanities scholars practicing in universities seem equally unconcerned. To be sure, the readers of this volume depart from the norm, but the reader may still grant that this is the prevailing outlook. Although some humanities scholars see a public mission of bestowing their expertise on a hungry public, this is a poor model for developing a new relationship between the humanities and public life.

But who are we to blame the humanities scholar for doing what seems to be so natural in a society that privileges objectivity? No longer do we think of human beings as essentially political beings. Our culture values individualism over political communities, and so education is seen as a way to further the individuals' freedom to pursue private ends. We have here the old chicken-or-egg conundrum: So long as our culture values objectivity and individualism, the humanities will aspire to specialization over educating for citizenship. Still, this may be a good time to try to break this pattern, especially that now after the Cold War the nation is reevaluating its commitment to higher education and the worth of the humanities is undergoing increasing scrutiny. Many scholars recognize a challenge to connect the mission of the humanities with the nation's aspirations and needs.

The Rise and Fall of the Public Sphere

Part of the chicken-or-egg conundrum involves the role of the public in political life today. As many people have noticed, even as the franchise has expanded, the public's role in deciding matters of common concern has diminished. Once upon a time — whether in theory or in fact — private citizens were able to join with other citizens through associations and through public conversations to make choices about public matters. In doing so, they created a sphere or realm sometimes called the public sphere or civil society. This realm exerted a force on government, a force that called the government to account in some way to this public.

In many political and theoretical circles, the term "the public sphere" has gained new currency. In large part this is due to the recent English translation of Jürgen Habermas' 1962 book, *The Structural Transformation of the Public Sphere*. In this work, Habermas traces the rise and fall of that political arena that is neither private nor governmental. The public sphere is that place where public opinion is formed. "A portion of the public sphere is constituted in every conversation in which private persons come together to form a public," writes Habermas. "Citizens act as a public when they deal with matters of general interest."

In his book, Habermas concludes that the public sphere has withered away. Robert Holub sums up Habermas' argument nicely:

> The public sphere, at least its bourgeois prototype, began to decline during the course of the past century.... The collapse occurs because of the intervention of the state into private affairs and the penetration of society into the state. Since the rise of the public sphere depended on a clear separation between the private realm and public power, their mutual interpenetration destroys it.... As we progress into the twentieth century, the free exchange of ideas among equals becomes transformed into less democratic communicative forms, for example public relations.[18]

Habermas analyzed the public sphere as both a historical development, which failed, and a normative ideal, which still holds sway today. As I see it, the public sphere is still alive today, though extremely malnourished. The public realm between the state and private spheres survives in community organizations, churches, labor unions, study circles, the National Issues Forums, and many other nongovernmental organizations in the United States and in countries abroad. The rise of civil associations in Eastern Europe helped bring down the Berlin Wall, and the few that exist in China exert an accountability force on the Chinese government.

---

[18] Robert Holub, *Jürgen Habermas: Critic in the Public Sphere* (New York: Routledge, 1991), p. 6.

Yet none of these public spheres fulfills its potential, in large part because public spheres are, at best, realms of solidarity, not objectivity. Vibrant public spheres will value public knowledge, the force of public opinion, and the importance of the public being the source of legitimacy for government. Yet, as we've seen, solidarity is hardly ever nurtured or valued in contemporary society.

Many today think invigorating this realm is vitally important. But many forces work against this, namely the same forces that favor disinterestedness, objectivity, and expert knowledge. The public sphere has little or no value in a model of politics that takes elite knowledge as its ideal. Just as my colleagues in policy school would never look to the public for guidance, those who value expert knowledge would just as soon there not be a public with which to contend.

In many respects, the plight of the public sphere is one with the plight of the arts and humanities. Neither is seen to have anything worthy to contribute to public policy-making. Their knowledge is suspect for being supposedly subjective, baseless, relative, arbitrary, and standardless. So the main task for a proponent of public knowledge is to defend its worth. To do this, let's look closer at knowledge.

Knowing What We Ought to Do

There are many ways of knowing, with different ways suitable for different purposes. This is an ancient distinction. In fact, one of the clearest — and still useful — expositions of the difference was made by Aristotle. He divided knowledge into three sorts: theoretical, productive, and practical. Only one of these is suitable for politics, for deciding what we as a community or *polis* ought to do on matters of public concern.

The Limits of Theoretical Reason: Description Not Prescription

The theoretical sciences aim at describing the world as it is. For Aristotle, this was the highest form of knowledge, since one engaged in it as an end in itself: knowledge for knowledge's sake. The theoretical scientist, according to this definition, wants to know how things work. The subjects of theoretical knowledge, for Aristotle, include metaphysics, physics, and mathematics.

Theoretical knowledge isn't concerned with action. It doesn't seek to change anything. In its proper scope, it has no ulterior motives and so has no moral or political concerns. This ancient definition is still apt today. Those interested in research for its own sake are aiming for understanding — not for putting this understanding to any particular use. In the theoretical sciences, whether in microbiology or in fractal geometry, researchers investigate how a system or entity operates. If the research produces knowledge that can be used, then the theoretician turns the results over to the technician. *Using* this knowledge takes us out of the realm of theory and into the realm of action.

The Limits of Instrumental Reason: Deciding Means Not Ends

While theoretical knowledge shuns action, other forms of knowledge embrace it. Aristotle called his second designation *productive knowledge*. This is the knowledge used to produce a given product. The physician uses her own knowledge to produce health, the chef to produce a delightful meal, the cobbler to produce shoes. Productive knowledge helps a practitioner produce some end, but it does not designate what the end ought to be. The end is given in advance, whether by an earlier choice of careers or the predetermined designations within a more traditional society. Productive knowledge helps one produce a particular end. It has nothing to say about what those ends should be.

Yet we have to be careful that production doesn't become an end in itself. As I noted above, the more theoretical knowledge produced, the more tempting it is to put this knowledge to use. In his critique of what he called technological society, Erich Fromm described the principle that seems to privilege means over ends: "the maxim that something *ought* to be done because it is technically *possible* to do it."[19] This violates the tradition that said

> that something should be done because it is needed for man, for his growth, joy, and reason, because it is beautiful, good, or true. Once the principle is accepted that something ought to be done because it is technically possible to do it, all other values are dethroned, and technological development becomes the foundation of ethics.[20]

In this century, productive reason has been put to such ill use. In fact, the logic of production — of instrumentality and technology — seems to have overridden the sort of reason needed in deciding ends.

Under this heading of productive reason, I'd like to include a more modern designation, that of instrumental reason. This is the term used by some twentieth-century philosophers to criticize the rationale that guides bureaucracies and other large systems. Wherever instrumental reason reigns, ends are generally predetermined and unquestioned. Reason works here to fulfill these often unacknowledged ends. It tackles the question of *how* to produce a particular end: whether the end is

---

[19]   Erich Fromm, *The Revolution of Hope* (New York: Harper & Row, 1968), p. 32.

[20]   Ibid., pp. 32-3.

amassing a fortune or winning a war. Sometimes the means seem to be ends in themselves. For example, efficiency is often idealized, but the most efficient society would not be the most humane one. As my former economics professor, Malcolm Gillis, said, the question of when and how to increase efficiency should never be decided by economists; it's a political matter that should be answered by the political process.

The sociologist Max Weber was one of the first to critique instrumental reason, saying that it was like an iron cage — not the liberating force that the Enlightenment promised. In response to his critique of reason, other philosophers — namely Jürgen Habermas — have tried to show that this reason was just one sort. He argues that there is yet another sort of reason that might fulfill the Enlightenment's promise of freedom and a more progressive society.

Deciding Ends: The Hermeneutics of Defining Meaning and Purpose

Both theoretical and instrumental reason are compatible with the objectivist approach. Theoretical reason seeks to understand some object or entity. Instrumental reason seeks the most efficient means to reach some predetermined end. But the third way of knowing that Aristotle defined calls on the self-reflective approach of solidarity.

Aristotle calls this third way of knowing *phronesis*. This term is generally translated as *practical wisdom*, but I'd like to broaden the translation to include practical intelligence or reason. *Phronesis* is the sort of wisdom or reason involved when acting, especially when deciding what to aim for. It is "the capacity for deciding what is good and advantageous" for oneself.[21] It is reason needed in deciding what one's ends should be.

> …production has an end other than itself, but action does not: good action is itself an end. That is why we think that Pericles and men like him have practical wisdom. They have the capacity of seeing what is good for themselves and for mankind, and these are, we believe, the qualities of men capable of managing households and states.[22]

Practical reason is a kind of legislation: "Practical wisdom issues commands: its end is to tell us what we ought to do and what we ought not to do."[23]

---

[21] Aristotle, *Nicomachean Ethics*, trans. M. Ostwald (Englewood Cliffs, NJ: Prentice-Hall, 1962), p. 152 (book six, chapter 5 1110a25-26). This section describes practical wisdom for an individual. Chapter 8 describes practical wisdom and politics.

[22] Aristotle, *Nicomachean Ethics* trans. M. Ostwald (Englewood Cliffs, NJ: Prentice-Hall, 1962), p. 153 (book six, chapter 5 1110b5-10).

[23] Ibid., 1143a7-9.

In the course of discussing practical wisdom, Aristotle also discusses political wisdom and deliberation. He says that there are two kinds of practical wisdom concerning the state: "the one, which acts as practical wisdom supreme and comprehensive, is the art of legislation; the other, which is practical wisdom as dealing with particular facts, bears the name which, [in everyday speech,] is common to both kinds, politics, and it is concerned with action and deliberation."[24] Here I am going to part company with Aristotle. Elsewhere (1112b11-24), he argues that we deliberate only about means not ends. His thinking seems to run as follows: The man of practical wisdom has the virtue of being able to know what the proper ends ought to be. He has this wisdom due to his experience and just nature. (A young man is too inexperienced to have this virtue.) There are times, though, when it is necessary to investigate the ways to achieve these ends. This is when deliberation is required.

I disagree with Aristotle's point that the man of practical wisdom just knows what the proper ends are without deliberating. For one thing, Aristotle simply makes this claim; he doesn't (as far as I know) give a reason for this claim. For another, in politics the proper ends aren't self-evident, even to someone with this wisdom. Rather, practical wisdom is the product of practical intelligence, and this intelligence would entail sorting through all the many proper ends or "legislation" to decide what coheres best with the group.

I agree with Aristotle that political wisdom requires deliberation, but I would add that in a democracy political deliberation is not a solitary venture (of "the man" of practical wisdom) but a joint venture of all the citizens who have a stake in the matter. Deliberation entails more than sorting through various options; it entails bringing together multiple points of view and concerns.

How would this sort of practical reasoning work? At present, there are various views. Some think it really isn't a *reasoning* at all, but rather a practice of interpretation. For these thinkers, *reason* implies some universal standards whereas a practice can be contingent and contextually defined. For my purposes, the distinction is not terribly relevant. The important point is that there is a way of thinking about ends that is neither purely theoretical nor instrumental. It is a way of taking into consideration the particulars, the context, the history of a community while making sense of what the community is and what it aspires to. It is a community thinking together about what its meaning is and its purpose ought to be. One name for this practice is *hermeneutics*, the art of interpretation, of opening up what was hitherto closed (think of the term, *her-*

[24] Ibid., 1141b24-7.

metically sealed). Hermeneutics is the practice of interpreting and making sense of something that might not have any objective meaning. One of the most influential practitioners of hermeneutics, Hans Georg Gadamer, argues that interpretations are never the final arbiters of meaning. Rather they are provisional, always subject to change. The same is true for communities. What we think is important and decisive one day may change the next. As new participants and points of view enter a community's conversation, new understandings will arise. The more open a community is to change — including this change in interpretations — the less exclusive and rigid it is, the less likely it is to become a homogeneous, uninviting place, and the more willing it is to adapt to new developments. The more hermeneutic a community is, the healthier it is.

Another take on practical reason is that it is, properly speaking, a form of reason not just provisional interpretation. This is the position that Habermas takes in his account of moral reasoning. Habermas argues that there is a form of reasoning that guides our communicative practice. To put it briefly, he thinks that all human beings hold certain rules about what kind of claims would be valid: namely, that our claims be comprehensible, true, spoken sincerely and appropriately. These are the preconditions for our taking part in conversation, including conversations about what moral and political ends we ought to seek.

> Just as an individual can reflect on himself and his life as a whole with the goal of clarifying who he is and who he would like to be, so too the members of a collectivity can engage in public deliberation in a spirit of mutual trust, with the goal of coming to an understanding concerning their shared form of life and their identity solely through the unforced force of the better argument. In such ethical-political discourses ... participants can clarify who they are and who they want to be, whether as members of a family, as inhabitants of a region, or as citizens of a state.[25]

This communicative reasoning is internal to our communicative practice, so it would seem to fit in nicely under the model of solidarity. Unfortunately, it does so only partially. One of the validity claims that Habermas believes everyone shares is that in order for a moral claim to be justified it has to be justifiable to everyone — within and without a community: "moral knowledge that raises a claim to universal validity must in addition detach itself from the contexts in which ethical knowledge remains embedded."[26] Habermas uses the term *moral* in a very spe-

---

[25] Jürgen Habermas, *Justification and Application: Remarks on Discourse Ethics*, trans. C. P. Cronin (Cambridge, MA: MIT Press, 1993), p. 23.

[26] Ibid., p. 24.

cific sense: as a universal claim. For claims that are only valid within a particular community, Habermas uses the term *ethical*. He argues that these claims can be reflective, which grants them a rational status. So we might follow Habermas up to this point. We might say (though there isn't room to make this argument here) that we all hold certain presuppositions about what moral or political claims are valid, that we can try to reach understanding and make choices together, but that we need not try to step outside our situatedness to justify these claims. After all, from the perspective of solidarity, there is no need to transcend our context. The only reason to try to universalize our claims is to have statements that are universalizable: an unnecessary tautology.

We need not depart from solidarity by going as far as Habermas does to describe a way of knowing in politics. Hermeneutics can fit the bill. Earlier, I noted the different ways of knowing between the sciences and the humanities. The first is really straight epistemology, which, as Richard Rorty argues, is based on the belief that "there are foundations to serve as common ground for adjudicating knowledge-claims."[27] Conversely, he argues, hermeneutics opposes this belief. As Rorty writes:

> Hermeneutics sees the relations between various discourses as those of strands in a possible conversation, a conversation which presupposes no disciplinary matrix which unites the speakers, but where the hope of agreement is never lost so long as the conversation lasts. This hope is not a hope for antecedently existing common ground, but simply hope for agreement, or, at least, exciting and fruitful disagreement.[28]

I take hermeneutic conversation to be a paradigm for a "community" political conversation, the ongoing deliberation devoted to deciding community direction and purpose. As I use the term, the "we" of community refers to the participants in that conversation. By community, I mean a contingent, evolving group of people. Rorty uses Michael Oakeshott's distinction:

> Epistemology views the participants as united in what Oakeshott calls an *universitas* — a group united by mutual interests in achieving a common end. Hermeneutics views them as united in what he calls a *societas* — persons whose paths through life have fallen together, united by civility rather than by a common goal, much less by a common ground.[29]

---

[27] Richard Rorty, *Philosophy and the Mirror of Nature* (Princeton, 1979), p. 317.

[28] Ibid., p. 318.

[29] Richard Rorty, *Philosophy and the Mirror of Nature*, p. 318. Rorty cites "On the Character of a Modern European State" in Michael Oakeshott, *On Human Conduct* (Oxford, 1975).

As Rorty puts it, *universitas* seems to imply a predetermined group with preexisting normative foundations and ends; *societas* implies that the group is brought together contingently, that its norms are contextually derived, and that common ground is irrelevant. I agree with Rorty on all this save the last point: While common ground is not determined in advance, it is relevant for the participants. In fact, common ground is what the conversation seeks to create. While *universitas* implies that common ground is waiting to be discovered, *societas* implies that it is contextually derived and created by the participants in conversation.

Here is the point: there is an immense difference between objective knowledge and public knowledge, but it is not that one is worthy and the other not. The difference is that the two have different criteria. Scientific knowledge is based on certain standards of rightness; public knowledge is judged on the basis of soundness. When we dismiss public knowledge, we dismiss the search for sound knowledge, knowledge about what course of action is most sustainable and consistent. Knowing what is a good end or purpose is political wisdom, the very wisdom that communities need in making political choices.

Who Can Know What's in the Public Interest?

I hope that by now I've answered the question with which I began. The kind of knowledge we need in politics, in order to decide what course of action is best, is the kind used in solidarity: practical reason, which involves interpretation and deliberation. So now I turn to a final question: Who is best suited to provide this knowledge? Certainly not those who claim to be objective and disinterested. Rather, we should look to those who are actively involved in interpreting, judging, and making their world: the public itself along with those who are schooled in interpretation, those in the humanities.

Why the public? Because it has the most at stake in political matters and it has the most knowledge about what should be done. Those who favor objectivity worry that particular, subjective perspectives are always partial ones, and that particular, special interests will override the public interest. Yet only insofar as partial perspectives remain partial will this be the case. The challenge is to bring these partial perspectives together, to engage the participants to weigh other points of view, to reconsider their own views in light of others. This is done when people come together in public conversations, in deliberation. (And this is why I brought Habermas' discourse ethics into the discussion.) Through deliberation, partial perspectives can be woven into a new whole. Each participant can bring to the table an array of considerations, and once at the table the participants consider views they might not have considered before. Through such deliberations, the public can articulate what the public interest is — far better than Lippmann's statesman ever could.

But because the public sphere and contextual understanding (solidarity) have been denigrated, the public may need an ally in this venture. What other field of inquiry shares so much with the public's way of knowing but the humanities? The process of creating sound public knowledge shares a great deal with the knowledge-making procedures in the arts and the humanities. These procedures include interpretation, judgment, imagination, and expression. They can be carried out well or poorly — we know the difference. Intellectuals in the humanities don't have the luxury of appealing to tried-and-true formulae; they must make decisions case by case, taking into consideration contexts and purposes, values and destinations. In short, they must do the very things that the public must do in deciding what judgment or course of action is best.

In this respect, then, the humanities scholars are natural allies for the public. They can speak for the value of contextual interpretation, which is much like public ways of knowing. And in doing so, in strengthening the public sphere, they can shore up their own place in a society that sees little need for them — that slashes funding for the arts and humanities, that endows chairs in engineering rather than the classics, that collapses and disbands whole departments in the arts and humanities. In short, the relationship between these intellectuals and the public sphere is mutual, a true inter-estedness, in the best sense.

But for this to happen, humanities scholars will have to modify or even abandon their aspirations for specialization — which narrows one's focus — and expertise, which is an attempt to "rise above" the layman's understanding. For the humanities to ally themselves with the public, they will need to see their work as closely bound up with the public's mission.

Writing from his Italian prison, Antonio Gramsci offered an alternative to traditional, disinterested intellectuals: "organic" intellectuals, intellectuals who are fully cognizant of their social and political roots. He saw a political need for this kind of intellectual who grows out of a political community. In describing this, he suggested a way in which intellectuals could be interested in public life: "The mode of being of the new intellectual can no longer consist in eloquence, which is an exterior and momentary mover of feelings and passions, but in active participation in practical life." This active participation meant being a "constructor, organizer, 'permanent persuader' and not just a simple orator." For Gramsci, an organic intellectual takes an active role in shaping society rather than just specializing in some arcane area of scholarship. By seeing themselves as organic intellectuals, humanities scholars could see their public origins as the wellspring, the purpose, and the gauge of their work as intellectuals.

This notion of organic intellectual may seem odd, for at first glance it seems that the humanities are quite separate spheres from the public. But this is an illusion borne of hundreds of years of specialization. What the humanities scholar studies is nothing more than the products of the public lifeworld according to the very vernacular of that lifeworld. The social and natural scientists might try to rise above that vernacular and perspective, but the humanities scholar, by choice of practice, has chosen them. It is only natural, then, for the humanities and the public to join forces: an alliance that will strengthen both the public sphere and democratic practice.

Alejandro Sanz de Santamaria

Education for Political Life

As a university professor, I am involved in two main activities. I teach (economics and management) and I undertake research (mainly in economics). And now I find myself deeply concerned about the kind of education for political life we provide through our teaching and research activities. I suspect that through these activities we are not educating people well to take their place in democracy.

For me, a central question is this: What is urgent and important if we are to provide people with a better education for political life? Should we generate additional education activities — additional to those currently being practiced in formal academic institutions — that are directly concerned with political life; or should we radically transform the current forms in which we carry out our educational practices in all subjects, so that they effect a different, better political education? The truth is that I'd be reluctant to argue against any of the efforts being made outside the formal education institutions to improve education for political life; yet I have a strong sense that these efforts consume immense energies merely to counterbalance the damaging effects that formal education, as it is provided in all subjects through existing academic institutions, is having on political life in our society. Thus my hypothesis is that it is more urgent and important to work as hard as possible to transform current formal educational practices in certain new directions than it is to create additional activities to improve people's education for political life. I think a transformation in the conventional social forms of education has to take place in the classrooms at schools and universities.

Just over a decade ago, I was invited to analyze the way in which local laborers' migration patterns, in the Colombian peasant community

51

known as Garcia Rovira, were affecting regional economic development, and to make appropriate recommendations on an economic policy that the government could enforce in connection with migration.   More recently, I have been engaged in evaluating the impact of a government economic development program that has been under way in the region for more than eight years.

A central feature of these two experiences was that the recommendations I was to produce had to be constructed from primary information collected through in-depth fieldwork and surveys. Thus in both projects the knowledge production process comprised, schematically, four "conventional" steps: a thorough analysis of available literature on this rural community; fieldwork in which different constitutive social agents of the community — peasants; landowners; merchants; state functionaries; local political, religious, and military authorities; etc. — were interviewed at length; a survey, designed and implemented in the light of the fieldwork; and, finally, the knowledge construction process itself, using all the information made thus available.

The experience was traumatic.

The available literature on Garcia Rovira when I started the first project was overwhelming: there was information on the agrological characteristics of the soil (soil qualities, steepness, altitudes over sea level, etc.), on local weather conditions (rainfall, humidity, winds, etc.), on water availability (rivers, streams, dams, and other irrigation facilities), on the regional population's size, growth rate and structure (urban, rural, age groups, etc.), on the most important crops grown in the region and the different labor processes practiced to cultivate each one of them (amount of labor time required, constitutive tasks of labor processes, production inputs needed, etc.), on the main characteristics of the markets within which the different products circulated (local, regional, national, and/or international markets), on prices per product, on rural development programs that had been enforced and were being enforced by the state and other institutions, on land ownership distribution, on productivity and levels of production per product, etc.

The abundance of this information meant that it was impossible for me to use it all in my own production of knowledge; yet, at the same time, I knew that this information would have to be taken into account by any research that proved effective in procuring economic development in this community. A troubling contradiction indeed.

Then, as I came into close contact with many individuals and households in the second step of my conventional knowledge production process — the in-depth fieldwork — this contradiction became increas-

ingly problematic. The richness and complexity of the innumerable natural and social conditions under which each one of the individuals and
households interviewed reproduced themselves over time, as well as the
impressive differences (the heterogeneity) of such conditions among
social units — which are often "homogenized" under the concept of
"peasant" — progressively undermined the possibility of producing a
conclusion that I could legitimately claim to be a "sound basis" for any
kind of recommendation. Recommendations could be formally constructed, of course. But I felt a moral impediment to doing so: in the
name of what "golden rule" was I to make the abstraction necessary to
produce my "knowledge" and make my recommendations about what
"ought to be done" to attain this community's economic development?

But I had to do it; there was a legal contract to which I had to
respond. Thus, I had to select a "principle of organization" — a theoretical framework, a symbolic space — with which I could select and relate
my "story" about Garcia Rovira. And so I did.

The complexity of the scenario I gradually perceived — of the
numerous intermingled social and natural processes in which the different individuals and households interviewed participated — turned the
experience of the third step of my work (the survey) into the most force-
ful and valuable evidence of the arbitrariness of the abstractions economists have to make. The design of the sample; the painful process of constructing the survey questionnaire; the even more painful process of col-
lecting the information — the pain one feels in this kind of research is, I
think, directly proportionate to how deeply concerned one is, as a
researcher, about the future of the community under study, about the real
social effects that the knowledge production process itself will have on
the community. How was I to design a sample survey of approximately
500 households that would be "representative" of this community as a
totality? I didn't have an answer then, and I still don't have it today!

But the sample was designed, the questionnaire was constructed, the
survey was carried out, and the collected information was "ordered" in
several computer files to be used as "raw material" to construct new
knowledge about the community. I proceeded then with the fourth and
final step of this conventional knowledge production process: to use all
this information, collected in the three preceding steps, for the construction of new knowledge and corresponding recommendations. But the
only firm conclusions I could draw from this exercise were confirmation
of my own "technical" incapacity unilaterally to determine what policies
would actually be effective in enhancing the development of these
households. This strongly reinforced the "moral impediment" I had felt to

making such "policy" recommendations. How could I unilaterally construct "knowledge" on such a complex totality, or recommend anything as "to do" in order to procure its development? On what grounds could I claim that the specific "options" I had taken throughout this long and cumbersome abstraction process were the "correct" options to procure such development effectively?

In the light of this experience, I found myself asking how was I, as a protagonist of this social process of producing knowledge, to ensure that the specific knowledge I was to produce was "adequate" for and would be effectively and successfully used in procuring its stated beneficial ends? The radical separation in space and time between the economic knowledge production process and the social uses made of the resulting knowledge allow for the social agents producing the knowledge to be different from the social agents responsible for taking action based on it (in this case, the state). Further, there is a still more radical separation between both of these two social agents and the people directly and radically affected by the production and use of knowledge — the "investigated" community itself (in my case, the rural community of Garcia Rovira).

It was clear to me that in these social forms of producing and using economic, scientific knowledge there was no communication whatsoever between science (myself as an academic economist) and society (the rural community of Garcia Rovira).

The question of the political legitimacy of conventional social forms of producing and using economic knowledge is, to me, strikingly similar to the question Paulo Freire, the well-known Brazilian educator, had to face when he called into question the legitimacy of "conventional" forms of education. For Freire, the "conventional" form of education, which he called "banking" education,

> becomes an act of depositing, in which the students are the depositories and the teacher is the depositor. Instead of communicating, the teacher issues communiqués and makes deposits which the students patiently receive, memorize, and repeat. ... Knowledge is a gift bestowed by those who consider themselves knowledgeable upon those whom they consider to know nothing. Projecting an absolute ignorance onto others, a characteristic of the ideology of oppression, negates education and knowledge as processes of inquiry.[1]

Similarly, the "conventional" social forms in which economists — uni-

---

[1] Paolo Freire, *The Pedagogy of the Oppressed* (New York: The Continuum Publishing Corporation, 1970), pp. 58-9.

laterally, not dialogically — construct knowledge, and the separation between the production and the use of economic knowledge, transform "knowledge" into a fetishized commodity whose "production," "circulation," and "use" can be separated in space and time. In the conventional forms of producing and using economic knowledge, the economists isolate themselves from the communities they investigate; the investigated community's perception of its realities is always abstracted by the economist in the name of an "objective, scientific knowledge."

This "separation," in turn, produces a political effect of the utmost importance: an authoritarian power is consistently exerted by social researchers on their investigated communities. Feyerabend was right when he denounced the intellectuals — in this case, economists — as people who

> have so far succeeded ... in preventing a more direct democracy where problems are solved and solutions judged by those who suffer from the problems and have to live with the solutions.... [They] have fattened themselves on the funds thus diverted in their direction. It is time to realize that they (the intellectuals) are just one special and rather greedy group held together by a special and rather aggressive tradition.[2]

To develop alternative social forms for producing and using economic knowledge, in which these separations are superseded, has meant for me in my more recent work, among other things, that my responsibility as a "development economist" in front of a community could not be limited to the conventional "academic" task of producing an economic knowledge and making a set of formal recommendations. I also had to be responsible for the use — or misuse — that would be made of this knowledge, and for the concrete social effects that the knowledge I was to produce would have (or would not have) on the community over time. In other words, my responsibilities as a development economist comprise the *political* problem (in the broadest sense) of how my activities as a social researcher will ultimately affect the living conditions of the community, not just the academic or technical problem of constructing knowledge to justify — in front of social agents different from the investigated community (the state, for example) — a set of formal economic policy recommendations. It has meant abandoning the comfortable position of being accountable only for "analyzing and recommending," to be held responsible, in front of the real individuals and households that constitute the community, for the concrete social effects that my produced

---

[2] Paul Feyerabend, *Science in a Free Society* (Norfolk: Verso Editions, 1982), pp. 85-6.

knowledge might have on their living conditions.

But I could not assume this new responsibility unilaterally. I had to develop radically new forms of knowledge production and use; I had to start a collective reflection process to identify and thoroughly analyze (understand) a few concrete problems: to start communication between the academic economist and the community, to achieve a collective and integrated process of knowledge production. The crucial contribution of this process has been to provide us — by "us" I mean the new community of peasants and academic economists that this process has been progressively engendering — with a collective experience, within which a collective knowledge about the numberless complexities of concrete problems has been constructed (by reflection) and used (in action). New channels of communication between science (academic economists) and society (the communities with which economists are doing impact evaluations of government development programs) are being constructed, out of which "new" knowledge is being produced. The conventional separation between subject and object in the production and use of knowledge has been superseded; thus, no totalitarian power is being exerted by science on society. And the knowledge itself that is being produced is not any more a commoditied "finished" product: it is now a permanently changing process that is increasingly becoming a constitutive element of the daily life of this "new" community.

The broader, most profound implication of this research experience as I have lived it — and made sense of it — is political: it has revealed to me the totalitarian nature of the exercise of social power that is ingrained in the conventional forms of producing and using economic knowledge. This pattern in the exercising of social power is embedded in the radical separation between, on the one hand, the few individuals who participate in the production and use of economic knowledge and, on the other, the masses of people who, in spite of being the most deeply affected by these processes, are maintained as nonparticipant objects in the production and use of this knowledge.

A second crucial matter I have learned has to do with the critical importance of collective participation by academics and the "investigated" communities in the process of production and use of economic knowledge that will affect the living conditions of the communities. Attaining this participation requires tremendous efforts in the construction of communication channels between science (economists) and society (the "investigated" communities). These communication channels can be constructed only if economists are willing to stop ignoring (abstracting), in their research practices, the cultural complexity of how the communities they "investigate" perceive their own realities. Communication between economic science and society will not be possible unless economists understand and fully accept in their research practices Feyerabend's striking proposition: "I am not looking for new theories of science; I am asking if the search for such theories is a reasonable undertaking and I conclude that it is not. The knowledge we need to understand and to advance the sciences does not come from theories, it comes from participation."

As for the role of the academic economist, this experience has taught me that it cannot be any more that of an "external" agent in charge of the limited and able task of "producing" knowledge to justify "recommendations." Such a role leads only to undesirable scenarios: the production and circulation of useless knowledge and recommendations that nobody takes seriously; or the use of knowledge and recommendations as weapons to exert subtle but violent forms of social power through science. This second scenario — the worst of the two — is eloquently described by Michel Foucault:

> In fact we know from experience that the claim to escape from the system of contemporary reality so as to produce the overall programs of another society, of another way of thinking, another culture, another vision of the world, has led only to the return of the most dangerous traditions.[3]

Alan Watts, in his book, *TAO, The Watercourse Way*, observes that:

> Government is simply an abandonment of responsibility on the assumption that there are people, other than ourselves, who can really know how to manage things. But the government, run ostensibly for the good of people, becomes a self-serving corporation. To keep things under control it proliferates laws of ever-increasing complexity and unintelligibility, and hinders productive work by demanding so much accounting on paper that the record of what has been done becomes more important than what has actually been done.[4]

In my long and intense research experience with economic development programs in so-called "underdeveloped" rural areas, I could clearly see happening what Watts describes. The well-intended efforts by the government's central offices to direct and control the actions of all the social agents involved in these programs — direction and control functions that are always exerted in the name of certain preconceived objec-

---

[3]   Michel Foucault, *Power/Knowledge* (New York: Pantheon Books, 1980), p. 46.

[4]   Alan Watts, *TAO, The Watercourse Way* (New York: Pantheon Books, 1975), pp. 81-2.

tives — led inexorably to the development of rules, norms, and policies of "ever-increasing complexity and unintelligibility" that suffocated everyone — including the government institutions responsible for the development programs to begin with.

But these programs generated even more serious problems at the social and political level. One that I could see very clearly was how government actions, as they are generally conceived and implemented in these "development programs," engendered profound paternalistic relationships that, paradoxically, reproduced and deepened human underdevelopment in those communities that were supposed to be the beneficiaries, as they were led (by these programs) to systematically expect others (e.g., governments, experts) to solve their problems — because they were led to see themselves as "ones who do not know."

Today, I can see no essential difference between this "expanded reproduction" of human underdevelopment, through paternalism in the government's "development" programs, and what we do in the classroom when we "teach" as we usually do. The role of the "development experts" with the communities on which they carry out their research is, in this sense, very similar to the role of the "teachers" with their students. In both cases, the relationship is governed by the alienating assumption that one has the knowledge that the other lacks and has to learn. This is why the concept of knowledge, and the use we make of it in both our teaching and our research activities, has become a significant political problem for me. Again, Watts writes:

> The game of Western philosophy and science is to trap the universe in networks of words and numbers, so that there is always the temptation to confuse rules, or laws, of grammar and mathematics with the actual operations of nature. We must not, however, overlook the fact that human calculation is also an operation of nature; but just as trees do not represent or symbolize rocks, our thoughts — even if intended to do so — do not necessarily represent trees and rocks.[5]

My conviction is that in our educational and social research practices we are permanently treating the concepts and ideas we "teach" and "use" as if they were "the actual operations of nature." Since in our educational institutions and research projects it is always assumed — even in many of those institutions that theoretically reject this assumption — that the teachers or researchers "know" and the students or investigated communities "don't know," the students and communities are never given

---

[5]   Ibid., p. 42.

opportunity to express and describe their own experiences and knowledge in their own ways and words. The education/research processes' objective is rather the opposite: to "teach" the student and communities to express themselves in the professors' and researchers' ways and words since they are, by assumption, "the ones who know."

Since the fall of 1988, I have been exploring different teaching formats trying to create conditions in which students can express themselves authentically. This has posed a serious challenge to my own capacity to listen to them. Both tasks — to create the conditions for them to be able to express themselves authentically and to develop my own capacity to listen to, and understand, what they want to express — have proved to be much more difficult and revealing than I could have expected: it has demanded a tremendous effort on my part to understand and transform my own biases, prejudices, and mental preconceptions as a professor, in both the content and the process of my teaching — biases, prejudices, and preconceptions that, as I have gradually discovered, pervasively obstruct communication with my students and their own personal development.

Thus, embedded in, and hidden behind these concrete day-to-day human relationships — teacher-student, researcher-researched, boss-subordinate, government-civil society — there is a deep, tough, invisible, political education process that we usually ignore and/or overlook. I call this invisible education process in which people learn so thoroughly — though mostly unconsciously — "political education by experience." I want to draw a sharp distinction between this invisible political-education-by-experience and what I would call a "visible process of political education" (to refer to what we usually do in the classroom — "teaching as usual"): *there* we take given, already constructed knowledge ("networks of words and numbers") about politics — contained in books, articles, or in professors' heads — and "teach" it to our students. This kind of visible education (and the same is true of research) process is, I think, starkly separated from concrete day-to-day human experiences; and it is my feeling that because of that dichotomy, this kind of education (or research) does more harm than good. It is inevitable that together with this visible political education process — intended to affect students' (or community members') intellects — there is also an invisible political-education-by-experience process that affects students' real life in the classroom (or a community's real life in the research experience).

I want to underscore that this invisible political education process is not explicitly and openly acknowledged as a constructive part of the education or research process. But life and mind *are* thus separated in the classroom and research practices; and this separation carries with it profound and harmful contradictions. For example, we often "teach" democratic theories in the classroom ("networks of words and numbers") while practicing, at the experiential level of teacher-student relationships ("actual operations of nature"), the nondemocratic exercise of power that is generally embedded in it. In other words, we "teach" one type of politics at the discursive level, and we "do" a different politics in our practices in the classroom. Because of this profound dichotomy between "discourse" and "practice" we lead our students to "learn" a very sophisticated "discourse" on democracy which they reproduce eloquently without changing anything at all in their day-to-day life to practice the democratic theories they are knowledgeable about. This is how, at the university, we end up producing tyrants who are intellectual experts on democracy.

Does it make sense for me to conceive, as one of my tasks, the education of others for political life? I find the notion of educating others problematic when the process of education is conceived and practiced in the conventional way — teaching as usual — of transferring a given, structured knowledge to other people through discursive means. An increasing number of experiences have shown me that when I practice this kind of education I alienate people, kill individual creativity, and bury extremely valuable knowledge and personal motivations. These kinds of educational practices operate on the assumption that the processes of "production" and "circulation" of knowledge, and then the "use" of this knowledge, are tasks that have to occupy separate moments in space and time, and be performed by different people. By doing so, by transforming knowledge into commodities, we separate the "knowledgeable people" from the "unknowledgeable people," and thus we create the conditions under which our teaching and research practices become, in themselves, nondemocratic practices in which a totalitarian exercise of power is systematically exerted by the "knowledgeable" on the "unknowledgeable."

I am more convinced every day that it is only through my own personal self-education for political life — conceiving self-education not as a process of accumulating discursive knowledge but rather as a continuous, endless practice in exploring new specific ways to relate to people in the classroom, in my research, etc. ("the actual operations of nature") — that I can effectively recruit others — my students, my peers, my bosses, my research assistants, the members of the communities I do my research with — to join with me in a collective, continuous, and open process of educating ourselves for political life.

My work as a teacher and as a social researcher is profoundly political. I may not deal with politics and political life as subjects to be studied in my courses or in my research projects: there are no readings assigned on this topic, no questions in the exams that require my students to "use" any formal "knowledge" on politics and political life. Yet, in the very processes of "teaching" and "constructing knowledge," when I give a class, coordinate a meeting, collect a survey, etc., I am teaching my students and the investigated communities — teaching them in a profound way, through the experience they live out in the classroom and in research activities — much more about politics and political life than I would if these topics were dealt with as "subjects" of study in the conventional way.

Peter Levine

Deliberation and Technical Reasoning: The Role of the Humanities in a Democracy[1]

In political debates, there often seem to be two potential paths to wisdom. The first is technical, employing the skills and knowledge of economists, scientists, lawyers, and other experts. The second arises from public deliberation, and is the result of an inclusive, democratic dialogue that focuses on values.

Technical discourse involves the application of general theories to particular cases. These theories, in turn, have been developed through a process of generalization and deductive reasoning. A theory is supposed to be testable, and usually it *has* been tested in a more or less rigorous fashion.

No one would claim that we can live without scientific and social-scientific theories. For instance, we are helpless in the face of environmental perils unless we understand the way that ecosystems and human activities interact — in large part, a scientific question. But this question assumes that we already know the *end* that we seek (environmental protection); science offers to show us the *means* that we must employ to reach that end. If we value two ends at once (say, environmental protection and economic growth), then science may be able to clarify the necessary trade-offs. But science does not pretend to teach us about values per se, nor about their relative weight.

Nevertheless, we need answers to normative questions: questions about ends or values. In this realm, we again seem to have two options.

[1] This article is a version of a chapter from my book entitled *Living Without Philosophy* (in manuscript). The original chapter places similar material in a different context and offers a more detailed reading of Plato's *Protagoras*.

The first is technical, and assumes that there can be a rough analogy between scientific reasoning and moral reflection. Adopting this approach, we would try to develop a technique that would tell us, in general, what is the right thing to do in any situation. Armed with such a theory, we could settle questions about ends much as scientists answer questions about means. This kind of technical solution to moral problems has been proposed over the centuries by many philosophers, theologians, and social scientists. Among the general rules of behavior that they have proposed are the following: "maximize utility," "give the proletariat control over the means of production," "obey the Ten Commandments," "never interfere with personal freedom," and so on.

So-called "ordinary people" — people who lack professional credentials — sometimes offer technical arguments when they participate in political deliberation about values. They may refer to general principles of a philosophical or theological nature. However, there is an alternative way of thinking about values that is far more common in public discussions. Unlike the technical approach, this method is open to everyone, without regard to special training or knowledge, although some people are better at it than others. It is more an art than a science, learned by experience rather than by the acquisition of facts or techniques. It is — to be more specific — a matter of describing particular actions or situations in a judgmental way.

A single act can be called many things at once: for example, a case of "squeezing a metal object" might simultaneously be an instance of "firing a gun," "killing a person," and even "a heinous murder." As we move from the "thinnest" vocabulary toward the "thickest" phrases, we find ourselves increasingly committed to value judgments. Squeezing metal objects is morally neutral; killing someone can be justifiable in certain contexts; but a murder is clearly bad. "Thick" descriptions support value judgments, and they are not arbitrary, subjective, or indefensible. In order to know that a particular instance of squeezing a metal object is also a case of murder, we have to describe the event in a broader context, explaining what happened in the light of other events, the participants' psychological states, their other options, the cultural background, and so on. Enough information of this kind can make a simple muscular movement look like a heinous murder — and appropriately so.

By describing acts, policy alternatives, and even whole social situations in "thick," value-laden ways, people support their beliefs and thus try to convince their fellow citizens about values and ends. The art of "thick" description does not invoke general theories or deductive reasoning; instead, it often makes use of narratives and rich, evocative depictions of reality. These techniques are the specialty of novelists, historians, visual artists, filmmakers, literary critics, and preachers — in a word, humanists. Therefore, the conflict between technical expertise and "thick" description resembles the ancient dispute between philosophy (which *tells* us what is right in general), and the humanities (which *show* us what is right in particular cases). For the purposes of this article, I will call defenders of deliberative judgment "humanists," in contrast to philosophers and other technical experts.

The conflict between these two approaches raises questions about the proper role of democracy. Technical arguments have clear solutions, like the answers to mathematics puzzles. Therefore, if we can solve moral problems with technical arguments, then we do not need inclusive public deliberation. On the contrary, if we include many untrained citizens in public debates, this may obscure the truth as it is known by technicians. Only a few technical experts are needed to arrive at the truth; everyone else might as well worry about other things. "Thick" description, on the other hand, must prove itself in public debate. Whether I have shown something persuasively through my rhetoric only becomes clear if someone else agrees with me. The more people agree with me, the more persuasive I am. Therefore, if thick description is the proper method for addressing questions of value, then deliberative democracy is indispensable — and the more of it, the better.

It is not easy to settle a debate between technical reasoning and deliberation, or between philosophy and the humanities, or between technocracy and democracy. We could make certain assumptions that would support one side or the other. For example, a defender of rhetoric may assume that a speaker's ability to persuade other people under fair conditions shows the moral value of his or her position; thus consensus is evidence of validity. But some philosophers have denied that agreement can tell us anything about truth: after all, Hitler won many converts through his rhetoric. Likewise, some people believe that all rational statements must be verifiable. Thus they may prefer "thick" descriptions (which can be supported by stories) over moral theories, which often seem unverifiable. But, under a different definition of "verification," theories may seem more verifiable than "thick" descriptions. In any case, all of this discussion is typically philosophical (i.e., abstract, theoretical, and technical), which means that it only carries weight if we are predisposed to favor philosophy in the first place.

Apparently, Plato realized that it is difficult to discuss the conflict between philosophy and humanism impartially. Nevertheless, he wanted to decide what role philosophy ought to play in public and private life.

Therefore, he worked out a profoundly illuminating synthesis, the Socratic dialogue, which incorporates elements of logical argument while simultaneously presenting participants as "thickly" described literary characters, whose methods and values can be judged morally. In the *Protagoras,* the quintessential philosopher, Socrates, debates a great rhetorician and democrat, Protagoras. They discuss moral education, the role of democracy and, above all, the extent to which moral questions are subject to technical solutions. The dialogue ends in a draw, and Plato neither tells us, nor clearly shows us, which contender he prefers. Nevertheless, he reveals what is at stake in their debate with unsurpassed clarity. At the same time, he presents us with a choice between two impressively wise characters, either of whom we can choose to imitate.

Historical Background

Protagoras was a Sophist. He and his colleagues studied history and literature, probably because they viewed these disciplines as repositories of moral, practical, and stylistic examples. As part of this project, they wrote some of the earliest books of literary criticism. In addition, they studied grammar and philology (Protagoras may have discovered grammatical moods and gender); and some even devised whole philosophies of language.

What defined them as a movement, however, was their profession as teachers. In Plato's dialogue, the character Protagoras describes his pedagogical method as follows:

> The works of the best poets are set before [children] to read on the classroom benches, and they are compelled to learn them thoroughly; and in these works are displayed many warnings, many detailed narratives and praises and eulogies of good men of ancient times, so that the boy may desire to imitate them competitively and may stretch himself to become like them.[2]

Against the Sophists, Socrates argued that a theory of the good was always necessary if people were to know whether an individual act that was described in a narrative was worthy of praise or contempt. In the *Phaedrus,* he remarks, "no one will ever be able to speak about anything appropriately, unless he has sufficient knowledge of philosophy."[3] But Protagoras wrote a book called the *Antilogiae (Contrasting Arguments),* in which he probably attempted to undermine the discipline of phi-

---

[2] *Protagoras,* 325e-326a. I translate all Plato passages from the Oxford Edition of J. Burnet (1958).

[3] *Phaedrus,* 261a 4-5.

losophy by offering arguments on both sides of each question.[4] Although he believed that philosophy was pointless, he had an alternative approach in mind, which he described in his famous aphorisms.

First, he said: "man is the measure of all things." He probably did not mean that things *are* just as each person sees them (a dogmatic philosophical theory). Instead, he may have meant that human beings and their experiences are the only available standard or criterion of truth, since philosophy cannot help us solve problems. In the *Theaetetus*, Socrates glosses Protagoras' man-is-the-measure doctrine as follows: "For whatever *seems* to be just and beautiful to each city, *is* such for that city, as long as the city considers it so; but the wise man causes the good — rather than that which is evil for each in each situation — to be and to appear."[5] Note that the protagonist in this sentence is "the city," not any individual; thus truth is a product of social agreement. There appears to be an inconsistency between the first and second parts of the formula: according to the first clause, anything that seems good, is good (thus "man is the measure of all things"); but then it turns out that a wise person makes what *actually is* good seem so. This inconsistency disappears if we assume that what is good is only identifiable as such if it succeeds in satisfying public opinion over the long term. Then the foolish person is the one who persuades people to adopt a wrong course of action, but — if the policy is wrong — then the error of their ways will soon become clear to them.

In short, the test of wisdom is pragmatic: the wise person produces enduringly popular results by promoting policies that are good insofar as they seem good over time. Protagoras was active in politics: he taught many prominent politicians and wrote a constitution for the new panhellenic city of Thurii. He was said to be of humble origin and a close advisor to Pericles, so he was probably a democrat. Thus he may have believed that truth was a product of democratic discussion, aimed at consensus.

In another phrase that is securely attributable to Protagoras, he said that one should "make the lesser reason *[logos]* stronger." In Aristophanes' parody of the Sophists, *The Clouds*, a character called the Wrong Reason actually engages the Right Reason in a brawl.[6] Many contemporaries seem to have thought that Protagoras wanted to play devi-

---

[4]   According to Seneca, letter 88, §43: "Protagoras asserts that it is possible to argue equally well on either side of any question, including the question whether both sides of all questions can be argued." I translate from the Latin text in C. D. N. Costa, ed., *Seneca: Seventeen Letters* (Warminster, 1988).

[5]   *Theaetetus*, 167c.

[6]   *The Clouds*, 890ff; cf. 112 ff.

ous, "sophistical" games in which the wrong argument was made to look right by the force of rhetoric. In fact, he never said that he could make false arguments appear true.[7] Rather, he wanted to support arguments (i.e., make them stronger), but without proving them to be absolutely true. He operated in the realm of rhetoric, but did not deny that some arguments could be made stronger than others. The best *logos* was the one that appeared strongest of all after efforts had been made to support every alternative view. Thus eristic, or competitive argument, was a device for testing truth; it was not a game.

Above all, people could try to persuade others of their moral vision by producing new works of literature and history, by making speeches laced with literary and historical examples, and by offering interpretations of poems and events. This, Protagoras thought, was the most pragmatically effective way to make the lesser *logos* stronger. At best, the process of comparing *logoi* might lead to the formation of a consensus, after adequate and well-informed discussion. As a result of this consensus, policies might emerge that would make the condition of the state *seem* better to its members — and this was all that Protagoras promised.

The Dialogue: Opening

Like many of Plato's works, the *Protagoras* is actually a dialogue within a dialogue. In the opening lines, Socrates is asked by an anonymous companion where he has been all morning. The companion assumes that Socrates has been pursuing the "very charming" Alcibiades. No, Socrates replies, he has discovered a "much fairer love" — Protagoras of Abdera, with whom Socrates has just had an encounter. So beautiful was Protagoras' intellect that it made Socrates completely forget Alcibiades, whom he describes entirely in physical terms. Socrates then proceeds to relate what happened between him and Protagoras.

This opening draws attention to the status of the work as a piece of literature narrated by one of the participants. This is not going to be an abstract philosophical tract; it will be a drama narrated from a contingent, immanent perspective. On the other hand, Socrates' preference for Protagoras over Alcibiades implies that *he* seeks pure intellectual insight, free from the contingencies of personality and circumstance. Protagoras is attractive not because of how he looks or even who he is, but because of the abstract content of his thought. But this sets Socrates somewhat at odds with the form of the dialogue, for Plato takes great pains to depict personalities as charming or obnoxious, and he carefully locates the work

---

[7] See Aristotle, *Rhetoric* II, 24 1402a23.

at a particular place and time.

Socrates' philosophical method (*techne*) is a central theme of the *Protagoras*. It is a method for measuring the objective value of actions and objects, so that we can make correct moral decisions free from all randomness and luck (*tuche*). Near the end of the dialogue, he says: "the art of measurement [*metrike techne*] would invalidate the effect of mere appearance and, showing the truth, would finally cause the soul to abide in peace with the truth, and so save its life" (356d). Socrates' metaphor of measuring suggests that the true value of everything is comparable on a single scale. Anyone who knows how to measure objective value can maximize the moral quality of his or her actions in a perfectly rational way. People who hold Socrates' view may distrust stories that employ rhetoric and "thick" description, and that are told from one participant's perspective; they probably prefer objective, detached arguments. Therefore, Socrates might disapprove of the dialogue in which he appears.

Socrates deliberately eschews the particular love of Alcibiades in order to discuss a general, abstract calculus of value. In general, anyone who believes in such a calculus must denigrate romantic love, because this means devotion to a particular person, i.e., devotion that is not exchangeable for any other value at any cost. Protagoras, on the other hand, later rejects the metaphor of measurement and the idea that all goods are mutually commensurable. Thus the basic issues to be addressed in the dialogue are as follows: First, is there a *techne* that can help us to make ethical decisions securely, universally, and with rigor? And second, who possesses the better technique for overcoming luck, Socrates or Protagoras?

Socrates visits Protagoras at the urging of a young man, Hippocrates, who hopes to study with the great Sophist. On their way to see Protagoras, Socrates and this young man conduct a philosophical discussion. Socrates uses their conversation to sow some doubts about Sophistic methods.

He first asks Hippocrates what he expects to learn from Protagoras. If someone wanted to learn sculpture, Socrates says, he would study with Pheidias; but what can a young man learn from a Sophist? Hippocrates is embarrassed by the obvious answer: that he would learn to be a Sophist. In the classical period, Sophists had a dubious reputation and an ambiguous social status. Socrates therefore rescues Hippocrates with another suggestion. What one can gain from a Sophist, he says, is an education that "suits a freeman and a layman" (312b). Sophists offer improvement for the soul, rather than specialized knowledge; they make their students into better people and better citizens. But Socrates is concerned that Hippocrates may not know in advance how to judge Protagoras' wares. If you want to buy a horse, you must first examine it to make sure it is sound. But education for the soul is a more important — and riskier — matter. Once ingested, a piece of knowledge immediately takes its irreversible effect, even if the recipient decides he would rather not accept the treatment after all.

Socrates sets the terms of his argument with Protagoras on ground best suited to his methods. Prior to any ethical education, he implies, is a true understanding of the good. Any ideas that Protagoras imparted would be either good or evil, depending on their relation to abstract moral truths. If philosophical analysis revealed that Protagoras was teaching good ideas, then Hippocrates should study with him; otherwise, he should shun the treatment. Thus, before anyone studies under Protagoras, he should first learn the skill that Socrates practices: philosophy. Socrates' analytic method has already reduced Hippocrates to confusion; and he plans to use it also against Protagoras. He plans to analyze Protagoras' methods to determine their consistency and correspondence to the Good as revealed by philosophy.

In general, Socrates believes that correct use of dialectic (a kind of technical reasoning), rather than majority opinion or personal experience, is the criterion of wisdom. However, at the end of his discussion with Hippocrates, he concludes that he cannot decide for sure whether Sophists are good or bad for the soul: this question lies beyond the reach of his dialectic. Therefore, he agrees to go with Hippocrates to visit Protagoras, giving two reasons for this risky decision. First, Protagoras and the other Sophists are old, whereas he and Hippocrates are "too young to decide such matters" (314b). Second, Protagoras is not alone, but is accompanied by many other Sophists. Thus, when it comes to the meta-question of whether moral issues should be addressed with humanistic or philosophical methods, Socrates at least initially gives a humanistic response. Like Protagoras himself (cf. 320c), Socrates asserts that age, experience, and majority opinion are criteria of truth — but only when the question is whether to rely on philosophy rather than experience and human consensus. At least so far, Socrates seems to agree with Plato, for Plato uses a humanistic vehicle, the dialogue, to address the conflict between philosophy and humanism. However, when Socrates actually encounters Protagoras, he will use his dialectical methods to criticize the Sophist.

When Socrates and Hippocrates arrive at the house where Protagoras is staying, a eunuch slave opens the door, sees the two men talking, and slams it shut again, mumbling, "Ha! Some Sophists! He's busy" (314d). The fact that the slave has already had enough of Sophists at dawn suggests that they are something like a cult: they are so obsessed with Protagoras' teaching that they have come to see him in large numbers when most ordinary people are still asleep. Upon finally gaining entrance to the house (which belongs to Callias, the richest man in Athens) the visitors see Protagoras strolling back and forth accompanied by numerous admirers, who hang on his every word. Distributed around the house are many of the most important thinkers of the day, engaged in their separate intellectual specialties; the scene looks like Raphael's "School of Athens." Plato weaves into this description several allusions to Book XI of the *Odyssey* (Odysseus' voyage to Hades), suggesting that the Sophists have something in common with dead souls. Thus the dialogue uses literary references to criticize people who take a literary approach to morals.

Socrates now approaches Protagoras and introduces Hippocrates as a young man of talent and political ambition. Protagoras seems wary of Socrates and slightly defensive. Without provocation, he gives a speech defending Sophism as an "ancient *techne*," and identifying many of the greatest Greek poets, musicians, and even gymnasts of the past as Sophists (316d). Homer, Hesiod, and Simonides, he says, were secret Sophists, afraid to bear the title publicly because of the odium attached to it; whereas he (Protagoras) is more honest and dares to advertise his profession openly. Thus Protagoras identifies his version of Sophism as a self-conscious form of the humanistic tradition that Homer founded.

Protagoras offers to speak with Socrates about his teaching methods. But Socrates says that he believes that Protagoras would rather hold forth in front of an audience, so he asks everyone to gather and listen to Protagoras' speech. It is difficult to tell whether Socrates is really trying to please Protagoras by assembling an audience, or whether he hopes to embarrass Protagoras publicly with his dialectical skills. The historical Protagoras apparently believed that the validity of an argument lay in its capacity to produce consensus; so he would have good reason to desire an audience. On the other hand, Socrates might want to imply that his method, too, can convince the many, although this is not his criterion of truth. In any case, Socrates begins the conversation over again so that everyone can hear. The purpose of his visit, he repeats, is to introduce Hippocrates, who "would be glad to hear what will really happen to him if he associates with you. That is all we have to say."

Protagoras directs his response to Hippocrates: "Young man," he says, "if you associate with me, on the day that you first converse with me you will be able to return home a better person, and better on the second day than the first, and each day after that you will grow ceaselessly better" (318a). Socrates politely replies that he is not surprised: Protagoras is old and wise, and anyone would be better off who was exposed to his knowledge. But, Socrates asks, what does Protagoras' wisdom consist in? What is the content of his teaching? Protagoras answers that he teaches "good counsel about domestic matters — how best to administer a household — and also about civic matters: how to speak and act most powerfully in the affairs of the state" (318e-319a). Protagoras thereby avoids answering Socrates' question exactly as asked. Socrates wanted to know the *content* of the Sophist's teaching (i.e., his philosophy, or what he believes), but Protagoras describes his pragmatic goal: the making of persuasive citizens. If Protagoras possessed a theory of the good, then being educated under him would be a simple and brief process; the student would just listen as he articulated his theory. Thus one would not grow "ceaselessly better" by studying under him; the whole process would be over and done with quickly. Socrates wants Protagoras to announce his theory, so that it can be debated. However, Protagoras does not claim to possess a theory of the good; rather he promises to fashion skillful citizens, a process that inevitably takes time. Socrates asks whether he means that he teaches the art of politics. Protagoras assents.

Socrates now states the thesis that he will defend through most of the dialogue: virtue, he says, cannot be taught. He supports this assertion by pointing out that everyone is allowed to argue in the assembly about moral matters, without being taught by experts in the "political *techne*," whereas no one can claim expertise in shipbuilding (for example) until he has had tuition under a master shipbuilder. This thesis puts Protagoras in an apparently difficult position. On one hand, he could say that virtue must be taught by an expert, just like shipbuilding, in which case no one who lacked a Sophist for a tutor could be a decent citizen. But this conclusion sounds implausible: Achilles and Theseus never had the advantage of a Sophistic education, yet they knew what virtue meant. Besides, this view would be undemocratic and might get Protagoras into trouble in Periclean Athens. Alternatively, he could admit that many people understand virtue without professional assistance — but then his own services would appear worthless.

Protagoras asks Socrates whether he would like to hear an answer in the form of a *mythos* (story), told by an older man to a younger, or whether he would prefer to continue the dialectical exchange. Socrates leaves the choice up to Protagoras, who opts to tell a story. Just by making this decision, Protagoras has already said something important about his methods. As a Sophist, he prefers to *show* people what he has learned as a man of worldly experience, rather than engaging in an *a priori,* logical exchange.

The "Great Speech"

Protagoras'"Great Speech"is a creation story, borrowed (with original additions) from Greek myth. In the beginning, the Titan Epimetheus gave all the animals except man means of defending themselves: shells, claws, or quick feet. Man had nothing — no "capacities" at all — until Prometheus recognized the mistake and provided people with knowledge of the arts and the making of fire. They then "discovered, by means of their *techne,* articulate speech and names," as well as religion, agriculture, and crafts (322a). If human beings had no capacities at all until they were given culture, then they *were* nothing without it. Protagoras says that Epimetheus had left man *acosmetos*: unorganized, unarranged, or unprovided. The Greek word means the opposite of "cosmos," which is a comprehensible order formed out of chaos. Thus one fairly clear implication of Protagoras' story is that there is no "human nature" that can be appealed to as a foundation for philosophical theories, and no coherent essence of humanity that is more fundamental than the diverse beliefs, techniques, and experiences of concrete human beings. If true, this idea would have dire consequences for Socrates, who is always trying to arrive at universal definitions of things like "man."

According to Protagoras, early human beings possessed religion and practical arts, but they did not know how to get along with each other, so they fell into fratricidal conflict. Prometheus had wanted to give them political wisdom, but this was hidden away in Zeus' citadel, where he could not venture. Fortunately, Zeus, fearing that the human race would perish, ordered Hermes to bring shame and justice to human communities (322c). Hermes asked whether these qualities should be given to only a few people. Zeus replied, on the contrary, that everyone should possess them; and those who didn't should be killed as enemies of the peace. Protagoras concludes that it is right for everyone to participate in peaceful political deliberations, even if their endowments of Promethean skills and virtues happen to be unequal. This is a basic principle of democracy: the assumption that people with different types or amounts of ability, aptitude, and education nevertheless possess equal political rights. Protagoras, after all, believes that moral and political questions have no correct answers that can be deduced by means of a specialized intellectual process, such as Socrates' dialectic. To practice medicine or to navigate a ship requires study of the relevant Promethean disciplines; but the truth about moral questions can only be ascertained as a result of an inclusive dialogue. The right answer *just is* the one that seems best to everyone, so everyone must be able to participate in political discourse.

Somewhat later in the dialogue (323b), Protagoras asserts that everyone always claims to be on the side of justice in an argument, whereas people do not falsely claim to be able to play the flute. This observation provides support for Protagoras' distinction between Prometheus' arts and Zeus' justice. It also reveals his understanding of the logic of democratic debate, in which participants must always state their own selfish interests in terms of general justice or universal interests, if they hope to achieve consensus. This is how they make the weaker argument stronger. The historical Protagoras apparently believed that the argument that appeared strongest of all at the end of a competitive debate was the best one, so he may have thought that a democratic argument in which everyone *pretended* to justice was an excellent means for discovering what justice actually required.[8]

Protagoras' creation myth may seem to be a kind of social contract doctrine, similar to the ones that Socrates outlines in the *Crito* and *Republic*. These theories treat justice as a natural fact, by suggesting that humans, in a state of nature, would inevitably choose to obey specific laws. But Protagoras forestalls this interpretation of his story, saying that people "do not suppose that virtue is by nature, or something automatic, but a thing that is taught and that is gained by taking pains" (323c). Human beings turned out as they did because Epimetheus happened to make an initial mistake; Prometheus failed in his effort to remedy his brother's error; and then Zeus decided to teach people a form of wisdom that he could have kept to himself. In short, our origins are *contingent,* and so is our continued survival as a species. In the beginning, Zeus need not have decided to educate mankind, and any generation of humans might fail to educate its children. Even if there is nothing natural or inevitable about political virtue, it is still a good thing to teach if we want to prevent anarchy of the kind that befell several Greek cities during Plato's lifetime. Protagoras (characteristically) refers to a literary work, *The Savages* by Pherecrates, to show how awful life would be if Greeks forgot to teach their children virtue.

Protagoras says that moral education takes place every day from birth to death. Parents, nurses, and tutors constantly tell a young child what is — and is not — just, noble, or pious; if the child does not heed them, they punish him. Later, the child is turned over to a schoolmaster, who enlarges his field of moral vision by exposing him to historical and liter-

---

[8] Allusions throughout the dialogue (e.g., 316c, 361d) identify Protagoras with Zeus, and Socrates with Prometheus.

ary texts. Just as his mother tells him that his own acts are good or bad, so the schoolmaster describes the deeds of heroes and villains as noble or base. The method remains the same, but the scope of experience grows larger. Finally, once the child is done with school, he continues to be taught morality by the city's laws, which incorporate the experience of past generations, and evolve to encompass the values of the present. Therefore, Protagoras concludes, knowledge of virtue is universal among Greeks, not because it is inborn, but because the mechanisms for teaching it are so widespread and pervasive. Can virtue be taught? You might as well ask (Protagoras says) whether Greek can be taught. The teachers of language are the same as those of virtue: the entire society. And yet, since virtue comes through experience, some people may be more knowledgeable about it than others, and that is why Protagoras' students "get their money's worth and even more" from him (328b). Protagoras concludes his myth by stating that the following three propositions are all true at once: (1) virtue must be taught; yet (2) virtue is universal among Greeks; yet (3) Sophists are valuable as teachers of virtue. Protagoras' position emerges not out of an *a priori* argument, but out of his "myth" and his detailed description of current social practices. He vindicates inclusive, public dialogue without denigrating education or the importance of the humanities.

Socrates' Technical Response

Socrates says that he is charmed almost out of his wits by Protagoras' speech. At first he does not realize that Protagoras has finished speaking — for a story, unlike a deductive argument, does not have to end at any particular point; there is no QED. Socrates praises Protagoras' beguiling rhetoric, but he says that there is "one tiny obstacle" in Protagoras' position that he is *sure* the great man can clear up, since he has explained so much already (328e). In fact, Socrates intends to use this "tiny" logical difficulty to undermine Protagoras' entire position. He says that Protagoras is better than such great rhetoricians as Pericles, who refuse to engage in question-and-answer but respond to every critical question with another long speech, "like great copper caldrons that reverberate at length when they are struck" (329a-b). Protagoras, in contrast, is capable of dialectic as well as beguiling rhetoric. Therefore, says Socrates, he would now like to engage in dialectic in order to discuss the "tiny obstacle" that he has identified in Protagoras' speech. The trap has been set, and Protagoras must walk into it unless he wants to admit that he is not very good at dialectic.

Socrates now asks how the various virtues (justice, piety, self-control) are related to each other. Are they, for example, parts of one thing, or different names for the same thing? Protagoras, playing along, says that all the virtues are one thing; but, in response to further cross-examination, he adds that they are all one in the way that many facial features can be part of one face. Socrates, however, wants to suggest that all the virtues are actually synonymous — that Virtue is the abstract universal that the various virtues reflect. If this is true, then Protagoras' speech contains an error, for it assigns a different (and contingent) origin to each virtue. Socrates proceeds to lead Protagoras through three technical "proofs," meant to demonstrate, respectively, the *identity* of justice and piety, of wisdom and self-control, and of self-control and justice. Having (allegedly) established these equations, Socrates can conclude that all the virtues are one. If so, then they could not have been given to man at different times and by different deities (one a Titan, the other an Olympian). Furthermore, if all the virtues were identical, then it would be easy to see how the good might be known *a priori*; it would be a single principle implicit in all of our genuinely ethical actions — one that we would recognize instinctively and that philosophers could clarify by means of analysis. Thus Socrates would be right and Protagoras would be wrong: there would be no need for an education in virtue.

The logical kernel of Socrates' first proof runs as follows:

1. Assume that no virtue is like any other (this is to be refuted).
2. Justice is like being just.
3. But holiness is not like being just (from 1).
4. Therefore, holiness is like being not just.
5. Therefore, holiness is like being unjust.
6. But it is inconceivable that holiness is unjust.
7. Therefore, holiness and justice are like each other.
8. Therefore, proposition 1 is false. QED.

As Socrates lays out this argument, Protagoras assents to every step, but he complains several times about the method. At one point, instead of answering "yes" to one of Socrates' questions, he says, "If you like — what difference does it make?" (331c). But Socrates refuses to accept this conditional answer and extracts a "yes." At another stage, Protagoras remarks that things must be more complicated than Socrates is making them seem; nevertheless, he continues to cooperate with the dialectical investigation. But even on Socrates' own terms, the logic of the argument is dubious. Reducing his proof to its skeletal form allows us to see how weak it is (e.g., in the transition from steps 3 to 4, which is an outright error), and how dependent it is on questionable axioms. No such paraphrase of Protagoras' Great Speech would be fair to the original, because its "beguiling" descriptions are essential to its content. But it seems fair to paraphrase Socrates' arguments, because he holds that logic is a matter of pure content, independent of its rhetorical form. However, such analysis makes Socrates' position appear untenable.

For his third proof — the demonstration that self-control and justice are identical — Socrates uses a different method. He begins to outline a theory that "the good" is one thing, and that therefore justice and self-control must be identical, because they both seek the good. Before he can express this view in so many words, he notices that Protagoras is "getting agitated and preparing for a contest and marshalling his forces for a reply" (333e). Given his chance, Protagoras responds that there is no such thing as the good-in-itself, only individual things that are good *for* various species; and he enumerates some examples. This is Protagoras' famous pluralism, used as a rebuttal of Socrates' moral absolutism. According to Protagoras, there is not one common denominator — "the good" — by which the good of all things can be measured; their value is rather contextual and relative to many scales of measurement. For example, Protagoras might say that, even in theory, it is impossible to weigh the value of poetry against that of good nutrition. If this is true, then Socrates' philosophical method would be unable to tell us what is right to do in every case, for some ethical dilemmas would involve incommensurable values.

A Debate about Method

But the argument quickly changes focus. Socrates, protesting a "bad memory," complains that Protagoras has outlined his position in a long speech. He demands shorter answers, i.e., dialectical cross-examination, which must be as free as possible from rhetoric. Protagoras says that he is famous for his long speeches, and that is how he intends to proceed. Socrates says that since *he* cannot engage in a rhetorical competition, he will have to leave. "If you desire to hear Protagoras and me," he tells his host, "you must ask him to answer briefly and keep to the point of the questions, as he did at first; if not, how can there be any dialogue? I was under the impression that there is a difference between coming together to have a dialogue, and making a public speech" (336a-b).[9]

In fact, Protagoras' last speech was not more than 200 words long. But Protagoras did raise numerous points and examples before Socrates

[9]   The word that I translate here as "making a public speech" *(demegorein)* is related to words meaning "the people," "democracy," and "demagogue." Socrates' antidemocratic attitude is manifest throughout the dialogue, and he consistently interprets Protagoras' humanism as democratic.

could respond to each one. Dialectic requires a subject to be analyzed down to its atomic propositions; each one is then assessed separately. But Protagoras' descriptive method demands a more continuous style. Thus Socrates and Protagoras are not merely squabbling about how to compete fairly; they have arrived at a substantial methodological difference. Philosophers like Socrates do not believe that real, human discussions are an ideal forum for discovering truth: they are too contingent, too dependent on the participants' skill, too random in their direction, and too vulnerable to rhetoric. Since philosophers must leave the realm of pure ideas to rejoin ordinary humans in their "cave," they must be willing to engage in real discussions. But, as far as possible, contingency should be banished from these discussions by the introduction of a rigorous method: dialectic.

After some debate about how to proceed, Socrates suggests that Protagoras should conduct the dialectical cross-examination, while he, Socrates, responds. In other words, he implies that the problem is not a conflict between two methods of argument, but simply a disparity in skill that can be remedied by handicapping Protagoras. His suggestion receives widespread approval, and Protagoras is forced to agree to it. Socrates says that there will be no need for a judge to ensure that Protagoras is playing by the rules and asking properly dialectical questions — *everyone* can judge together.

Socrates has successfully won the many over to his side. For Protagoras, consensus is the criterion of truth, but Socrates has persuaded the audience to consider only the degree to which each side is playing by his rules. This is what they are to arrive at a consensus *about.* Nevertheless, Protagoras still has a card up his sleeve: he suggests that "ability in poetry is the most important part of education," and that this ability allows the reader to distinguish ethically "correct" works from "incorrect" ones (339a). Thus Protagoras proposes to continue talking about virtue and to adopt Socrates' dialectical style, but to make literature and literary interpretation the subject of their discussion. In this way, Protagoras presumably hopes to inject some elements of humanism back into an otherwise technical conversation. More specifically, he suggests that they should interpret a poem by Simonides, his "Eulogy to Skopas," because it contains a discussion of virtue.

Simonides and the Problem of Contingency

Socrates and Protagoras do not quote the whole "Eulogy" in their debate, and no other surviving source gives us a complete text of Simonides' poem. All we have are the following lines, which appear in the *Protagoras:*

1   To become a truly good man is difficult:
     Built without a blemish, square in feet and hands and mind.
     [...]
3   And although it comes from a wise man, it does not ring
     true to me,
     The saying of Pittacus that: "It is hard to be good."
5   A god alone has this excellence; and a man cannot help but be
     evil
     If he is overpowered by calamity, and impotent.
     For if things go well, all men are good,
     But all are evil in adversity,
     And those whom the gods favor are most likely to act nobly.
10   Therefore, I will never throw away a portion of my allotted
     life
     Seeking a futile hope, something that cannot be:
     A man wholly without fault among us who take fruit from
     the broad earth.
     But if I find one, I will send you the good news.
     I applaud all those, and love them
15   Freely, who merely commit no atrocity; for even the gods
     Never battle against necessity.
     [...
18   ...] for I am no lover of censure;
     I am satisfied if
20   Someone is less than good, but not too incompetent —
     If he knows the law that benefits the community —
     A sensible man. Such a man I will never
     Reproach. For the race of fools
     Is boundless;
25   And everything is beautiful in which no outright atrocity
     is mixed.[10]

In some respects, Simonides' perspective is as far removed from that of Socrates as possible. Socrates assumes that there is always just one right thing to do in any case, and that this choice is made clear by his philosophical method. No matter what situation arises, however tragic or unlucky it may seem, we always face a moral problem that we can solve; we can always do what is best. Although bad luck can reduce our prosperity, our longevity, our health, and our status, it cannot affect our moral-

---

[10] I translate from J. M. Edmonds, *Lyra Graeca* II (London, 1924), p. 285 n. 2.

ity. Moreover, just people are those who derive happiness from their own morality, which means that they can always be perfectly happy. In any situation, they can be perfectly moral by doing whatever reason demands. In *The Republic,* Socrates describes the proper way to respond to bad luck: "As in a throw of the dice, we should reckon our affairs according to the results, as reason proves to be best, rather than grasping at the calamity like children and wasting time wailing, and should always accustom the soul to engage as quickly as possible in healing and correcting what has fallen and is unsound, eliminating dirges [threnody] with the art of healing" [X.604b-d]. A rational or philosophical response to calamity is, according to Socrates, impossible for those who think in a poetic fashion. Poetic descriptions often make situations look genuinely tragic — i.e., sufficiently horrifying as to paralyze us and devoid of any rational solution. For Socrates, poetic "dirges" are childish; and maturity means a rational art of calculation.

But Simonides (whose surviving works include several "Threnodies") thinks that it is impossible to be a perfectly good person, because necessity rules human affairs and makes us imperfect (see lines 5-9 of the "Eulogy"). This is not just a cynical view of human nature. Simonides even believes that the gods never battle against necessity (line 15), so he seems to be saying that, in principle, there is no escape from contingency. Perhaps he doubts that there is always one right choice, a correct decision demanded by reason. Anyone who believes in tragedy thinks that some situations have no satisfactory solution. Simonides has precisely this tragic perspective, which is most evident in his "Dirges." For example: "All things come to one terrible Charybdis / even great virtues and wealth." Or: "There is no evil / that men should not expect, for in short order / god turns everything upside-down."[11] Nevertheless, Simonides says that he finds beauty in lives that are not truly infamous. One function of his poetry is to make tragic situations appear beautiful. Perhaps this is the meaning of his aphorism: "In necessity even harshness is sweet."[12] The theme of his eulogy to Skopas is the glory of a human life that is lived *as well as possible* in a world of inescapable necessity.

Plato is deeply aware of the conflict between a tragic and a philosophical outlook; he even has Socrates ban tragedy from the ideal republic. Not only a tragic view of life, but also a commitment to pluralism would rule out Socrates' belief that there is always one right thing to do in any case. A tragic view rests on the assumption that some situations

---

[11] Ibid., pp. 28, 33.

[12] Quoted by Plutarch, *Life of Aratus,* 45, in Edmonds, II p. 263.

are *true* dilemmas in which no choice is good. And pluralism assumes that some values are not mutually commensurable — there is no common coin with which to compare them — so reason cannot always tell us which good to choose. Plato presents Socrates as a literary character who is almost supernaturally immune to contingency, who has brought his life under the control of a philosophical *techne* that allows him to measure the true worth of any choice. But in the process, Socrates has lost sight of the complexity and tragic struggle that is celebrated by Simonides; his life is in some ways sterile. If Simonides is right, and there is no rational technique that can ever guarantee happiness or morality, then literature gains a crucial function. For literature can help us to depict one choice as more attractive than another in a difficult situation, although without dialectical certainty. It can also find beauty in the plight of human beings who must make tragic choices between two unpalatable decisions.

Protagoras invokes Simonides' poem, but he does not make it work as well as he could for his own position; he treats it as a kind of philosophical text, and a flawed one at that. By failing to quote any lines (and perhaps stanzas) in which Skopas is described, Protagoras and Socrates make the "Eulogy to Skopas" appear more abstract than it probably was. The success of the original poem would have depended on its portrait of a particular man who was necessarily less than perfect, but still admirable. But Protagoras is perhaps not wholly at fault in mistreating the poem, for Socrates has established rules to govern the debate that require Protagoras to ask dialectical questions — and dialectic is inappropriate to literary interpretation. First, Protagoras asks Socrates whether the poem is "beautiful" and "correct" (339b). Socrates says that it is. Protagoras then asks whether a good poem can contain a contradiction; when Socrates denies this, Protagoras points out an apparent inconsistency between lines one and four of the poem. In line one, Simonides says that it is difficult to become good; but in line four, he says that he disagrees with the aphorism that it is difficult to be good. Protagoras' intention is to use cross-examination to reveal an error in Socrates' judgment, and he is rewarded with partisan cheering that makes Socrates "feel faint, as if I had just been hit by an excellent boxer" (339e).

Socrates now asks whether he may instead lay out a reading of the entire poem in some detail. Although Socrates is violating his own rule that the discussion must remain dialectical, no one complains, and he proceeds. He says that in Sparta and Crete, there is an esoteric tradition of wisdom that is embodied in the pithy sayings of sages like Pittacus. One of these sayings is that it is difficult to be good. Socrates construes

Simonides as rebutting this aphorism by claiming that the difficulty is not to be good, but to be perfect: "built without blemish, square in hands and feet and mind." According to Simonides, it is not merely difficult, but actually impossible, to be perfect. Socrates says that this may be true, in part, because "to be" means to remain permanently in a given state, yet experts in individual arts and crafts are always overcome by bad luck sooner or later. Even doctors and other intellectual specialists — who are "good" because of what they know — inevitably forget their knowledge over time.

Everyone (Simonides, Socrates, and Protagoras) agrees that specialized, Promethean arts do not guarantee durable goodness. Therefore, Simonides favors a moderate kind of civic virtue, which can serve in place of Pittacus' unrealistic standard of perfection. His goal is to avoid outright antisocial behavior and to build a political system in which *satisfactory* results can generally be achieved. Socrates does not state his response to this view immediately, but he prepares the ground for it. He will argue later that there is one supreme Promethean *techne*, the philosophical art of measuring objective value, that allows us to escape luck permanently and decisively.

Socrates implies that the debate between Pittacus and Simonides is an ancient version of his own quarrel with Protagoras. Pittacus used the same style of speaking, *brachylogia* (terse speech), that Socrates claims for himself. He was a philosopher, not a Sophist. Further, according to Socrates, Pittacus' wisdom was best understood and appreciated in Sparta and Crete. These states were known for their heroic asceticism, their "laconic" style of speech, their xenophobia, their distaste for public debate, and their totalitarian opposition to pluralism and contingency. We might imagine that these traits resulted from anti-intellectualism, or even from downright ignorance. However, Socrates asserts that the Spartans and Cretans were actually wise, but they kept their wisdom to themselves. Pittacus was a tyrant, but a benevolent one. As a philosopher, he knew what was objectively best for his subjects, so they had no need for democratic debate.

By contrast, Simonides argued in public; he defended a pragmatic or realistic approach to ethics; he was a cosmopolitan; and he debated competitively, trying to beat Pittacus and thereby enhance his own reputation. Simonides was a particularly successful teacher, an epistemological skeptic, and a pioneer in the study of language. He was also a friend of the democratic leader, Themistocles, just as Protagoras was Pericles' friend. His belief in the democratic, deliberative process may account for his statement that "the city teaches man."[13] Unlike the ancient Spartan sages, he had a reputation for wordiness and digression. In all these respects, Simonides resembled Protagoras, who earlier in the dialogue claimed him as a Sophistic forebear (316d).

Although Socrates' interpretation of Simonides' ode is implausible in places, he speaks eloquently and makes the poem appear relevant to his debate with Protagoras. On the other hand, he fails to advance the discussion of virtue. Protagoras had tried to show his mettle by catching Socrates in a purely logical inconsistency; Socrates escaped the trap by means of a skillful exercise in literary criticism; but by that time, the original point was lost. Socrates might say that points *typically* get lost in real conversations that lack dialectical rigor. The fault would then lie with Protagoras, who introduced a poem into the discussion, thereby making it necessary for Socrates to offer lengthy speeches and a historical narrative. In short, Socrates was forced to become a humanist in order to provide a persuasive reading of the poem — but the result (he implies) was a waste of time. Socrates believes that he has struck a blow against literature by his very success in offering a literary interpretation. Even though he makes the poem sound like a defense of Protagoras' position, he suggests that the ode does Protagoras no good, for poetry cannot advance a debate. At the same time, he scores a point against Protagoras, for the Sophist had introduced Simonides' poem in order to show that it was flawed. Socrates argues that it is actually consistent and that it embodies Protagoras' point of view — but also that there is no point to arguing about literature. "It seems to me," he remarks, "that conversation about poetry is too much like the wine-parties of superficial and vulgar people. These people — since they are too uneducated to entertain each other with their own voices and ideas while they drink — pay a fee for flute-players, hiring for great sums another's voice (the flute's), and entertaining each other with this voice" (347b-d).

Here Socrates offers a rhetorical analogy of literature to uncouth parties. According to him, the "vulgar" people who rely on poetry lack self-control and are subject to luck, for they have hired other people to do their talking for them. The word that I have translated as "vulgar" *(agoraios)* is derived from *agora*, the town square and public forum of a Greek city-state. The word connotes someone or something (presumably distasteful) that might be found in the *agora;* but it also alludes to the political realm, and consequently some classical authors used the word positively. Thus Socrates' rhetoric is subtly antidemocratic, as well as antipoetic.

[13] Edmonds, *Simonides*, p. 95.

So far, Socrates' own argument against poetry has consisted in a skillful deployment of similes; it is an exercise in "thick" description, intended to make poetry seem vulgar. He then remarks that interpreting literature is futile, because the poet is never present to answer; so any reading is as reasonable as any other. He says that the best people, instead of pursuing a futile and vulgar discussion of poetry, "talk with each other, offering and testing their own arguments. And it seems to me that it is better to imitate these people, you and I, setting aside the poets and conducting the conversation according to our own ideas, seeking the truth and testing each other" (347e-348a).

This speech convinces the audience, and ends the "humanistic" section of the dialogue. Instead of understanding virtue by imitation of literary classics (as Protagoras had suggested), the company decides to imitate an ideal philosophical conversation. But Socrates gains his victory over poetry by rhetorical means, not by setting forth a philosophical argument. Moreover, the poem of Simonides remains in the background as an alternative view, compatible with Protagoras' humanism and unrefuted by Socrates' philosophy.

An Uncertain Victory

Socrates now tries to restore the dialectical rigor of the conversation by asking once again whether all the virtues are one. Protagoras has a new answer to Socrates' question: wisdom, self-control, justice, and piety are all one, he says, but courage is something else, because a person can be courageous in acting unjustly or impiously. Socrates must prove that courage equals knowledge, which requires several pages of exposition. He wants to begin this intricate argument with an axiom: pleasure equals the good. However, Protagoras says that this claim needs to be investigated. Socrates therefore backs up even further and suggests a new starting point: people, he says, always seek pleasure, and therefore pleasure must be the good. This thesis is often called "eudaimonism."

John Rawls argues that the fundamental assumption behind eudaimonism is the idea that all goods are mutually comparable; they can be measured on a single scale, which the eudaimonist calls "happiness." According to Rawls, hedonism "attempts to show how a rational choice is always possible, at least in principle."[14] In contrast to this view, Rawls (like Protagoras) argues that there is not always one morally correct and rational choice. Only in the *Protagoras* does Socrates adopt a view that seems so close to hedonism, or the unequivocal embrace of pleasure. But

---

[14] John Rawls, *A Theory of Justice* (Cambridge, MA: Belnap Press, 1971), p. 555. In general, see sections 83 (Happiness and Dominant Ends) and 84 (Hedonism as a Method of Choice).

if the real issue in the dialogue is the conflict between Socrates' *techne* and Protagoras' pluralist vision, then perhaps Socrates adopts eudaimonism largely as a way of getting around pluralism. In other words, what attracts him to eudaimonism is its promise of a single scale on which all goods can be measured, and the most plausible scale is that of happiness.

Socrates suggests that "the many" disagree with the thesis that people always seek the good; they believe that people sometimes know what is good, but still do the wrong thing because they are overcome by pleasure. Socrates believes that there is no such thing as being overcome by pleasure when one is pursuing the good, in part because he has defined the good *as* pleasure. When people appear to seek pleasure rather than the good, he thinks, they are actually seeking an immediate pleasure rather than a deferred one. In other words, their error comes not from choosing pleasure over the good, but in failing to measure correctly: they take a distant pleasure to be "smaller" than a more immediate one, through an illusion of perspective. Things are good or evil (i.e., pleasurable or afflicting) in themselves, but people rely on perspectival appearances, and are thereby misled. Socrates' philosophical "science of measurement" promises to provide true measurements of the things in themselves.

There are several ways to criticize this position. For instance, someone could say that things are not good or evil in themselves, but that their value depends on context; or that some things have value that cannot be measured against other things, for they are mutually incomparable. Protagoras was just beginning to express the view that value is relative to context when Socrates complained that his speeches were too long, and the discussion then turned to Simonides' poem. So Socrates is never challenged in his assumption that the value of all things can be measured by a single standard. This assumption serves as the foundation of his "proof" that courage equals knowledge.

In the last section of the dialogue, the conversation at last becomes perfectly dialectical. Socrates asks simple questions that demand yes or no for an answer; each question is logically linked to the next. After Protagoras obediently answers 17 of these questions, the conclusion that courage is knowledge seems to emerge. Once it is clear that he is going to lose the argument, Protagoras at first refuses to answer Socrates' questions. At last he says: "It is very contentious of you, Socrates, to make me answer." But, being a man of grace, he states "very reluctantly" that courage has been proved to equal wisdom, and then he praises Socrates' skill in disputation.

Socrates appears to have won the argument, but it is not at all clear that he deserves the victory. His logic is assailable on numerous grounds; he has left Simonides' tragic perspective unrefuted; and he has persuaded Protagoras to argue dialectically only by using nondialectical methods, such as his caricature of literature as a vulgar wine party.

Socrates points out that he and Protagoras still have to decide whether or not virtue can be taught, and he suggests proceeding methodically this time, by first asking what virtue is. But Protagoras is in no mood for any more rounds of argument with Socrates. He states that he is not of a base nature and is therefore not envious of Socrates' skill; he is willing to acknowledge its excellence. But he would rather talk about something else. Socrates says that for his part he should really leave, since he is late for a prior appointment — and so the dialogue abruptly ends.

Conclusion

This sudden finish suggests that Socrates and Protagoras *could* continue their discussion. Socrates' arguments contain logical flaws, but he could try to fix them; after all, philosophers have debated moral theories for 3,000 years. For his part, Protagoras could invoke new stories or poems or draw more content from the "Eulogy to Skopas." Plato's dialogue is, if nothing else, an invitation to continue the debate.

But Plato also implies something else: that the proper tribunal in which to judge the rival claims of philosophy (or technical reason) and deliberative judgment (including rhetoric and literature) is a public deliberation. A purely technical discussion of this issue will beg all the important questions: it will have to *assume* criteria of valid argumentation that are biased in favor of either philosophy or rhetoric and literature.

If we want to decide whether Socrates' way is better than Protagoras', we must examine how each man actually operates; and that means describing them in a "thick," judgmental way and then deciding where we stand as individuals and as a community. In the end, we may choose technical reasoning, at least to some extent and for some purposes. But our method of reaching that conclusion will have to be deliberative rather than technical. Thus Plato indicates that an inclusive, rhetorical, nontechnical, democratic, public dialogue is ultimately sovereign, even if the public decides to leave some room for Socrates and his *techne*.

PART TWO

THE PUBLIC WORK
OF THE HUMANITIES

Jamil S. Zainaldin

The Realm of Seriousness:
The Public Role of the Humanities Scholar[1]

We shall not cease from exploring, and at the end of the exploration, we'll return to where we started and know the place for the
first time.

— T. S. Eliot

I'd like to indulge in a little autobiography. When I began as a graduate student in history in 1970, I could not possibly have separated my
motivation for going into history from my personal need to know more
about American society, a society that at the time was at war with itself.
Ironically, given my preoccupation with the current scene, I chose during
my first year of study a specialty in colonial history — actually, colonial
legal history. It was not possible to become more specialized in a single
discipline than I was; it was not possible to move farther away from contemporary America than I had and still be an American historian. Perhaps
for this very reason, somewhere in my recesses there gnawed at me a
need to justify myself, to "apply" my history to society, to connect with
society through my craft.

I taught for four years at two midwestern universities, and left full-
time university teaching in 1980. Looking back, I now know that
throughout that period I was daily, if not so self-consciously, connecting

[1] I would like to thank the following individuals whose critiques improved on an earlier version
of this essay: James Banner, Douglas Greenberg, Alicia Juarrero, Esther Mackintosh, Margaret
McMillan, Page Miller, and Charles Muscatine. Any errors or omissions that remain, and the
viewpoints contained herein, are my own responsibility.

my craft to society as a teacher. And I know that the subject matter that I specialized in as a scholar (early American history, public policy, law, and the family) was in no small part a reflection of my preoccupation with contemporary public affairs. Still, I felt an uneasiness that may have grown from the apparently seamless way my graduate school experience slid into my new role as a faculty member, each phase sharing a sense of apartness, a sense that life was something that happened around me and not to me. I attributed this anxiety to the removed life that I fancied I was leading.

Let me say at the outset that this was my own problem. There is nothing in the life of the academy that intrinsically makes it cloistered or apart from the rest of society. Yet the real questions about the significance of the scholarship that I was so busily working at left me feeling that somehow I had not been prepared for my induction into the life of the mind.

In retrospect, I see that my problem was in how "life of the mind" was defined. My years of graduate training were ordinary: I attended two well-respected graduate institutions, and not once was the subject of teaching mentioned publicly in class, though I was every day on the receiving end of some brilliant demonstrations of it. And not once, not even *once*, did the subject of public service come up in class.[2] I do know that some of my friends who dropped out of the graduate program, and even some who did receive their Ph.D.s, ended up in places where public service was a more dominant theme. I eventually ended up in one of those places too, (a nonprofit organization outside the walls of the university).

In the past ten years, I have been serving as an adjunct faculty member at a Washington-area law school, plying my academic trade, legal history; but my employment in Washington, D.C., has been spent more or less where I intended it to be when I left the academy: at the convergence of scholarship, public policy, and public affairs. My professional home is now the Federation of State Humanities Councils, a nonprofit membership association of the state humanities councils. The humanities councils, 56 in number (one in each state, the territories, and the District of Columbia), are governed by boards made up equally of scholars and public members who employ small professional staffs. They receive congressionally mandated support from the National Endowment for the Humanities. They also receive support from state legislatures, private donors, and foundations and corporations. Their mission is to help make

---

[2]   My two mentors, Stanley Katz and David Flaherty, are both something of an exception because both created their own exceptional roles as scholars: they were, and still are, actively involved in public policy and national affairs.

the humanities a part of everyday life, and they do so by funding and conducting projects in support of film, library reading programs, interpretive museum exhibits, lecture series, Chautauqua performances, community symposia, seminars for high school teachers, and other projects as well. Many of these programs involve scholars working with the adult public.

I think of the humanities councils as part of a "movement" because they stand for the proposition that the humanities belong to all people, that people create the humanities in the lives they live, and that the scholarship of the humanities takes its ultimate significance from its capacity to serve people, ordinary people, who, like scholars, use the tools of the humanities to make sense of their lives.

While I feel very gratified by what I'm doing, there is something unfortunate about the way that we seem to define "scholar," the way that people like myself come to our kinds of jobs, and the role that is assigned to "scholars" in the humanities.

I was struck by a second unfortunate fact when I recently bumped into a colleague in history. We had not seen each other in years. He knew I was with the federation, and he knew also that humanities councils fund and conduct public humanities programs. He asked, and I think with the best of intentions, what is it about humanities programs that appeals to folks in communities? I mean, what do people *really* do in those programs? Are they antiquarians? Phil simply could not imagine anything of any seriousness that could happen in a humanities program "for the public." I think he respected me well enough to think that there must be something to "humanities council work," but he simply was not prepared by his professional work or his professional role as scholar to know what that could be. And this is the misfortune: that my friend, a leading scholar, a person of great and strong opinions about politics, a person whose political views are sensitively interwoven through his well-respected scholarship — a person, in short, who readily understands the complexity of the relationship between politics and his scholarship but who apparently had not thought much, or maybe at all, about the relationship between *his* scholarship and his *public* role as a scholar. I had encountered in Phil the shadow that worried me as a fledgling academic: an apparent split between my role as scholar and my role as citizen (a citizen with important historical information at his fingertips!). I will return to Phil in a moment.

Civic Values of the Humanities

Humanities council programs indirectly empower members of the public by giving them access to a unique realm. We can all agree that we live in different realms of life, sometimes in many realms at the same time. One realm is that of work. We do it because we have to, and need to. Some of us love what we do, but do we must. Another realm is that of entertainment. When we have a beer; when we watch a show on television, or a football game; or play a game; or watch a movie; or listen to music; or entertain our friends or be entertained, we are pausing for pleasure. American society is good at promoting these realms, and it is exceptionally good in promoting entertainment. We are world leaders, in fact, and our culture has made many of us believe that experiencing pleasure is an end in itself.

Our society is not so good at promoting the more serious realm of meaning. We need to look hard to find it and much of this work is done, as it were, privately. I like the way Susan Sontag has described the purpose of this realm as well as her own role in it: "to keep alive the idea of seriousness." It is where we get down to the business of thinking about life itself, and this business is every bit as essential to the living as bread and water.

Many of us could not live without having a serious "space" where we can talk, and think, and write, and ponder, and listen, and debate what living is about. This is timeless, obviously, and the pursuit of seriousness comes in many forms: the spoken word, the written word, music, visual and performing arts, memory, moving images. For many people, it is this realm that religion occupies. It is also a realm that higher education inhabits. In this realm, the humanities also preside: it is a home for the scholar-humanist. It was this need for meaning that led me to graduate school and drew me to history as a young person. I believe that this sphere where the "idea of seriousness" is unchallenged is what draws most if not all humanities scholars into their professions.

It is also the lifeblood of the work of the humanities councils: to help expand in society that realm of seriousness, that space for the pursuit of meaning, and in this work to invite the scholar to join with the public in a common search. It is my own belief that scholars who take part in this activity qualify as heroes, even though "heroes" are people who surpass themselves, and these scholars are simply carrying out their role. They qualify because our entertainment culture seems almost at war with attempts to explore the depths. We allow some seriousness to occur over the airwaves (public radio and public television, and some commercial television programming); here and there we support monuments to seriousness (libraries, museums, historical societies, symphony halls, theaters); on occasion the print media pays it a nod (some newspapers, magazines, and popular journals honor it); and in the world of books and education, seriousness finds a solid and steady home. But seriousness is not much rewarded in our society, and that is nowhere so painfully evident as in popular attitudes about education and, in particular, higher education and scholars.

I want to unite these two ideas — the humanities council and the scholar as a social force who together contribute to a public humanities movement — and say something about specific ways this movement meets social ends in our society.

The humanities councils, when they fund or conduct projects, make a noteworthy contribution to society. This is a contribution made full by the expertise of humanities scholars working with people at the local level and through local institutions: libraries, museums, historical societies, town halls, civic centers, civic clubs, heritage sites, local and state government bodies, colleges and universities. It is also a contribution made full by the public's participation, for it is the genius of the councils' work to elicit thought from nonscholars. There are at least five distinct services in council programs.[3]

First, council programs offer a unique kind of "forum." The humanities give us a medium for communication where language, disagreement, ideas, values, where "reasoned analysis," where discussions of what constitutes "a fact" can become part of a discourse that is deliberately outside of the political context that prevails in a city council, the hall of Congress, the state house floor, or in one's own community where positions have been made rigid by "opinion." A discussion, through the humanities, can get us away from the tyranny of opinion and into perspective and context. This "forum" will not give us answers; it will give us an intelligent way to talk about the whole, with a better-than-even likelihood that something *important* can be said and learned. Also explicit in the forum idea is the notion of inclusion: it is open to everyone.[4]

This forum implies a method of discussion as well that is suited to the humanities: free exchange, tolerance, mutual respect, and listening. This is more than an issue of process, though. It is also "civility" which Charles Muscatine has described as,

> not just norms of decent public behavior toward each other, but also something deeper, that web of understanding and feeling

---

[3]   See Esther Mackintosh, *Strengthening Community: Achievements of the State Humanities Councils* (Arlington, VA: Federation of State Humanities Councils, 1992) and Esther Mackintosh, *Remaking America Together: The Work of the State Humanities Councils* (Arlington, VA: Federation of State Humanities Councils, 1993).

[4]   It is in this spirit that Catharine Stimpson describes humanities council programs as part of a "republic of discourse." Catharine R. Stimpson, *The Necessities of Aunt Chloe* (Washington, D.C.: Federation of State Humanities Councils, 1989), p. 9.

which bind people into a civilized society. It is in knowing each other, appreciating our differences, and celebrating our sameness, our sharing, that we become a civilization.[5]

Second, humanities council programs preserve and assert the moral worth of "seriousness." Humanities councils stand for the proposition that within communities there must be occasions, times, and places for discussing meaning. These discussions take place elsewhere too, and nowhere so earnestly as in one's own heart and head, but serious discussion is always vulnerable because it is perceived to be neither necessary nor entertaining (though it can be), and because sometimes it presents a danger to the society of which it is a part by introducing contrary values, facts, moralities, and views of power.

Third, humanities council programs foster local and community history. This may be one of the most important products of council programs that connect scholars with communities. Americans learn history in various forms as we work our way through school: neighborhood civics at first, some state history, a very little U.S. history, and on occasion world history. We may have no history at all beyond twelfth grade. While history is a modest priority in public and private education, we know, as human beings, that our identity, our direction, our self-worth and understanding, our relations with others, our ability to perceive and comprehend — these are all attributes of knowing who we are and where we come from. They are attributes of history, and community history "gives back" to communities a formal, thoughtful, shared record of the past that promotes a sense of belonging, a sense of connection with others. And nowhere does this empowerment have such depth and value as in communities who have felt abandoned by history itself, victims of the industrial revolution, or transportation revolutions, or out-migrations, or economic dislocations, or neighborhood transitions.

It is worth looking at one local history project in some detail to see what can be accomplished when working with the people of a community. The project site is in Etowah, Tennessee, an Appalachian community that was thriving in the early twentieth century as the L&N Railroad regional headquarters and the home of railroad car works. When the railroad died, according to James Ward, a historian who evaluated the project, "the community that remained lost its principal economic connectedness with the larger world." It also had "little connection to the widely taught and understood history of the South, with its focus on the old agricultural South and the modern South of sprawling cities." However,

---

[5] Mackintosh, *Remaking America Together*, p. 4.

this project gave the citizens back a history of their own. Under a grant from the Tennessee Humanities Council, professional historians worked with former L&N employees and other longtime residents of this 73-year-old company town to collect, preserve, and give meaning to their stories. These talks, according to Ward, "helped to place Etowah's recent economic, culture, political, and social conditions in perspective, and the entire project will have lasting effects upon Etowah."[6]

An exhibit grew out of the project and now has a permanent home at the restored train depot. "Dominated by the images of hard-muscled railway workers caught by the camera at their tasks," Ward notes,

> the exhibit illustrates a measure of the dignity and dirt inherent in working for a railroad in the days of steam locomotives and wooden cars. Conspicuously absent are the usual paeans to the town's "first-families." The permanent exhibit concentrates almost wholly on the experience of working people, both black and white. It pays special attention to their working and living conditions to present a sense of what it was like to claw a living from skill and sweat in the early twentieth-century industrial South. It also emphasizes the depot's social importance when it was the center of the little town's existence. . . .

The depot itself has been made a new center of the town's life. It is a functioning building with office space and rooms for meetings, and there are areas set aside for the community

> where receptions, family reunions, political meetings, and celebrations marking the passing of individual lives are regularly held. It stands as a constant reminder that Etowah is a living historical entity, always changing, always valuable. Its story is on full display for all who attend wedding receptions and retirement parties, reminding them that they, too, are adding to Etowah's historical records.

Perhaps most important, Ward concludes, is the fact that the people of Etowah have come to an understanding of "what it all meant."

What is remarkable about many council programs, like the Etowah project, is that scholars and members of the community, together, are engaged in a reconstruction of the past. In fact, it is the shared work that makes the recovery of history, the recovery of a valuable identity, so potent; when those who have experienced the history are also those who, with scholars, have helped to recapture it, then people become, to use Sheldon Hackney's elegant phrase, "the subjects of history rather than

---

[6] Quoted in Robert Cheatham, Testimony Presented in Behalf of the Federation of State Humanities Councils, before the Subcommittee on the Interior and Related Agencies, Committee on Appropriations, U.S. House of Representatives, May 12, 1993.

its objects." This is a powerful process to behold whether it occurs in a southern industrial community, or in a Native American community in New Mexico, or in a mill town in New England, or in a once-thriving coastal fishing village on the eastern shore of Delaware, or in a working-class multiethnic neighborhood in Cleveland.

A fourth function of humanities council projects is that of promoting storytelling. Storytelling comes in many forms: as poetry, as forms of history, as oral history, as remembrances. Storytelling can also take place through fiction, of course, and it is the power of story, pure and simple, to connect us with others — not simply other human beings, but human beings who seem profoundly different from ourselves. Eudora Welty described it this way in *One Writer's Beginnings*:

> It is our inward journey that leads us through time — forward or back, seldom in a straight line, most often spiraling. Each of us is moving, changing, with respect to others. As we discover, we remember; remembering, we discover; and most intensely do we experience this when our separate journeys converge. Our living experience at those meeting points is one of the charged dramatic fields of fiction.[7]

These lines are about individuals; they are also about human community. The D.C. Community Humanities Council has been supporting an oral history project in a public housing unit for senior citizens ("Potomac Gardens") located in one of the poorest sections of the city. The residents of the project, working with scholars, told their stories and, in the process, learned about and from each other. The experience for the residents was one of unimagined revelation that actually gave birth to a new community. Thelma Russell, a senior citizen resident of Potomac Gardens, reflected on the project:

> Program after program, we began to learn more and share more about what we remember and what we experienced. We have talked about religious traditions; migrating to and growing up in the city; working as domestics; and living through the depression and later the riots in Washington. These programs have helped us listen to one another and to learn from each other. The education most of us received taught us as though black people did not exist, let alone contribute anything worthwhile to our city and our nation. [This project] is filling in the gaps and showing us that we are a part of history — our lives and experiences are important.

---

[7] Eudora Welty, *One Writer's Beginnings* (New York: Warner Books, 1985), p. 112. The universal power of story is discussed in Betty Sue Flowers, "Mythmaking and the Civic Spirit" (Arlington, VA: Federation of State Humanities Councils, 1993).

Just as important, we are learning how much we have in common with each other. We were strangers before; now we understand that our common ground is the African-American heritage that we share.[8]

The records and oral histories created by the residents of Potomac Gardens, trained by area historians, have been preserved as part of a collection on the history of the District of Columbia and will be used by scholars writing histories of the District's neighborhoods.

A fifth function of council projects is problem solving at the community level. These are not ordinary projects, but every state has funded programs that seek to create a forum where disputes in the community can be "worked through." In Zion, Utah, a council project allowed polarized factions in the village of Zion, located at the entrance of the renowned national park of the same name, to discuss their differences over economic and environmental development through panels made up of a philosopher who was also a city mayor (Daniel Kemmis of Missoula, Montana), a rancher-turned-novelist (William Kittredge), a literary scholar (Tom Lyon), and a psychologist (Jordan Paul of the Center for Community Partnership). Constructive conversation had broken down entirely by the time the project began. What the townspeople and city leaders found at the end of the five-week series of programs was common ground; the immediate issue of development was no less divisive, but the healing had begun.[9]

All of these programs are educational. And a great many council programs are not so easily contained in the simple rubric I've adopted above. A school curriculum project, a seminar for high school teachers, a reading and discussion program in a local library, a community lecture series, a book festival, a Chautauqua program — in all these activities there is the simple joy of learning something new, of extending one's horizon, of engaging an idea. However, I have pinpointed these five functions because they brightly illuminate the essential civic purpose behind the humanities.[10] And they demonstrate a public role of the scholar that, like

---

[8]   Agencies, Committee on Appropriations, U.S. House of Representatives, May 12, 1993.

[9]   Mackintosh, *Strengthening Communities*, p. 15.

[10]   See: James Veninga, "Scholarship and Citizenship in the Humanistic Tradition," in *Contemporary Essays on Greek Ideas: The Kilgore Festschrift*, eds. R. Baird, W. Cooper, E. Duncan, and S. Rosenbaum (Waco, TX: Baylor University Press, 1987), pp. 277-94; James Veninga and James Quay, "Making Connections: The Humanities, Culture, and Community," in *National Task Force on Scholarship and the Public Humanities*, ACLS Occasional Paper, No. 11 (1990), pp. 1-29; William Leuchtenburg, "Charles Frankel: The Humanist As Citizen," in J. Agresto and P. Riesenberg, eds., *The Humanist As Citizen* (Washington, D.C.: National Humanities Center, 1981), pp. 228-54; and Merrill D. Peterson, *The Humanities and the American Promise* [Report of the Colloquium on the Humanities and the American People], (Austin, TX: Texas Committee for the Humanities, 1987).

my own first inklings as a graduate student, seems not only natural but inseparable to the task of *being* a humanist.

The role of the scholar in a public program is not a wholly autonomous one. The most successful council programs involve scholars as participants in a public dialogue. It is a fact that scholars are experts in some subject matter, but it is also a fact that the subject matter of much scholarship is life itself, albeit life explored through academic disciplines and analytical treatment. A truly great council program is one that begins conversation, one that acknowledges that we are all learners, and that what the scholar brings to discourse (thoughtful, reflective, learned, analytical study) is absorbed and enlarged by, in the words of Robert Coles, "the lives of ordinary people who have their own ways of struggling for coherence, for a compelling faith, for social vision, for an ethical position, for a sense of historical perspective."[11] It is akin to what Harold Best has described as the difference between "thinking about music" and "thinking in music."[12]

For the scholar, the implications of this dialogue are not insignificant. There is, first, the existence of the discourse itself: a true dialogue with a public often invites the scholar to reconsider central questions. A true dialogue often knows few academic disciplinary bounds. There is no required attendance for a public program, and so there is a further challenge to the scholar to consider what she, the audience, and the subject matter have in common. In some states, particularly the western states, council programs have helped nurture a public audience for indigenous forms of literature that draw from a powerful "sense of place," which in turn has fueled new scholarship about the region. There are dozens of examples of such symbiosis between public and scholar. "Relevance" has no dominion here. The opening pages of J. Huizinga's classic, *The Waning of the Middle Ages*, uses as a metaphor of meaning the ringing of the bells, an incessant and ubiquitous ringing that connected all villagers. Any rural community in America, where sense of place is so powerful, could talk meaningfully and endlessly with a medieval historian — or an Emily Dickinson scholar or a Jeffersonian scholar or a Homer scholar, too.

Scholars regularly report that their teaching and scholarship can greatly benefit from their interactions with the public. A survey of all humanities scholars taking part in council-funded or conducted programs in California (384) revealed that 90 percent reported a positive

---

[11] Robert Coles, *Times of Surrender: Selected Essays* (Iowa City, IA: University of Iowa Press, 1988), p 266.

[12] Harold M. Best, "Evolving Relationships Between the Arts and Humanities," in *National Association of Schools of Music 68th Annual Meeting Proceedings*, p. 80.

influence on their scholarship, and 82 percent a positive influence on their teaching.[13] For scholars truly *engaged* in a public program (hit-and-run doesn't count), enrichment is practically inevitable.

I want to return to my opening two stories. The first is my own, where I have come to learn that history has power for solitary individuals and for society as a whole. And that professional history has great power because it preeminently honors the value of free inquiry in pursuit of truths. I regret that I have not been able to continue as a productive research scholar in my chosen academic field of specialty, but I feel nevertheless that I am working at being a citizen whose public role grows naturally from my subject of expertise, American history. My humanistic background is shared by the executive directors of humanities councils, many of whom are scholar-citizens in the same sense as I apply that label to myself (and some productive research scholars as well), and they, too, feel the civic value of their work. Robert Cheatham, executive director of the Tennessee Humanities Council and past chair of the federation board, has aptly captured this spirit of humanities council work, and the good sense of doing good:

> There are, perhaps, inevitable chasms between scholarship in its purest forms and the public who want to have reasons why everything they pay for exists [referring both to public funding of NEH and universities]. I think our survival depends upon bridges over these chasms, where we come to speak to each other, where the larger community utters its needs to us, and where we say and show how [the] humanities can fulfill those needs. I can think of no better builders and tenders of these bridges than the staffs of the state humanities councils who, under guidance from the yearnings, wisdom and experience of their diverse boards, have built remarkable bridges and tended them with thoughtful, loving care.[14]

Phil, on the other hand, sees things differently, I'm sure. The puzzle I have with Phil is that he is successful as a productive research scholar; he is at home in his world of politics; he fully understands how his views about trends in culture and society subtly shape his scholarship. But he makes a radical separation between what he does as a scholar — a teaching scholar full of ideas about public, public power, values, and history — and what he does as a "citizen," a sphere that for Phil is private. I realize now what I should have said to Phil, when he asked me what scholars in public programs *really* do:"Scholars in public programs agree to be them-

[13] "CCH Scholars Survey," California Council for the Humanities, November 1, 1993 (unpublished).

[14] Personal correspondence: Robert Cheatham to Jamil Zainaldin, November 9, 1993.

selves in the company of others." My point is simply that Phil has something important to say to the public *as a scholar*. I want to go a little further: the public will want to hear from him, needs to hear from him, and, if it does not, society's discourse is the poorer for it, and Phil himself has lost some of his power to help shape public discourse on matters of importance to him and society. Possibly, Phil is the poorer, too. This is anything but a private matter.

I've lightly pressed the civic values of the humanities; I want to press harder still. Because they are so life bound, the humanities have the capacity to speak to many of the problems we're experiencing in late twentieth-century American society. It has been said that democracy depends on "faith in strangers," and we are a society, it would seem, with little faith and many strangers.[15] We are beset by problems in the body politic — racial and ethnic antagonisms, rising xenophobia, troubled communities, violence and hatreds, distrust. We have before us a prospect of limited economic growth, if there will be growth at all, and a government that seems taxed in the extreme in its capacity to "solve" social problems. Indeed, the government cannot heal us. It is our instrument, not our soul. The healing must begin within.

We can no longer afford to be "innocents" in a world of experience as philosopher Stuart Hampshire has put it. The dilemmas of existence that face us at the end of this century are not susceptible to quick or easy solution. We cannot wipe them away, or declare them gone, but we can at least seek to understand them, and we may be forced into making hard choices. To do so, Hampshire reminds us, will require "something of 'the cunning of the serpent' … which Aristotle claimed that both rogues and statesmen needed." But cleverness is not enough. We will also need, in Hampshire's words, "the ingenuity of worldly wisdom" — the resources of knowledge, thought, understanding, meaning.[16]

As a humanities scholar, I have found a way to contribute through my involvement with the humanities councils. But Phil, I must confess, is a challenge because he is a chair of a department in a university. There are others, many others, who are major figures in academic history, and literature, and philosophy, who give unstintingly of their time (or of their words)[17] to

---

[15] Taylor Branch, "Democracy in an Age of Denial," *Federation News* (May/June, 1992), p. 8.

[16] Stuart Hampshire, *Innocence and Experience* (Cambridge, MA: Harvard University Press, 1989), p. 172. Hampshire attempts to come to terms with the essential truth that Machiavelli presented in *The Prince* without sacrificing the nobility of purpose that seems, at the same time, to be a necessary ingredient of wise leadership.

[17] There are many historians who write as scholars, and not necessarily for a public audience, but whose scholarship is of such significance, moment, and clarity that it becomes embedded in the public's understanding. The work of southern historian C. Vann Woodward would come within this category.

the public and who personally define their roles as scholars to include a public dimension — who believe that part of the privilege of being truth seekers, knowledge makers, information transmitters is the obligation to give back to society. This is not an obligation that many institutions impose on faculty. Rather it seems to be more privately held.

This has not always been the case. In the first half of the nineteenth century there was an easy equation between the purposes of education and republican citizenship that continued to fuel educational expansion into the twentieth century. Prior to World War II much of higher education rested on a civic foundation whose broad mandate was to serve and "affect intimately the lives of the people."[18] In the field of history, between the two World Wars, there were historians like Charles Beard, a scholar-icon in the historical profession, who saw their roles as including a public dimension. For Beard, being a scholar-historian included extensive involvement in secondary school education, curriculum development, textbook writing, and teacher training. The circle of history was more widely drawn then to include school teachers, college faculty, learned librarians, archivists, students, local historians, and patrons committed to "historical progress." Though in truth this circle was being constantly winnowed and professionalized throughout the first half of this century, it was in the decades after World War II that the process gained momentum. The emergence of the research model was complete by 1960.

While I cannot imagine what history or our imagination would be like without the new knowledge created by the growth of higher education in postwar America, I lament that the older public clothing of the scholar seemed so awkward a fit. It was put aside, at least in an official sense, and a price is being exacted. Phil is not the exception and, if he prevails, the future of higher education and the vitality of that realm of seriousness that is so essential to our well-being as individuals and as communities will be at risk.

Perhaps it is here that I need to enter an important qualification. While I am pushing both for an expanded conception of the scholar and a recognition of the essential civic nature of the humanities, I recognize also that in the pursuit of knowledge, not all knowledge is or will be useful; indeed, we may not even know the uses of knowledge. Clearly, there is an imperative to protect the pursuit of knowledge from "worldly intrusions" for reasons that have to do with the intangible value of knowledge itself. I am intrigued by Herman Melville's own somewhat mystical mus-

---

[18]   Clara M. Lovett, "To Affect Intimately the Lives of the People: American Professors and Their Society," in *Change: The Magazine of Higher Learning* (July/August, 1993), p. 37.

ing on this subject. In *Billy Budd*, Melville contrasts two kinds of knowledge, one of which he calls "knowledge of the world," and the other, "knowledge of human nature." Billy Budd's story leads us to contemplate the nature of evil and goodness, and in the passage below, Melville asks if the "knowledge of the world" — practical knowledge — can help us better to "know" the mystery of Claggart, the ship's master-at-arms whose obsessive hatred of the youthful Billy ("the sweet and pleasant young fellow," Claggart calls him) seems to plumb some unknowable darkness beyond ordinary comprehension. Melville answers his own question by replying that worldly knowledge is

> superficial ... serving ordinary purposes ... Nay, in an average man of the world, his constant rubbing with it blunts that fine spiritual insight indispensable to the understanding of the essential in certain exceptional characters, whether evil ones or good. In a matter of some importance I have seen a girl wind an old lawyer about her little finger. Nor was it dotage of senile love. Nothing of the sort. But he knew law better than he knew the girl's heart. Coke and Blackstone [both lawyers who also were renowned legal thinkers] hardly shed so much light into obscure spiritual places as the Hebrew prophets. And who were they? Mostly recluses.[19]

The Tradition of Scholar Citizen

I carried out a survey of humanities councils to learn something about how the reward structure operates in the public humanities. Recognizing that this is not a scientific survey because it includes a good deal of impressionistic information, here is what I learned:

1) Most scholars participate in council programs because they want to. Most are not rewarded for these efforts, except psychically, of course, and occasionally by humanities councils who now publicly honor citizen-scholars in their states with prizes or awards.

2) Institutional encouragement of public programs follows no particular pattern. There is some evidence to indicate stronger participation on the part of public universities, though scholars from private institutions are also present. College or university leadership is important in faculty decisions to participate in programs, it would seem. In some states, community college faculty are very active participants in public humanities programming, and elsewhere would be more so except for the demands on their time in their home institutions.

---

[19] Herman Melville, *Billy Budd and Other Tales* (New York: The New American Library, 1961 ed.), pp. 36-7.

3) There are "enough scholars to go around" for most councils, but if councils programs were to expand in scope — funding permitting — there would not be. Several councils, in fact, have indicated that they are hampered in programs that they can plan because they cannot attract scholars to carry out the work and cannot afford to hire scholars on a full-time basis either.

4) There seems to be no pattern in who, among scholars, participates in council programs. Certainly, younger scholars not yet tenured are rather unusual, but they are in evidence. Younger tenured scholars are in evidence too, and some of the most distinguished humanities scholars in the nation are active participants in council-funded programs in their states. It seems to be the case that the more established scholars take part in council programs generally, however. One conclusion from this hodge-podge is that the chief reason for taking part in a council-funded program is personal, and therefore that the reward is in the doing.

What portion of the university-based population is like Phil? There is no certain way to say, since noninvolvement in a public program can also be attributed to not being asked, to being quite busy and in fact overburdened with existing duties, and other factors as well. Moreover, one must be careful about generalizing from state to state, since humanities councils in small population states in the West have a history of involving almost every humanities scholar in their states. However, I must report that many of my colleagues in the councils see very little "official" home-state support for scholars who take part in their programs or for the work of the councils — this despite the fact that college presidents, deans, and department heads are frequent members of humanities council boards. Overall, though, the apparent lack of official institutional rewards seems not to have materially hampered the efforts of humanities councils to carry out their programs.

This picture of higher education, neither hostile nor particularly supportive, seems reflected in other evidence. Of the 91 current campus initiatives on file with the American Association of Higher Education relating to faculty workloads, assignments, and rewards in research universities, comprehensive universities, and liberal arts colleges, I found few that addressed issues of service, and only one was noted that offered a systematic definition of service to include scholarship in the community. And presumably, these are the reform-minded committees.[20] AAHE's 1993

---

[20] See "Master List of Campus Documents," in *Resource Packet* (AAHE/Forum on Faculty Roles and Rewards, 1993), [Part III] pp. 1-28. See also Russell Edgerton, "The Reexamination of Faculty Priorities: Discussion Paper," in *Resource Packet* [Part I], p. 5: "'Service,' in all this," concludes Edgerton, "is typically treated like the country cousin. The status and definitional issues of service are as muddled as ever."

report on how liberal arts colleges evaluate professors more or less bears this indifference out. In a ranking based on the "percentage of liberal arts colleges that consider each criterion a major factor in evaluating overall faculty performance," public service ranked last in the list of eight criteria.[21] There was, however, a slight improvement in score since 1983. Yet another vantage is a survey of disciplinary faculty (American historians) conducted by the editor of the *Journal of American History* in which respondents were asked to register their agreement or disagreement with the following statement: "The academic reward system encourages historians to write for academic audiences and discourages historians from reaching out to multiple audiences." The result: 38 percent of the respondents strongly agreed, and 43 percent agreed.[22]

To paraphrase James Joyce, do we have an open gate — something you can put your fingers through — or a closed door? Do we have a foundation on which to build a public role for the scholar, or not?

There is visible concern on the part of public and private university leaders about the reward structure generally, the role of teaching, and the relations between the university and the public. There is cause for concern. Tax revolts in western, midwestern, and Plains states have done palpable damage to state universities. Eastern institutions have been suffering for years. The rounds of school, scholar, and university critiques that have been building in strength in recent years are seriously eroding public confidence in all forms of education.[23] There have been scandals here and there, financial ones especially, that make quick headlines in newspapers. Still, I think the answer to the question is "yes," we have some promising foundations on which to build.

There are now a number of higher education leaders and thinkers taking a visible stance on the importance of reconnecting universities with society, on putting universities in touch with the needs of people in the state, on rethinking the reward structure. In urban universities, according to Blaine Brownell, Lowe may have oversold our capacity to solve problems in the community when those problems are intractable. This is giving way to a new dialogue in higher education that is focusing on the uni-

---

[21] Peter Seldin, "How Colleges Evaluate Professors: 1983 v. 1993," in AAHE *Bulletin* (October 1993), p. 7.

[22] David Thelen, "Preliminary results of a reader survey conducted by the *Journal of American History*, Indiana University, 1993, unpublished. These percentages are based on 961 responses. Final percentages may vary, since responses were still being tabulated as this essay was written.

[23] An excellent brief review of the important literature appears in Clara Lovett, "A Select Bibliography of Recent Works," in *Resource Packet* [Part II], pp. 2-5.

versity as moral leader, "a bridge" that can "help restore a sense of *civitas*."[24] There are now ample examples of these programs involving departments and schools within a university working cooperatively with the residents of a city or county, or sometimes the state, in response to local planning needs, health needs, business development, teacher training, environmental protection, and school improvement. Building on the traditions of the land grant system, there is promise here for a more solid, long-standing grounding in the institutions and processes of community life.

The tradition of scholar-citizen does exist today as a model, and it is practiced by some of the most distinguished scholars in the humanities professions. Moreover, some of the elected leadership of the humanities disciplinary organizations are beginning to question the posture of some members of their profession and, in language that is strong, sometimes verging on judgmental, are prodding a greater involvement with the public. Other organizations like the Organization of American Historians and the American Historical Association are reconnecting with their own activist tradition in secondary education. Definitions of scholarship are also being affected. Some national disciplinary associations in the humanities, such as participants in the Syracuse project, are working on statements about scholarship that are inclusive of public activities.[25] Stimulated by the work of Ernest Boyer, Eugene Rice, and others, this is a dramatic step in the redefinition of a faculty role that, if it continues, has the potential of connecting to developments at the state level and setting a more encouraging tone for public scholarly involvement of the professoriate.

An awakening to the importance (or should we say, reality) of public authority is in evidence by the growing activism of humanities organizations in relations with Congress — often coalescing around funding, policy, and regulatory issues connected to the National Archives and Records Administration, freedom of information laws, records classification, programs for international exchange and education, portions of the National Science Foundation, the National Park Service, and the National Endowment for the Humanities. Many of these disciplinary organizations are actively involved in lobbying through coalitions created specifically

---

[24] Blaine Brown, Address delivered at the Conference on Metropolitan Universities, University of North Texas, March 28, 1993.

[25] Some of these statements are reprinted and analyzed in Robert Diamond and Bronwyn Adam, eds., *Recognizing Faculty Work: Reward Systems for the Year 2000* (San Francisco, CA: Jossey-Bass, 1993).

for this purpose, an unthinkable activity 15 years ago.[26]

National disciplinary organizations are also paying closer attention to the public dimension of their profession's work. The American Council of Learned Societies, a membership organization of humanities learned societies, has worked closely with my own association, the federation, to explore ways of strengthening ties between scholars and humanities councils.[27] The Modern Language Association includes in its survey of its members questions about fostering public appreciation and use of the humanities. Interestingly, in 1990 MLA learned that fully one-third of the respondents had taken part, as scholars, in public programs.[28] There is some evidence that these tended to be the more "established members of the profession." In the same 1993 *Journal of American History* survey cited above, among the statements that readers were asked to respond to was the following: "Good historical scholarship engages multiple and diverse audiences," 40 percent "strongly agreed" with the statement, and 42 percent "agreed." A mere 7 percent disagreed on the importance of reaching a broader audience.[29] These are significant findings that eventually, I hope, may place Phil in very select company.

There is also the national example of NEH Chairman Sheldon Hackney, previously the president of an Ivy League university, who has announced that broadening the humanities to reach more of the American public is one of his highest priorities. He also announced his goal of establishing a "partnership" with the state humanities councils, the

---

[26] The major lobbying organizations are the National Coordinating Committee for the Promotion of History (Washington, D.C.), composed of history and archival organizations; the National Humanities Alliance (Washington, D.C.), composed for the most part of the constituent societies of the ACLS; and the Consortium of Social Science Associations (Washington, D.C.), composed of social science disciplinary associations, including history, linguistics, anthropology, sociology, political science, and "hard" science and mathematical disciplinary associations. The Federation of State Humanities Councils likewise advocates for the humanities, but it is not affiliated with any disciplinary organization; its board includes members of discipline-based associations such as the AHA, MLA, and OAH, members of the public, and staff of humanities councils. The federation is a coalition member of the NCC and NHA, and an affiliate of the ACLS.

[27] *National Task Force on Scholarship and the Public Humanities.* ACLS Occasional Paper, No. 11 (1990). The vice president of the ACLS, formerly Douglas Greenberg, routinely sends out the following letter to executive directors of state humanities councils and corresponding letters to scholar recipients of ACLS fellowships: Dear [executive director]: In accordance with ACLS's determination to work closely with the Federation of State Humanities Councils, I enclose the names of residents of your state who have been awarded fellowships and grants by ACLS during the past academic year. I have informed them that we will be sharing their names with you, and I have urged them to take part in public programs. I hope that you will call upon some of these people should your programs require their expertise. Sincerely, [D.G.]

[28] Bettina J. Huber, "The 1990 Survey of the MLA Membership: Data Collection Procedure, Sample Representativeness, and Respondent Characteristics," (New York: Modern Language Association, 1992; revised and expanded, 1993), unpublished, p. 41.

[29] See note 22.

first chairman to do so, and has launched "a national conversation" in which the humanities can be infused into a new national discourse about the direction of the nation. Again, it is the public dimension of the humanities that is being emphasized. In Mr. Hackney's case, the emphasis makes great sense, not only because of the contemporary imperatives of heading a public tax-supported agency, but because Congress' original vision in founding the endowment in 1965 directly correlated the "investment" in humanistic scholarship with a "return" to the public weal: nothing less than the "orderly continuation of free society."[30]

There is yet other evidence of a growing regard for the public. Using the early work of German philosopher Jürgen Habermas, *The Structural Transformation of the Public Sphere* (1962), the scholarship of literature, and of history, is showing a new appreciation for the dimension of a "public sphere" as an intellectual concept in the United States. Scholars in each of the humanities disciplines are also seeking a broader audience for their work, and some for the specific purpose of joining an already public debate (see *Wild Orchids* and *Trotsky: Messages from American Universities*, edited by Mark Edmundson, 1993) or in order to enter a discourse that will make academic thinking more accessible to the public and its decision makers, as Yale historian Paul Kennedy has now done in two best-selling books (*The Decline and Fall of the Great Powers* and

---

[30] The example of the National Endowment for the Humanities is itself a case study in the dynamics of public-academy relations. The endowment receives its annual appropriation and its multiyear authorization through a process that requires close congressional oversight. Appointments to NEH's national council also must be approved by the Senate. Within these set-pieces are played out some of the societal tensions between citizens and scholars. The bloody fight over Carol Iannone's nomination by President Bush to serve on NEH's national council is a case in point. The more recent confirmation troubles of Sheldon Hackney as Chairman of NEH is further evidence of the potential volatility. In both cases, some senators charged that humanities scholars, and higher education generally, were inappropriately political in their scholarship and teaching and therefore "out of touch" with ordinary Americans. "Political correctness" entered the popular American lexicon through the press' reportage on the Iannone nomination in the summer of 1991; it resurfaced with Hackney's nomination in 1993. In the case of the Iannone nomination, the nastiness of the attacks on the academy were wildly out of proportion to the "offense," which was no more than several scholarly organizations taking a position on a presidential nomination—anything but an unusual event in Washington. Lynne Cheney, then chairman of NEH, was active, visible, and effective in "framing" the terms of the debate that was waged in the press, and even on the television news. In Hackney's case, events taking place on his campus were picked up and attached to some quite one-sided reportage on his "qualifications" to chair the agency. Far more serious than these "culture wars," as the media has dubbed such squabbles, is the persistent indifference of more than a few lawmakers to funding for humanities. As of this writing, the House and Senate are considering amendments to reduce funding for the NEH by two percent a year for the next five years, justifying such action on the grounds that NEH grants mainly support "higher income people."

On the "populist" and "elite" tensions that characterized the early years of the endowment, see Stephen Miller, *Excellence and Equity* (Lexington, KY: University of Kentucky Press, 1984), pp. 38-59.

Preparing for the Twenty-First Century).[31]

One particularly important initiative related to the public is being launched by the Center for History Making in America, housed in Indiana University. The center, working with several humanities councils and with funding from NEH, is conducting a national survey to learn more about how ordinary people perceive, use, and understand history in their daily lives. Recognizing that there is an extraordinary gap between the voluminous production of scholarship on the one hand, and where the public gets its information about history on the other, the center is, in a sense, opening up the difficult — and very sensitive — question about the consequences of specialization.

The debate within the academy over conceptual developments in humanistic scholarship and pedagogy itself has a very public ring: arguments about the literary canon are front-page media fare because the public — and journalists — instinctively know that large issues are being debated about values, personal identity, and national direction. Much the same thing can be said about "the new Western history," feminist literary studies (and publicly waged counter-arguments), and "bottom up" history. Not unlike the rock and roller who records on a country-and-western label, scholars like Henry Louis Gates in literature, and Cornel West in religious studies, who actively pursue a more public voice now have their own label: "the crossover academic."[32] "Culture wars" and "political correctness" are not terms that describe a scholarship in retreat from issues of public significance.

Still, the cost of indifference to public attitudes has been dear. There is a pervasive sense among defenders and critics that higher education has done poorly in explaining itself to its constituencies and that scholars (the defenders speaking now) must "take back" from the media and public critics the power of defining who and what the academy is. Inevitably this will include reforming some part of the scholar's role. It is not the reform that is new; what is new is the ensconced model of today's research scholar that has broken off the rhetoric of public from

---

[31] Thomas Bender, *Intellectuals and Public Life: Essays on the Social History of Academic Intellectuals in the United States* (Baltimore, MD: Johns Hopkins University Press, 1993), and Bruce Robbins, ed., *The Phantom Public Sphere* (Minneapolis, MN: University of Minnesota Press). See also: Scott Helter, "Humanists Renew Public Intellectual Tradition, Answer Criticism," in *Chronicle of Higher Education* (April 7, 1993), p. A6.

[32] Scott Heller, "In Effort to Reach Broader Audience, Scholars Ask: What Is Public," in *Chronicle of Higher Education* (April 7, 1993), p. A12.

the traditional role.[33]

In summary, the public role of scholar can be talked about in two ways: the unofficial role inherent in being a truth seeker, and the official role that is recognized and rewarded by higher education institutions. The problem is in the latter category, and while there are changes occurring in the official language of "reward structure," they are minor at best where public service is concerned. In spite of this, scholars are taking initiative in a whole range of activities — writing books for public distribution, writing op-ed columns in national newspapers, contributing to magazines and book review supplements, appearing on radio and television talk shows, speaking before large audiences. What information we do have available suggests these numbers are growing, or at least, that there are changes in the attitudes of the membership organizations that educators and scholars belong to. There is the example of the American Association of Higher Education and its creation of the Forum on Faculty Roles and Rewards for evidence of a ferment that will not be contained.

Implications for the Reward Structure

There are at least four options and, additionally, some considerations of strategy, for addressing public service scholarship in the reward structure.

One is to modify the definition of service in the reward structure so that the application of one's scholarly expertise in service to the community is recognized and rewarded. This model has been elaborated with great care and persuasion by Sandra Elman and Sue Marx Smock.[34] It would require evaluation and documentation. This seems a perfectly log-

---

[33] See Charles Muscatine, "The Public Humanities and the Academic," Chair's Report Presented to the Membership of the Federation of State Humanities Councils, October 18, 1993 (unpublished). An eminent literary scholar (emeritus) whose education spanned the World War II years, Muscatine joined the Berkeley faculty in 1949 and retired in 1991. His own career, not unlike many others of his generation, reflects a commitment to multiple scholarly roles: teacher, scholar, education reformer, and civic activist. In his address, Muscatine lamented the direction of much of the humanistic research in his field and urged that "the academic examine his or her profession from the perspective of the public good." He called on the academy to address itself to the people of the twenty-first century, bourgeois or not, inhabitants of untenable cities and endless suburbs, who will be neither smug nor certain, and who will desperately need a humanities that promotes communication, alleviates alienation, and exemplifies the possibility of human community. Muscatine, however, does not believe that the answer to reengaging the academy with the public rests with "the reward system for promotion and tenure, if by that we mean setting out bait to attract the same careerists." He continues: "The answer is to get another kind of person, and another conception of academia, into our colleges and universities." What is particularly powerful about Muscatine's head-on critique is that, unlike other critics of higher education, he is an insider, an internationally eminent scholar and a feminist in orientation who has welcomed the broadening of his profession to include minority groups and their perspectives. Obviously, his assertions ring like "a fire bell in the night."

[34] Sandra E. Elman and Sue Marx Smock, *Professional Service and Faculty Rewards: Toward an Integrated Structure* (Washington, D.C.: National Association of State Universities and Land Grant Colleges, 1985).

ical way to discuss the public role of the scholar. However, one criticism raised against putting public service scholarship in this category is that it would need to overcome the baggage and marginality that the current "service" category seems consigned to in the minds of most.

A second model is to recognize that the public role of the scholar involves elements of teaching and scholarship and, to the extent that these can be documented and evaluated, they can be rewarded within the present structure. The greatest challenge posed by this model is expanding one's understanding of what comprises scholarship and teaching. The theoretical foundations already have been laid by Boyer and Rice, and practical applications have begun to appear in the reports from the Syracuse project.

A third option is to admit that the "research model" for the reward structure is more appropriate for some institutions than others. The challenge this approach is open to is that of elitism: it implies an inverse relationship between quality and scholarly service. It is also not logical, since research can be research regardless of how the results are presented (journal article, museum exhibition, presentation at a scholarly conference, presentation before a convention of nonscholars).

A fourth option is to ignore the current reward structure and allow "market forces" to work. Voting with one's feet would include the individual decision by a number of scholars to engage the public without regard for peer-conferred rewards. In incremental fashion, the reward structure eventually might begin to accommodate changes in the professorate's attitudes and behavior. This is contingent, however, on an assumption for which there is no solid evidence: that the propensity to become involved as a scholar with the public is not influenced by one's age or generation.

There are the strategic options for how best to promote reform. Through the disciplinary organizations? Through reform organizations? Through the membership organizations of institutions? Through other vehicles? Certainly, any effort to modify the reward structure, or even to acknowledge the value of a public role for scholars, will have to account for what is taught in graduate education. It is here that we learn what it means to be a scholar, and it is here, at the point of recruitment, that we can explore the universal question of what it means to be part of a profession.

And from over my shoulder I hear the haunting voice of my friend and colleague, Charles Muscatine, wise, gentle, an educator, a scholar's scholar with a long view, an intimate of university life with 40 years of campus battle scars (some he won),[35] and a citizen who has taken stock and a stand:[36] "If, as has been repeatedly said, academia will never reform itself, then the informed public must help reform it, with all the means it has."

Summary

There are many public spheres, and it is the public work of scholars close to home, the low visibility trench work of laboring in one's own community that humanities councils specialize in — schools, libraries, historical societies, local museums, historic sites, civic clubs, local government, neighborhood associations, residential housing sites, literacy programs, factory lunchrooms, and the Chautauqua "big top." This is action that can make a difference because it takes place *where people live and work*. And it is at the local level where ordinary people can be touched and absorbed into a discourse of meaning.

Even unordinary people. I recently heard a radio interview with former Secretary of Defense Robert McNamara. It spoke volumes about lost opportunities and tragedies, and the essential, primal, personal value of the humanities that cannot be separated, either, from public roles. Near the end of the interview, and with the ghost of Vietnam eerily present, National Public Radio's "Morning Edition" host Bob Edwards asked, "At what point did you determine that not everything had a solution?" McNamara, laughing, replied, "Well that's a very good question." He went on:

> Rather recently I might say. And it's very hard for me to say it, I'm a problem solver whether it be at Ford or the World Bank or Defense, but I am gradually learning as I suggest some problems don't have solutions. Moreover, even if they do, I'm not wise enough to know them. I want to suggest to you, I'm going to start this book [his memoirs about the Vietnam war] by quoting four lines from T. S. Eliot that my wife, who was one of God's loveliest creatures, brought to my attention about thirty years ago, and the lines are these. Eliot wrote, "We shall not cease from exploring, and at the end of our exploration, we'll return to where we started and know the place for the first time." Now I haven't finished my exploration, I haven't returned to where I started, and I don't know

---

[35] In 1949, Muscatine refused to sign the loyalty oath required for all faculty on the campus of Berkeley. He sued, and emerged victorious. He was active in the free speech movement at Berkeley and was principal author of the widely regarded report on *The Status of Education at Berkeley* that grew out of that turbulent era (the "Muscatine Report"). He was the founder of Berkeley's experimental Strawberry Creek College program, which, despite its remarkable success, failed to win the support of the university system.

[36] Muscatine, "The Public Humanities and the Academic," p. 4.

the place yet, which simply means I am quite clear on my limitations, and I don't have solutions for all the problems.[37]

There does seem to be a permeable gate for reform. The public dimension of the scholar's role, perhaps for the first time since World War II, is under very serious scrutiny, at large and within the walls of universities. I believe there is a great deal at stake in opening that gate, for it is in the realm of seriousness, the realm of T. S. Eliot, that McNamara came to late in life, the realm that a great many scholars believe they occupy, that we can make our strongest appeal for the public's support, and not with the goal in mind of solving problems, but with the goal of seeking to understand so that we, scholar and community together, may act with wisdom and with heart.

---

[37] Transcript, "Morning Edition," National Public Radio, September 10, 1993, p. 30.

Tomas N. Santos

On Listening Deeply:
The Moral Imperative of the Humanities

Academic truth and political truth turn out not to be fundamentally different. Politics and inquiry converge in the quest for better truths. Such a notion of truth may make us uneasy — both as academics and as citizens — but it may also make it easier for us to be at once academics and citizens in a democracy.

— Thomas Bender

If, as Thomas Bender suggests, the unity of academic and political truth makes us uneasy, it is probably for good cause. It may very well be that humanism and civility are strange bedfellows. A humanist is — typically — an academic, one who has chosen not to be in politics. A politician is one who has chosen not to be in the academy. As Machiavelli would say: "One can save one's soul, or one can found or maintain, or serve a great and glorious state; but not always both at once." To paraphrase loosely: one can teach and help to enlighten others, or one can lead and help the state; but not always both at once. We realize, of course, that Machiavelli's observation worked on the customary separation of the religious (saving one's soul) and the secular (serving the state). The separation of offices to accord with one's function in society is a throwback to medieval times: the clerk was not to be confused with the reeve.

The phrase "town vs. gown" is almost equally antiquated. It's a worrisome oversimplification because it misrepresents the current relationship of scholars and officeholders to publics. What's closer to the truth is that both scholars and officeholders have little to do with publics. Humanities scholars spend their lives in school, first as students, then as teachers. Their professional commitment is to the disciplines they teach. Once their classes are taught, they withdraw to their offices or to libraries to do research. Officeholders are currently the object of much anger and dissatisfaction among the electorate who feel disenfranchised by government. In their detachment from publics, scholars, and officeholders — in effect — become disconnected, isolated, private citizens.

Private citizens constitute publics when they engage in activities that are participatory; furthermore, publics (at least where the state guarantees the right to free speech and assembly) mediate between the state and society.[1] These publics may be constituted informally, as in discussions that take place at the local coffeehouse, or formally, as in a town meeting. While humanists and officeholders may constitute different publics, the public discussions that take place in both spheres share the same purpose: the common good. Even though a different perspective and even a different methodology arises, in either case, the goal is the same.

Ways of Knowing

The most significant commonality between humanities and publics is in the degree to which both subscribe to similar ways of knowing. We begin by distinguishing between public and scientific ways of knowing. For over half a century, the model for research in higher education has been scientific research, with its data gathering, its carefully circumscribed experiments, its cautiously worded findings, its slow but certain progress toward the betterment of our quality of life. Its steps toward progress are quantified in the number of grants acquired and articles published. The social sciences and the humanities, though hard pressed to replicate the methods and purposes of the sciences, nevertheless produce a reasonable facsimile of scientific research. There is data gathering, there is an identifiable "field" for research, negotiations between intellectual and social realities, engagement of quality of life issues. And there is the measure of grants and publication.

Yet the model of scientific research has wreaked havoc on the humanities, and — to a certain extent — the social sciences. Scientific research, because it is objective, analytical, and experimental tends to sep-

---

[1]   See Jürgen Habermas' ideas on the public sphere ("the domain of our social life in which such a thing as public opinion can be formed"), refined in such texts as *The Phantom Public Sphere* (Bruce Robbins, ed.).

arate subject from object, the knower from the known. Humanistic discourse is about human experience with all its vicissitudes. The humanities do not produce data that is objective, quantifiable; nor do they deal in replicability and prognostication. Questions having to do with value, ethics, virtue, morals, and community are not quantifiable. These questions bear on different realities and on varying degrees of subjectivity than those found in ordinary scientific inquiry. More significantly, they bear on ways of knowing that implicate the subject in the very questions s/he asks.

Writing about Giambattista Vico (1668-1744), Isaiah Berlin (in *Against the Current*, 1980) discovers "a sense of knowing basic to all humane studies."

> This is the sort of knowing which participants in an activity claim to possess as against mere observers: the knowledge of the actors, as against that of the audience, of the "inside" story as opposed to that obtained from some "outside" vantage point; knowledge by "direct acquaintance" with my "inner" states or by sympathetic insight into those of others, which may be obtained by a high degree of imaginative power....

Berlin argues that Vico's emphasis on participatory experience, on "inner" knowing, marked the "divorce between the sciences and the humanities." But Vico clearly does more than create a separation between one way of knowing and another; he allows for the possibility of interrelated, participatory knowing. In *Exploring Reality*, a book that examines interdisciplinary approaches to "factual" judgment, Michael Leahy says that all theories of knowledge must acknowledge the participating observer:

> ... human beings are in any case not mirrors. Historians will try to prove each other wrong, scientific explanations make reference to abstract entities like laws and theoretical particles.... An alternative theory of reality, if it is to avoid the unsatisfactory outcome of the positivistic model, must take seriously the role of participating observer, not the merely passive.

The participating observer is intimately linked with the process of knowing — not as subject, not as object, but as both simultaneously, as knower and known. How a nonobjective epistemology operates is through narrative, through a respect for the uniqueness of voices, through the cultivation of a complex equality.[2] By listening, we partici-

---

[2] For a more elaborate description of complex equality, see Michael Walzer, *Thick and Thin*, 1994. He claims that two types of moral argument, the thick-and-local and the thin-and-universal, need to be accepted simultaneously for a culture to celebrate its uniqueness and its members' oneness with the rest of humanity.

pate in narrative process; and what we hear is the voice of another.

Vox populi, or the public voice, is that which comes about after many have expressed their views and shared their experiences. It is a product of deliberation rather than debate, discussion rather than argument, of storytelling rather than oratory, of "thick descriptions" rather than dialectics. The deliberative process finds its allies in a most unlikely place: the Sophists whom Plato was wont to satirize. Protagoras, for instance, always looked befuddled in the face of Socratic dialectics. Dialectics works in terms of polarities, "either/or," "yes/no," and does not permit the exploration of gray areas. Logic rules. With thick description, complexity is in the particulars — not in logical turns of thought; argument is difficult to identify. The descriptive style is more akin to Homeric narrative and shows continuities between story and culture.[3] In his essay for this volume, Peter Levine contrasts Socratic dialectics with the thick description of Protagoras; he argues that Socrates pretends to be skeptical about virtue in order to adduce it (the desired reply: it cannot not exist) whereas Protagoras simply accepts that virtue does exist and gets on with the business of teaching it. Levine's point is that Protagoras is a humanist because he advocates action and civic responsibility, whereas Socrates is a philosopher who is content to contemplate theory.

Robert Coles sees narratives as a way to learn morals and to open ourselves to the richness of human experience. He describes how he veered away from scientific methodology:

> What I've had to do is leave the realm of social science, which strives for predictability, consistency, and theoretical amplification. … Anyone who has gone through the years that I went through of psychiatry, child psychiatry and psychoanalysis develops a theoretic mind. While I've had to hold on to some of those virtues, I've also had to leave behind much of that way of thinking in order to turn toward what I think stories offer us — an appreciation of complexity, irony, ambiguity, inconsistency, fate, luck, chance, circumstance.

In *The Political Life of Children* and *The Call of Service*, Coles favors the idiosyncrasies of narratives over the consistency of scientific observation in order to infer the larger sociopolitical narratives.

"Knowledge is not the same as science," says Jean Francois Lyotard (*The Postmodern Condition: A Report on Knowledge*), and with this he

---

[3] The *Odyssey*, for example, illustrates the ethical battle within Odysseus, his struggle with duty and desire, responsibility and revenge. In epic narrative, conflicts are resolved not by dialectics but by living through the conflicts, hence the high degree of realism in Homeric narrative. Story, not argument, discloses another path to insight.

draws distinctions between denotative statements (the stuff of scientific observation) and other kinds of statements that come out of a narrative tradition. Lyotard's distinctions are useful because they call attention to a broader range of knowledge beyond the scientific: there is "know-how" *(savoir-faire)*, there is "knowing how to speak" *(savoir-dire)*, and finally there is "knowing how to hear" *(savoir-entendre)* — the latter I read as indistinguishable from "listening" *(savoir-écouter)*. These types of knowledge, which he calls "competences," are necessary to the lives of ordinary citizens but are not critical to scientific process. Scientific methodology depends only on self-legitimating criteria that determine the truth value of denotative statements. Such competences as "knowing-how-to-speak" and "listening" involve a different pragmatics.[4] They define how we do things as members of a group; and they are defined by social narratives.

Narrative in Lyotard is writ on a grand scale: we are all part of an ongoing story that is always changing, formulating itself moment by moment. We take narrative in its etymological sense (from *gnarus*, knowing) as the process by which something is known or made known. Culture, for instance, is the story that people tell about themselves; it is a narrative based on consensus. Society is also an evolving fiction, a product of "play" that is not unlike "language games." A citizen is referent, addressee, and sender all in one. She is a referent even before birth because the child already has a position in the story of the family; when the child receives knowledge about her family, she is the addressee; and when she tells her story to others, she becomes a sender. Lyotard's language demonstrates his interest in process. By using words such as "rhythm," "reference," "formation," "networks," "relation," "deliberation," and phrases like "fruitful exchange," "a unity of experience," and "common disposition," he avoids eristic modalities (the language of debate — as in: "to the contrary," "conversely," "in opposition"). A recent work, *Peregrinations*, is a personal narrative about critical inquiry.

Narrative, then, is the basis for our unification of disparate ways of knowing. Stories, whether they are history or metanarrative, allow us to remember and reassess experience, and offer us the privilege of creating ourselves in the process of their making.

The Production of Knowledge

What is it that narratives teach us? Perhaps this: how to listen. How to read our story, which presupposes the universality of my story. My

---

[4]   Pragmatism is a theory of action, and as such, owns the task of disabusing itself of philosophy. Richard Rorty would add that pragmatists do not require a metaphysics or an epistemology. They view truth as what is good for us as a community to believe. For pragmatists the gap between truth and justification is the gap between actual good and the possible better. See *Objectivity, Relativism and Truth*, 1991.

publicness. The *personal* character of "public politics." Narratives produce community just as they are produced by community. And if we say that narrative operates on ways of knowing that are different from those of traditional science, then it must also be the case that narrative concerns sentiments that move beyond the language of denotation. Literary narratives are exemplary. The poem, for instance, relies on imagery, on a turn of phrase or wordplay to entice the reader to see the world differently and to invite the audience to share in the creative act. Novels describe the human condition and ask questions about our values, how we relate to one another, and even urge us to take action. If a story does not reach a specific conclusion, then it is perhaps to a higher end that the story aspires: the creation of connections that ultimately forge community. This connectedness is based on sharing, empathy, fairness, compassion, the need for nurturance, cooperation. Robert Penn Warren (in *Democracy and Poetry*) says that literature conduces to moral thinking through the paradoxes of finding the self in selflessness and discovering self-fulfillment within the community or the group. The link between ethics and literature is persuasively established by Martha Nussbaum, who says that novels have forms and structures that offer adequate and complete investigations of ethical ideas.

> A view of life is *told*. The telling itself — the selection of genre, formal structures, sentences, vocabulary, of the whole manner of addressing the reader's sense of life — all of this expresses a sense of life and of value, sense of what matters and what does not, of what learning and communicating are, of life's relations and connections.

Her pursuit of moral philosophy leads her to investigate all forms of deep and sympathetic expressions, expressions that allow us to compare major ethical alternatives with our active sense of life. Literature extends our experience of life and allows us to see how choices are made and to evaluate the consequences of those choices.

The bridge between ethical thinking and action is the subject of public knowing and knowledge. As publics, we are aware of the imperatives of interdependence and moral judgment. Hannah Arendt advocated thinking-as-the-other, thinking in place of everybody else;[5] she called this faculty an "enlarged mentality," one of the grounds for judgment. Judgment is distinct from thought in that it requires interaction; it needs the presence of others to be valid. Judgment about "the Good Society" or

---

[5] Cf. Kant's idea of reflective judgment—that faculty which operates in the absence of universal law and requires the ability to imagine other viewpoints.

"the Good" depends on communal ways of knowing and on a discussion of ethical standards based on consensus.[6] Knowing is the basis for the production of meaning in the community as well as the prerequisite of judgment. Benjamin Barber goes so far as to say that judgment is already part of what we do: the political actor operates in a frenzy of activity involving collaboration, discussion, and conflict with others; he writes: "common civic activity is constitutive of what we mean by political judgments."

Public knowledge is in constant flux. As new ideas emerge and others are discarded, this process parallels the manner in which, say, scientific paradigms are supplanted by new ones. But unlike scientific paradigms, or even the scientific method, the nature of empirical knowledge in the realm of publics has much to do with subjective experience. The following from Bitzer is illustrative:

> … the remote and disinterested observer of a child wasting from disease observes a purely factual condition, while the mother whose love embraces the child witnesses real tragedy. The mother's love, existing in her and nowhere else, is precisely the condition or element which transforms bare facts into personal facts; the personal facts would not exist in the absence of her loving participation (85).

I'd like to take the example a step further to demonstrate the mediating effect of narrative in the creation of public knowledge. If the disinterested observer were to report about the child, s/he would use language different from the language used by the child's mother were the latter to speak about the tragedy in her life. Yet, in either case, the fact that something is told produces the kind of knowledge that a public can act on. The narrator, whether reporter or mother, mediates between personal experience and public knowledge.

The connection between the humanities and public politics is forged on both the level of thought (as in common ways of knowing) and the level of action (as in significant products). The difference between dialectics and deliberation is the difference between self-reflection and judgment, or between insight and choice, or further: between thought and action. The dynamics for the reconciliation of polarities has been described as a back and forth movement, an oscillation between the

---

[6] Consensus is especially important in the face of cultural relativism. In a forthcoming book (*Nietzsche and the Modern Crisis of the Humanities*), Peter Levine discusses the Nietzschean distinction between morality and moralities. The idea of one morality is naive; the idea of moralities is so problematic as to be futile; the third option Levine offers is to "develop ethical standards through a universal discussion that is aimed at consensus."

polarities of private and public, between philosophy and rhetoric, thought and action.[7] Narrative mediates between experience and knowledge, and acts as a catalyst for public deliberation.

Projects

Patrick Parks, an English professor at Elgin Community College in Illinois, has connected the world to his students by supporting their effort to produce a book of poems, essays, and fiction entitled *Sarajevo: An Anthology for Bosnian Relief.* Sales of the anthology have raised $20,000 for Bosnian relief.

Max Reichard, a professor of American history, sees his work at Delgado Community College in New Orleans as a natural outgrowth of his scholarship. "It's our responsibility as academics," he says, "to engage the community in dialogue about public issues."

My colleague at the University of Northern Colorado, Rita Brady Kiefer, poet and currently director of the Women's Studies Program, spends two nights a week working at a shelter for battered women; she urges the women to write as a way of healing.

These are only a few instances of the civic dimension of the humanities. There are better publicized examples: the late A. Bartlett Giamatti, Yale English professor and major league baseball commissioner; Claudia Card, philosopher and feminist at the University of Wisconsin; Robert Coles, Harvard humanities professor and child psychiatrist. But the less publicized ones are the more engaging because their public work is done quietly and without a view to rewards or recognition.

Some of us have just begun to move outward from our academic compartments. At the University of Northern Colorado, I was part of a group of faculty from different departments to propose a new humanities program. This was the first time many of us had gone outside of our disciplines to team-plan and team-teach courses. Courses with titles such as "Ideas in Conflict," "Search for Meaning," and "Value Issues in the Political Economy" allowed us to cut across departmental lines. Lecturing was deemphasized or minimized to allow for a vital exchange of ideas in the classroom. Professors became facilitators; in some cases, we became students again. We all sat in a circle. The product of our effort was extremely rewarding for the teachers and, consequently, for the students.

The most remarkable effect on the teachers who participated in the project was the invigoration they felt from moving out of their disci-

---

[7] *Sprezzatura* is the term identified by Lanham (661) from Castiglione's *The Book of the Courtier.* It means "perpetual oscillation" between separated terms: ideal vs. real, Truth vs. truth, One vs. the many. The idea is not to favor one term over another but to work within the tension created by these oppositions.

plines. Recently, we developed a humanities course for multicultural studies called "Confluence of Cultures." The course took two years to plan, and it brought together faculty from Black Studies, Hispanic Studies, Anthropology, History, and Literature. Faculty shared their expertise and learned from one another. This, I believe, is the initial step we need to take: to move beyond academic compartmentalization in order to realize community within the college or university. The next step is easy to imagine but hard to make. It means having to break free of the university itself. Charles Muscatine, in a 1993 speech to the Federation of State Humanities Councils, "The Public Humanities and the Academy," says:

> People who deal with the humanities not only as ends in them-
> selves but also as essential to our common life force on the aca-
> demic humanist another point of view; they demand (up to now
> mostly implicitly) that the academic examine his or her profession
> from the perspective of the public good. They ask the academic
> this question: "Your patrons — mostly the public — have provided
> you haven, security, libraries, and time for study; what are you pro-
> viding in return?"

The return is for the teacher to realize a public role and to surmount the differences between discussion (which promotes self-reflection and insight) and deliberation (which emphasizes judgment and choice). As subject fields become interdisciplinary, discipline-based expertise slowly gives way to competences that are conversant across disciplines. Knowledge is the transformation of relations. We may not even need to distinguish between humanist and scientific knowledge. Recent theories of discourse (Reiss) and language (Kumar in *Exploring Reality*) indicate that all materials developed in a culture produce meaning; in other words, literary, artistic, and scientific products are interrelated, and are all part of social transformation. In the postmodern era, nobody has a hege-mony on truth; but everybody has the responsibility to seek it. These competences are not far from Lyotard's view of "know-how" and "listen-ing." Perhaps there is no better place to begin than in the community that is the university. In his plea for civility on college campuses, Ivan Strenski insists that "The university is not apart from the 'real world' where seri-ous matters are considered. The university is the 'real world' — of uni-versality, intellectual creativity, and rigor."[8] Scholars have the knowledge that goes beyond science; they know how to speak, and they can teach themselves how to listen. It wouldn't be too far of a stretch to say that

---

[8]   The argument has been made that teaching is public humanities. Charles Muscatine, for
      instance, says this is the case because eventually students become part of publics. Other texts
      connect pedagogy and politics, as in Patricia Bizzell's "The Politics of Teaching Virtue."

the best teachers at our colleges and universities are excellent discussants because they are well spoken and they listen. These are the teachers whose classes are characterized by intensive discussion and group involvement, whose classes are considered to be the most challenging and thought provoking.

Sheldon Hackney, chairman of the National Endowment for the Humanities, has issued a call to humanities scholars to join in the public conversation on cultural diversity and other issues facing their communities. Just as a partnership was formed between government and the public humanities through NEH, a new opportunity arises for a partnership between the academic humanist and the public. This partnership is possible because both share similar ways of knowing, similar ways of producing knowledge, and the partnership ensures that neither humanist nor public is put in the service of the other.

To promote the national conversation, schools need a committed core of faculty. It is clear that not all scholars will be drawn to public projects. Robert Grudin (*The Grace of Great Things*) speculates that the reason the university has not encouraged public service scholarship is that humanists are "constitutionally wary of undertaking social criticism or making value judgments." Humanists such as Stephen Greenblatt have justified the relevance of the humanities (or of teaching Shakespeare) to contemporary life but, I think, miss the point because of their paranoia about academic freedom. The issue is not whether literature professors are relevant, or leftist, or that they need to justify their scholarly mission. The issue is whether they can go beyond insights about diversity, to choices about diversity, whether they can go beyond a description of the diaspora to the ethics involved in immigration policy. The question of relevance is moot; what isn't moot — and arrives with a certain urgency — is the question of belonging, of having community, solving problems, realizing a civic role.

Literary critics like Edward Said and Homi Bhabha have suggested that the critic's role is to stand outside, or in between, thought and action. It is a theoretically unassailable position: it liberates the critic to be political without being involved in political action, to be humane without being involved with people. Thus, for the critic to be *of* the public, s/he must be simultaneously within and outside it. This seems to be the ultimate form of self-marginalization: existence on the fringes as a justification for noninvolvement. It has been further observed that language used to explain the paradoxes of commitment-without-involvement is so abstract as to alienate the public. Russell Jacoby observes that, "Unlike past American intellectuals, who saw the educated, nonacademic public as their main audience, today's leftist intellectuals feel no need to write for a larger public."

The task of the scholar is nothing less than this: To listen deeply, to ask for involvement without preaching, to see compassion as no different from the exercise of it, to grasp that, in the sphere of moral responsibility, understanding and judgment are one.

Common sense dictates that we think of the humanities and publics as already unified. Both care about the same things — happiness, the pursuit of the common good, the recognition of individual and social responsibility. Both are grounded in the same struggle to reconcile discernment with judgment, cognition with values, thinking, and choice. Both produce the kind of knowledge that is determinative, referential, personal. Both subscribe to a methodology based on acts rather than systems, ethics rather than science. And both enterprises require not so much a justification of their separateness as a program for their unification.

When Machiavelli entertained the possibility that a person could be clerk and reeve — "both at once" — he marked the shift from the medieval to the Renaissance worldview. The Renaissance ideal was for the humanist and the leader to be one and the same. As in the classical age, there was once again no difference between humanity and humaneness, or between the scholar and the good citizen, or between the good citizen and the responsible leader. Francis Bacon, for instance, saw Humane Philosophy as a branch of Knowledge that combined the study of classical languages, and the study of man and society. The word "civil" combined humanity and politics because it denoted ethical norms such as empathy, cooperation, kindness.

A new Renaissance awaits us.

Works Cited

Arendt, Hannah. *Between Past and Future.* New York: Penguin, 1954.

Barber, Benjamin R. "The Politics of Judgment." Rev. of *Political Judgment*, by Ronald Beiner. *Raritan*, Fall 1985: 130-43.

Bender, Thomas. *Intellect and Public Life: Essays on the Social History of Academic Intellectuals in the United States.* Baltimore: Johns Hopkins University Press, 1993.

Berlin, Isaiah. *Against the Current: Essays in the History of Ideas,* ed. Henry Hardy. New York: Viking, 1980.

Bitzer, Lloyd F. "Rhetoric and Public Knowledge." *Rhetoric, Philosophy, and Literature: An Exploration,* ed. Don M. Burks. West Lafayette: Purdue University Press, 1978.

Bizzell, Patricia. "The Politics of Teaching Virtue." *ADE Bulletin,* Winter 1992: 4-7.

Cohn-Sherbok, Dan, and Michael Irwin, eds. *Exploring Reality.* London: Allen & Unwin, 1987.

Coles, Robert. *The Call of Service: A Witness to Idealism.* Boston: Houghton, 1989.

_____. *The Political Life of Children.* Boston: Atlantic Monthly Press, 1986.

Greenblatt, Stephen. "The Best Way to Kill Our Literary Inheritance Is to Turn It Into a Decorous

Celebration of the New World Order." *The Chronicle of Higher Education,* 12 June 1991.

Grudin, Robert. *The Grace of Great Things: On the Nature of Creativity.* New York: Houghton, 1991.

Habermas, Jürgen. *The Structural Transformation of the Public Sphere: An Inquiry into a Category of Bourgeois Society.* Trans. Thomas Burger. Cambridge: MIT Press, 1992.

Jacoby, Russell. "The Ivory Tower Obscurity Fetish." *Harper's Magazine,* September 1994: 22-8.

Lanham, Richard. "The 'Q' Question." *South Atlantic Quarterly* 87 (1988): 653-700.

Levine, Peter. Draft copy of "Moral Education (*The Protagoras*)." *Living Without Philosophy.* In press.

_____. *Nietzsche and the Modern Crisis of the Humanities.* SUNY Press, forthcoming.

"Looking at the World Upside Down: An Interview with Robert Coles." *The Christian Century,* 1 Dec. 1993: 1,208.

Lyotard, Jean-Francois. *Peregrinations: Law, Form, Event.* New York: Columbia University Press, 1988.

_____. *The Postmodern Condition: A Report on Knowledge,* trans. Geoff Bennington and Brian Massumi. Minneapolis: University of Minnesota Press, 1984.

Machiavelli, Niccolo. *The Prince.* Vol. 1 of *The Chief Works and Others,* trans. Allan Gilbert. 3 vols. Durham: Duke University Press, 1965.

Muscatine, Charles. "The Public Humanities and the Academy." Address. Annual Business Meeting. Federation of State Humanities Councils. Washington, 17 October 1993.

Nussbaum, Martha C. *Love's Knowledge: Essays on Philosophy and Literature.* New York: Oxford University Press, 1990.

Reiss, Timothy J. *The Uncertainty of Analysis: Problems in Truth, Meaning, and Culture.* Ithaca: Cornell University Press, 1988.

Robbins, Bruce, ed., *The Phantom Public Sphere.* Minneapolis: University of Minnesota Press, 1993.

Rorty, Richard. *Objectivity, Relativism, and Truth.* Cambridge: Cambridge University Press, 1991.

Strenski, Ivan. "Recapturing the Values that Promote Civility on the Campuses." *The Chronicle of Higher Education,* 23 June 1993.

Walzer, Michael. *Thick and Thin: Moral Argument at Home and Abroad.* South Bend: University of Notre Dame Press, 1994.

Warren, Robert Penn. "America and the Diminished Self." *Democracy and Poetry.* Cambridge: Harvard University Press, 1975.

Jay Rosen

Public Journalism:
A Case for Public Scholarship

"**N**ew York University: A Private University in the Public Service" —
that's what my department letterhead says. A few years ago I decided to
take those words seriously, particularly the key word "public." While I'm
proud to call myself a professional scholar and consider service to my
profession important, what I mean — and what I hope my university
means — by "public service" is a little different. Here, the ideal to be
served is democracy, understood the way John Dewey understood it: as
an entire way of life, rather than a form of government.

What kind of intellectual work best promotes democracy as a way of
life? "Public scholarship" is the answer I would offer. By "public scholarship" I mean the quest to know things that can only be known with others in the public arena.

Currently my chosen arena is a movement to change the way the
American press does things and sees things. It's called "public journalism," or in some cases "civic journalism," and it is primarily a group of people within the profession who realize that something has gone seriously
wrong in journalism lately. What's gone wrong is suggested by a 1994
study by the Times Mirror company showing that 71 percent of
Americans now think the press "gets in the way of society solving its
problems." Public journalists are people who take that sort of finding
seriously, who understand that the press is implicated in the sad state our
public life has reached, and who are trying, within the constraints they

face, to reform themselves and their colleagues.

I helped coin the term "public journalism"; I run a foundation — a funded project that supports the movement; and I am working directly with journalists who are trying to figure out what this new approach is and how to make it work. That means I spend a lot of time on airplanes, in hotel ballrooms, and in conversation with professionals in the field, many of whom do not yet accept this approach.

I came to this work from a deep sense of dissatisfaction with the various identities available to me as a scholar interested in the press and public life. With only a brief career in journalism, I did not feel qualified to pass along the secrets of the craft to young people. Besides, I had come to the conclusion that the craft was dangerously adrift. What it needed was not new practitioners but new practices. That put me in the role of critic, but I was wary of the inward turn that social criticism and media theory had taken in recent years. Much of the best work, while thoroughly sophisticated, had only one location where it was discussed: the campus. That wasn't public enough for me.

Journalism, I thought, needed a new and stronger public philosophy. But with little sense of intellectual adventure within the profession, and with scant contact between academic thinkers and the craft of journalism, there seemed to be no room for the kind of conversations that might lead to reform. What was happening to the press, what was happening to public life, what was happening to democracy, what was happening to citizens, what was happening to work and leisure — all these had to be discussed together, under the premise that they were mutually dependent. But unless such a conversation was linked to reform, it would have no lasting value.

I was still struggling with my approach to this problem when I had one of those "never again" experiences. In 1990, I found myself at a university think tank, in a room with six newspaper editors and six social scientists. The meeting had been called so that the journalists could get the benefit of what the academics knew about political alienation, voter turnout, and related themes. All of the social scientists were people steeped in survey research, and they immediately took over the discussion, exchanging sophisticated interpretations of the polling data as if they were at an academic meeting. I have a Ph.D. and took my mandatory course in statistics, but I had trouble following the discussion, and the editors, of course, were lost. Intimidated by the seeming blunt superiority of academic knowledge, they withdrew into an angry silence.

I found this whole scene embarrassing for the editors and for myself as a scholar, and I've been brooding about the episode ever since. What made it possible for the academics to virtually deny the humanity of the editors, people sitting right across the table from them? What left the journalists helpless to speak up for their own way of knowing? How should we have been talking if we wanted to get somewhere by reasoning together? As journalists and scholars, what was our common problem, our common work, our common language? And finally, what was I doing there? I had done a dissertation on the idea of the public and its relationship to the press, and while I thought I knew something about the subject, I too remained lodged in a frustrated silence, listening to the data pour forth.

What I call "public journalism" and some call "civic journalism" is, in a way, an attempt to overcome this scene, to build a conversational space that has not emerged from professional training on the one hand, social science on the other, or the culture of academic critique on a third. Public journalism, then, is a way of studying the press in common with journalists, where they are not the objects of inquiry, or targets of an academic critique, but coproducers of a form of understanding that could not exist without them. This, to me, is the heart of public scholarship — it is reasoning with, rather than knowledge about, others. It has a critical element of solidarity in it. And it is best practiced in public settings, where common languages must be used.

Defining Public Journalism

So, what exactly is public journalism? It's at least three things. First, it's an argument about the proper task of the press. Second, it's a set of practices that are slowly spreading through American journalism. Third, it's a movement of people and institutions.

What the argument says is this: Journalism cannot remain valuable unless public life remains viable. If public life is in trouble in the United States, then journalism is in trouble. Therefore, journalists should do what they can to support public life. The press should help citizens participate and take them seriously when they do. It should nourish or create the sort of public talk that might get us somewhere, what some of us would call a deliberative dialogue. The press should change its focus on the public world so that citizens aren't reduced to spectators in a drama dominated by professionals and technicians. Most important, perhaps, journalists must learn to see hope as an essential resource that they cannot deplete indefinitely without tremendous costs to us and them.

The argument public journalism makes is derivative of academic theory. It is borrowed from the work of German philosopher Jürgen Habermas on the public sphere, from John Dewey's great book, *The*

Public and Its Problems, and from the writings of James Carey, perhaps the leading journalism educator in the United States. What is distinctive about the argument is not the ideas in it, but the simple fact that journalists are helping to create the argument.

As an example, I offer my working relationship with Davis Merritt, Jr., the editor of the *Wichita Eagle*. Merritt is my partner in crime. I consult with him weekly, we have shared many platforms together, and he is identified with the rise of public journalism to visibility within the profession. He has written a book on the approach and is trying to practice what he preaches. Merritt brings more than 30 years of journalism experience to the table and is persuasive to his colleagues in a way that I could never be. By doing something he's willing to call "public journalism," by urging his colleagues to try their own versions, he prevents the idea from becoming merely "academic."

Public journalism is also a set of practices, most of them experiments by local newspapers trying to connect with citizens in a more useful way. For example, the *Charlotte Observer* in 1992 abandoned the approach to election coverage known as the horse-race angle. Instead, it sought to ground its coverage in what it called a "citizen's agenda," meaning a list of discussion priorities identified by area residents through the paper's own research. When candidates gave an important speech during the campaign, the contents were "mapped" against the citizen's agenda, so that it was easy to tell what was said about those concerns that ranked highest with citizens.

This may seem like a modest reform, but it involved a fundamental shift in the mission of campaign journalism. The master narrative changed from something like, "Candidates maneuver and manipulate in search of votes," to something like, "Citizens of Charlotte demand serious discussion." The Charlotte approach has become widely known and widely copied because it addresses long-standing frustrations with a campaign dialogue dominated by political professionals and the cynicism they engender.

A second kind of public journalism initiative is under way at the *Norfolk Virginian-Pilot*. There, the editors have created something called the "public life team," which is a group of reporters assigned to cover politics and government in a "more public" way. Previously, these reporters would have been attached to institutions like city hall, and this attachment would have provided them with their lens on politics. The public life team is charged with inventing a more bottom-up orientation to public affairs reporting — one that includes city hall but doesn't originate there. Among the techniques they employ is the use of small deliberative forums, what they call "community conversations," not to ask people what they want to read, or to survey their opinions, but to discover how nonprofessionals name and frame issues. This then becomes the starting point for the paper's political reporting, replacing the usual sources — the machinations of insiders or the maneuvering of public officials.

In effect, Norfolk is trying to routinize the shift in narrative strategy that the *Charlotte Observer* undertook in its campaign coverage. As the public life team learns how public journalism is done — and they are very much inventing it as they go — they teach what they know to other teams of reporters. I recently assisted the editors of the *Virginian-Pilot* in a weekend retreat intended to jump-start the process of changing routines. Fifty participants devoted three days to thinking through the shift in consciousness and technique that public journalism demands. The editors and I agreed on a price of admission to this retreat: a rather lengthy reading list of works in democratic theory and press scholarship, including essays by political scientist Robert Putnam of Harvard, along with excerpts from Daniel Yankelovich's important work, *Coming to Public Judgment*, and Tocqueville's *Democracy in America*. Officials of Landmark Communications, the company that owns the newspaper, chose to attend and they did the reading, too.

This retreat meant creating a public space for intellect within journalism. When 50 working journalists take time out to spend the weekend struggling with the implications of democratic theory and press criticism for their own work, when they do so under the expectation that they will reform their routines accordingly, when the executives within their company are joining them in this adventure, I hope you can see how a new kind of space has been created. As far as I know, nothing like it has been attempted in American journalism. This is public scholarship and public journalism brought together.

Other public journalism practices have involved creating public forums that show citizens engaged in deliberative dialogue. The forums, sponsored by a media partnership in Madison, Wisconsin, model democratic habits of mind and conversation. In several places, like Boulder, Colorado, and Olympia, Washington, newspapers have intervened in a lethargic public climate, bringing together civic leaders, experts, and groups of citizens to chart a long-term vision for a community, which is then published and debated in the newspaper. There have been various efforts to focus political reporting on the search for solutions to public problems: and a variety of measures have been adopted to heighten the visibility of citizens in the news by, for example, telling the story of individuals who get involved and make a difference. There have been campaigns to get people to vote, including some that allowed people to register in the lobby of the newspaper. There also have been other efforts to engage citizens as participants — for example a "Neighborhood Repair Kit" published by the *Star Tribune* in Minneapolis, which sought to give residents the information and incentive they needed to improve their neighborhoods.

The third form public journalism takes is as a movement. In the classic American tradition of public-spirited reform, this movement is trying to recall journalism to its deepest mission of public service. The movement is primarily drawn from professionals within the press, along with a smaller number from the academic world, and several institutional players. I would estimate its core membership at perhaps 200 or so, with several hundred others expressing sympathy with its general aims.

Most (but not all) are daily newspaper journalists, typically from small and medium-sized cities like Charlotte, North Carolina, or Wilmington, Delaware, although we do have a tiny foothold in larger precincts like Boston (the *Boston Globe*). The institutional support comes from projects like mine, funded by the Knight Foundation; from the Pew Center for Civic Journalism, supported by the Pew Charitable Trusts; from the Poynter Institute for Media Studies; and especially from the Kettering Foundation, an operating and research organization in Dayton, Ohio, which was the incubator of the idea.

As a reform movement, public journalism tries to provoke discussion within the profession, spread the lessons of practice, and put like-minded people in touch with one another. At this stage, it is very much a minority impulse, rooted primarily in the regional press. But it is on the radar screen of the entire press, and has been debated everywhere. The practices that correspond to the argument are not very far advanced; they are experiments at best, and it will be five to ten years before we know what their real potential is. We are just at the beginning of a long process of cultural change within journalism, and there is every chance that the movement will be marginalized, or defeated by the forces of reaction or by its own failure to grow and mature.

Resistance to Public Journalism

Even within those organizations led by editors committed to the approach, public journalism is resisted in the name of traditional values — especially the imperative of distance and detachment. It is called a fad or gimmick by some who see any attempt to "connect" with citizens as equivalent to a marketing approach, pandering to readers, surrendering professional judgment.

Another kind of objection is more telling. Recently I debated public journalism with Leonard Downie, editor of the *Washington Post*, who — not surprisingly — rejected the suggestion that journalists were public actors of any sort. Since they were not actors, they did not need a philosophy of action, which is one thing public journalism is. Therefore, according to Downie, public journalism is either a waste of time or a dangerous intrusion of "advocacy" into the politically neutral space of the news.

Downie's objections show how underdeveloped is the journalist's political or public identity. Once questioned about it, journalists find themselves bereft of any means of understanding, defending, or sharing that identity with others inside or outside the profession. Within the American press, "identity politics" means the vehemently advanced denial that doing journalism has anything to do with doing politics. According to this understanding, journalists are never actors, always observers. They are also exempt from what may be the thorniest problem in twentieth-century thought: how to handle the insight that the knower is incorporated into the known, without falling into a mindless solipsism or retreating into naive empiricism.

Without saying how they have done it, many in the press seem to consider the problem effectively solved. They stubbornly maintain that their portrait of the public world is not constructed; rather it reflects the world as it is. Journalists, they insist, are not implicated in public life even though they affect it. They are truth-tellers, but not truth-makers. They are also watchdogs, critics of the government, but this to them is not a political identity or a political art. It is a professional role performed in a more or less neutral fashion. Others have agendas; journalists merely ask questions and gather facts.

In my own writings on public journalism, I press hard on this point, which I consider the key point in a whole architecture of professional denial. But the difficulty I have in this endeavor is a measure of the university's failure to transport the discussion of the knower and the known into public arenas where it has daily relevance. Journalists, I have found, rely far too much on the claim to "objectivity," which tends to be ridiculed in the academy as hopelessly naive or deliberately evasive. But ridicule is easy; relationships are hard. Whatever modest progress I've made in persuading some journalists that they are at least implicated in public life is due to the relationships I maintain with them, which allow me to see how they see the problem of the knower and the known.

So here is the accommodation we have come to: to acknowledge a political "identity" as a public journalist is to agree that you have a stake in public life — that you are a member of the community, and not a mechanism outside it. This does not mean that the press can become a partisan or advocate. But neither is it to withdraw into a stance of civic exile, where what's happening to the community somehow isn't happening to you as a professional.

Public journalists see themselves as conveners of public talk, aids to a more active citizenry, modelers of deliberative dialogue, supporters of a healthy public life. They are willing to assume a kind of political identity, but are not willing to join the struggles at the heart of left-right-center politics — except the very important struggle for a more vital public sphere, a better conversation, a public life that might earn our respect.

But isn't this the struggle we want the university to be engaged in? In this sense public journalism is very much an academic concern, but what it requires of the academic is to give up the one thing we often defend most vigorously: our claim to expertise. As soon as I become the expert in public journalism, I know I have failed, for public journalism has to be what journalists say it is, what they decide to do with it. I can try to persuade them that the interesting work lies in this or that direction; I can try to offer a vocabulary for their use. But the test of this vocabulary always lies with journalists themselves, and in a deeper sense, with the communities where public journalism is practiced.

What my colleagues in the academic study of the media think is an adequate philosophy or an important critique is relevant only if some journalist somewhere can be persuaded to share it and to employ it in reforming his or her work. That act of persuasion is at the heart of scholarship as engagement, along with a willingness to be persuaded, in return, by people without Ph.Ds. Indeed, public scholarship begins with a recognition that the most important thing you can know is not knowable through your relationships with other scholars. In my case, the thing I most needed to know was: Where are the openings for a stronger public philosophy to emerge in the professional culture of the American press? The only way to answer this question is to experiment with that culture, to become conversant with it, to test where its own resources lie. That's what I'm doing — I think.

That's a quick sketch of public journalism. My own role within this movement is to discover the philosophy lying, as it were, within the practices that also illustrate it; to organize meetings, public spaces, where journalists interested in this approach can mingle and learn together in concert with a few intellectuals; to research the relevant experiments through the project I direct; to get on airplanes and spread the word about public journalism to any journalism group that will hear me; to defend the need for this approach against the criticism it receives and requires; and to think strategically about where the movement can go next. Eventually this work must be turned over to the profession itself, for if public journalism cannot live within the craft and become normalized, then it will have failed.

Scholarship and Public Journalism

I want to add a few remarks here about scholarship as engagement. As a professor of journalism, what I "do" is not theory, research, or criticism. What I do now is relationships — and these relationships with journalists are the proving ground for the ideas about democracy that matter to me. To the degree that these relationships work, public journalism lives. To the degree that the relationships falter, the approach is faltering.

Picture the territory that separates intellectuals who think about democracy from journalists who operate within the democracy as it exists "out there." Suppose we imagine this territory — the distance between us and them — as a political space. What makes it so? Well, one thing that makes it so is that we're in this together. Whatever is going to happen to democracy is going to happen to all of us — journalists, scholars, officeholders and government officials, citizens, exiles, left, right, center, or margin. Another thing we have in common is this: if markets replace publics as the only relevant arena in contemporary society, we're all sunk. What we do won't matter, what they do won't matter. Only the TV ratings will matter.

Many in the academy have profound differences with practicing journalists over a whole range of questions, from the myth of objectivity to competing visions of a just society. Differences are what make for politics, of course, and when they don't — when there's no political space in which to negotiate our differences — we know we have failed somehow in our pretensions as democrats. Public journalism attends to this failure, tries to take it seriously. It worries about the silences, the conversations that don't happen when intellect traps itself too cleverly within an academic frame.

In a sentence I find myself returning to again and again, the political philosopher Michael Sandel writes, "When politics goes well, we can know a good in common that we cannot know alone." Here is the intellectual opportunity afforded by the political challenge I just outlined. What can practicing journalists and critical scholars know in common that they cannot know alone? The only way to answer this question is to try to make the politics between us "go well," to assume that we're "in this together," to ask, as the comedian Joan Rivers used to put it, "Can we talk?"

For an academic accustomed to operating within a discipline or "field," the first challenge is preeminently one of language. Keeping the conversation going takes priority over making the conversation go the way you need it to go for your expertise to matter. Maintaining relationships becomes more important than maintaining your position. What you can only know in common with journalists is privileged over the knowledge you have only because you are a scholar of the press. The public sphere, for this purpose, is not what Habermas or his critics say it is. It is the "field" you can manage to create, in association with others who have very different ideas and very different professional lives. What's true is what works in maintaining the relationship and moving it forward, which is another way of saying that public journalism is pragmatism in the William James and John Dewey sense. It is also frustrating in the way that democracy is frustrating, risky in the way that democracy is risky.

What are some of the advantages of working in relationships? Well, it immediately changed my view of journalists. I now see them as people struggling to preserve a connection to the public sphere amidst two kinds of pressures. One kind obviously is market pressures coming from the media industry. The other is the pressures that come about from the evaporation of public life, the general disgust with politics, the rising tide of cynicism, the weakening of community ties that also weakens the interest in journalism, the decline of civic capacity, the erosion of literacy and competence.

Trying to understand these pressures as they come to bear on journalists in newsrooms has taught me to distinguish the media from journalism. If we conflate these things we miss the threat to journalism posed by the media. We give up too quickly the rhetoric of public service and First Amendment values that still clings to the journalism profession. The fact is that journalists need our support if we're serious about creating a workable public sphere. The media threaten them just as much as they dismay some of us.

I also look at media companies in a different way. Some still have room for the values of the public sphere; others are squeezing that space. Their corporate cultures now look like distinct entities, whereas before I might have collapsed them under a category like "global capitalism." Widening the available space for public interest journalism within these companies is something journalism professors should be helping to do — unless, of course, we know that there is no such possibility. The only way to know that, I think, is to be in relationship to working journalists and to observe the forms of autonomy they do and do not haste.

Another thing I have discovered is the importance of rootedness. The journalists most attracted to public journalism tend to be those who have something to defend beyond their professional status. They have put down roots in the communities where they work. They have tried traditional journalism and found themselves frustrated that problems kept getting worse. Those who dismiss public journalism most quickly are journalists passing through on their way to Washington and New York. They romanticize the figure of the journalist as hard-boiled detective, ferreting out lies and corruption and moving on to the next town. Public life doesn't interest them — exposure does.

Finally, I discovered how far we have to go in reforming journalism education. Several years ago I gave a talk at one of the elite schools of journalism. My visit came in the twelfth week of the semester. To my standard speech on public journalism the reaction was 90 percent hostile. The mere suggestion that there was a responsibility to the outcome of public life was enough to turn almost everyone in the entering graduate class against the idea. This year I returned to the same school and gave the same speech to a new class during its second week in school. This time, the reaction was only 50 percent hostile, with genuine divisions opening up between those who saw in public journalism the reason they had chosen the field, and others who stared at their classmates in disbelief.

What explains the two different reactions? My answer is this: between the second and twelfth weeks of the term the professional ideology of the press takes over and students learn that they should have no political identity if they're going to be serious professionals. In other words, they assimilate the stance of civic exile, and it is the university teaching it to them! The journalism school as it now exists works against public journalism, when it should be the strongest home of the idea. For me, the most immediate result is that I have more support in newsrooms around the country than I do inside my own faculty. But I am hopeful I can change that as my colleagues grapple with what is at stake — the character of journalism as a public profession.

Drawing journalists (and scholars) out of the stance of civic exile, getting them to invest in the fortunes of public life, is a political project for which only one form of politics will do: politics as conversation, mutual persuasion, and as an experiment in public learning. The knowledge uniquely available to this work is the knowledge of possibility: the possible meanings of the public sphere, the possible journalisms that remain, the possible identities journalists can have as citizens, and those that scholars can have outside the university's walls, but fully within its animating ideal.

I close by borrowing a line from the philosopher Jean Bethke Elshtain who has written a wise book called *Democracy on Trial*. In the introduction she remarks on her complex feelings about Richard Nixon on the occasion of his death. Looking back on the past 20 years, she says she's surprised by how easy it was for her to hate. "I don't hate anymore," she writes. "I have joined the ranks of the nervous." What she means, of course, is that she is nervous about the future of democracy, about our ability to solve the problem of living together, about Rodney King's profoundly political question: "Can we all get along?"

This, finally, is why I now deal in relationships. With Elshtain, I have joined the ranks of the nervous.

Max R. Harris

A Surplus of Seeing: Bakhtin, the Humanities, and Public Discourse

In his presidential address to the annual meeting of the American Academy of Religion in 1986, Nathan Scott spoke of "the myriad disjunctions that fractionize and disunite cultural discourse in our period, making all our forums a scene of babel." Far from advocating a return to a simpler time, in which all (or, at least, all those with the power to shape the dominant discourse) spoke with a single voice, Scott warned against "any effort at bullying the world into granting its suffrage to some unilateral position which is claimed to be foundational in respect to the rest of culture and therefore capable of adjudicating the claims of all other points of view." Rather, he said, "given the pervasive cultural fragmentation of this late time," we are "irrevocably committed to an ethos of encounter, to the stance of attentiveness and listening."[1]

Although the fear of fragmentation has intensified in the decade since Scott thus measured "the larger cultural atmosphere"[2] in which we live, there has been no concomitant increase in attentiveness and listening. Instead, the prevailing form of public discourse seems to have become, to borrow a phrase from William Raspberry, one of "simultaneous shouting."[3] Fearful of a radical loss of identity amidst the growing multitude of

[1] Nathan A. Scott, Jr., "The House of Intellect in an Age of Carnival: Some Hermeneutical Reflections," *Journal of the American Academy of Religion* 55 (1987), p. 7.

[2] Ibid., p. 3.

[3] William Raspberry, "Needed: A Conversation about Race," *Washington Post,* 24 March 1995, A23.

voices demanding attention, we are prone to greet misunderstanding or dissent, like the proverbial American tourist in Paris, by raising our voices and repeating ourselves.

Consider, by way of example, the very "pluralism" which, according to Scott, is "the name of the game we are fated to play."[4] Pluralism is a term little suited to a discourse of simultaneous shouting, for it still bears traces of an original ideal of unity. *E pluribus unum* is, after all, the foundational motto of the United States. It is significant, therefore, that pluralism has been largely superseded in popular parlance by a word that has come to bear more divisive connotations: multiculturalism. For this is a word that signals to those on one side of the aisle a concerted attack on the traditional values of Western civilization and to those on the other side an opportunity to flaunt all that will not readily assimilate to those values. The merits of multiculturalism depend, I suppose, on your point of view.

In fact, the defining characteristic of multiculturalism itself and of our period as a whole may well be the widespread conviction that all things do assuredly depend on one's point of view. And, amidst the clamor of voices competing for attention in the cultural marketplace, it is this very conviction that both emboldens those on the margins to demand a hearing and scares into fierce rear guard action those whose claim on the center has been declared untenable. How, then, are we to think and speak, in such a fractured state, if we are not simply to resort to the cacophony of simultaneous (and sometimes armed) shouting? And what part might the humanities play in making such thinking and speaking not only possible but (dare we hope) habitual?

The Validity of Multiple Perspectives

There are those, of course, who will cry out in horror that to grant any credence to the validity of multiple perspectives is nothing more than an invitation to relativism. They will at once reassert the objectivity of their own particular perspective and demand that all others conform to their way of seeing things. But, if those who are tempted to respond in this way would but raise their index finger at arm's length from their eyes and then focus through it on a small object some few feet away, closing first one eye and then the other, observing that the relationship of the object to their finger shifts as one or the other eye is closed, they would notice that even the two eyes in their own head have different points of view. Or, if they were to wander round a European cathedral during liturgy, viewing the congregation and the celebrant and the details of the ancient building from several vantage points, their view blocked at one

---

[4] Scott, p. 7.

point by this pillar and at another by that arch, they would surely agree that what they see depends on where they stand. Or, finally, if they were to speak, as I have done in my capacity as a Presbyterian pastor, to Christians troubled by the traditional language of theology, they would realize that human responses to the image of God as an omnipotent Father are unconsciously shaped by childhood experiences, good and bad, of human fathers, and that even our view of the invisible depends, at least in part, on where we stand emotionally. To invalidate multiple perspectives is not to resist subversive ideology; it is to ignore a fact of life.

Then, too, there are those who apparently abandon claims to cultural hierarchy and embrace the virtues of difference only to insist, after all, that distinct cultures are profoundly incapable of assimilating to or even communicating with one another. According to a recent United Nations report, it is this that fuels the frightening resurgence of racism in Europe. Neoracist ideology, the report claims,

> emphasizes the unique nature of the languages, religions, mental and social structures and value systems of immigrants of African, Arab or Asian origin … in order to justify the need to keep human communities separate. It even goes so far as to contend that preserving their identity is in the interest of the communities concerned. By asserting a radical cultural pluralism, the new racism based on cultural difference tries, paradoxically, to look like genuine anti-racism and to show respect for all group identities.[5]

This is the dark side of enlightened multiculturalism, which has moved so far to the left as to circumnavigate the globe, as it were, and reemerge on the right. And, I am afraid it is also sometimes the position taken by members of previously oppressed groups, who in their desire to take pride in their own heritage, assert that their own culture is inherently incomprehensible to anyone of a different skin color, gender, or ethnic heritage. They, therefore, retreat into cultural ghettoes of their own making from which all others are excluded. Even so ardent an advocate of marginal perspectives as Tzvetan Todorov has renounced this cultural "apartheid," which, in its concern to avoid the presumptions of "ethnocentric universalism" swings to the opposite extreme, renouncing "the very idea of shared humanity," and thus abandons the possibility of dialogue between different points of view.[6]

And, finally, there are those whose discourse is so guarded as to

---

[5]   United Nations, Commission on Human Rights, Sub-Commission on Prevention of Discrimination and Protection of Minorities, *Elimination of Racial Discrimination: Measures to Combat Racism and Racial Discrimination and the Role of the Sub-Commission*, E/CN.4/Sub.2/1992/11 (New York: United Nations, 14 July, 1992), p. 3.

[6]   Tzvetan Todorov, "'Race,' Writing, and Culture," trans. L. Mack, *Critical Inquiry* 13 (1986), p. 175.

exclude all personal commitment from the public square. George Marsden has complained at length in *The Soul of the American University* of the degree to which religious belief is excluded from intellectual engagement in this country.[7] One might add that, in certain circles, it is not merely religious belief but conviction of any sort that is greeted with a hermeneutics of suspicion. Academic discourse, for example, routinely insists that unqualified declarative statements be ascribed to others and surrounded with quotation marks to signal their inherent subjectivity; and that the object of study not be the world itself but reported perceptions of the world. The reader will note that, without planning to do so, I have conformed the second and third sentences of this paragraph to such a guarded style. In the one, I ascribe opinion to a colleague rather than own it myself and, in the other, I twice qualify the concluding observation with "one might add" and "in certain circles." While such careful discourse makes a welcome change from the simultaneous shouting of which Raspberry complains, it is not, on the whole, conducive to heartfelt investment in the well-being of civic society.

What is needed, then, is a way of thinking and speaking that accepts the validity of multiple perspectives and treats the other with dignity as a subject to whom it is worth listening rather than as an errant object at whom one feels compelled to shout; that, amidst a multitude of differences, allows the possibility of genuine communication; and, that, for all its care not to take refuge in unqualified dogma, is yet not afraid of personal investment in the discourse at hand and in the world to which that discourse, however obliquely, refers. If, in the process, we should also learn something fresh about the world in which both we and our distant neighbors live, so much the better.

The Surplus of Seeing

This, I believe, is where Mikhail Bakhtin comes in. Bakhtin was a Russian literary critic who labored in considerable obscurity during a half-century of Stalinism. Toward the end of his life, he achieved a certain recognition in Russia and, since his death in 1975, his writings have acquired a substantial influence both at home and abroad.[8] Bakhtin wrote under a regime that sanctioned only a single, official point of view, a condition that Bakhtin called "monological," because, as in a monologue, only

---

[7] George M. Marsden, *The Soul of the American University* (Oxford: Oxford University Press, 1994).

[8] The best introductions to Bakhtin's life and thought in English are Katerina Clark and Michael Holquist, *Mikhail Bakhtin* (Cambridge, MA: Harvard University Press, 1984) and Gary Saul Morson and Caryl Emerson, *Mikhail Bakhtin: Creation of a Prosaics* (Stanford, CA: Stanford University Press, 1990). Much of what follows is adapted from several passages in Max Harris, *The Dialogical Theatre* (New York: St. Martin's Press, 1993).

one point of view was allowed expression. Against what he called the monological pretensions of official culture, Bakhtin championed the diversity of ethnic cultures, the multiplicity of languages, dialects and jargons, and the possibility of genuine dialogue or, as two of his biographers have phrased it, "communication between simultaneous differences."[9]

Bakhtin's view of languages will serve as a good illustration of his celebration of diversity. Human society, according to Bakhtin, is blessed with a multitude of tongues. There are languages that generate their own dictionaries and manuals of grammar; and, within "any single national language," there are "social dialects, professional jargons, generic languages, languages of generations and age groups, tendentious languages," "bland languages," "languages of the authorities" and of the oppressed, and languages "of various circles and of passing fashions." This happy state Bakhtin calls "heteroglossia."[10] Bakhtin welcomes such profusion because, as he sees it, each language embodies in some measure a different ideology or point of view. One person's "freedom fighters," for example, are another's "terrorists," "mujahedin," "holy warriors," "martyrs," "bandidos," "guerrilleros," "nationalists," "republicans," "Bolsheviks," or "barbarian hordes." The coexistence or, even better, the interanimation of different languages bears witness against the presumptions of what Bakhtin called "monoglossia" and guards against the imposition of a single, "official" point of view. Whereas most scholars interpret the story of the Tower of Babel conventionally as an account of "the fall of language into multiplicity,"[11] it becomes in Bakhtin's scheme of things the gracious gesture of a God who knows the political value of variety.[12]

Bakhtin's insistence on the necessity of multiple points of view was not, however, merely a way of resisting totalitarianism. It was, he believed, written into the very nature of human beings. Just as I have illustrated the phenomenon of multiple perspectives from a single pair of eyes or from the different positions an individual might take within a medieval cathedral, Bakhtin illustrated the same phenomenon from the positions that might be taken by two individuals. One may observe very simply, he wrote in one of his early essays, that no two bodies can occupy the same space at the same time, and that no two viewpoints can therefore be identical:

When I contemplate a whole human being who is situated outside

---

[9]   Clark and Holquist, p. 9.

[10]   Mikhail Bakhtin, *The Dialogic Imagination*, trans. Caryl Emerson and Michael Holquist (Austin, TX: University of Texas Press, 1981), pp. 262-3, 295-6.

[11]   Michael Edwards, *Towards a Christian Poetics* (London: Macmillan, 1984), p. 55.

[12]   Bakhtin, *The Dialogic Imagination*, p. 278, compares "the Tower-of-Babel mixing of languages" to "the unfolding of social heteroglossia."

and over against me, our concrete, actually experienced horizons do not coincide. For at each given moment, regardless of the position and proximity to me of this other human being whom I am contemplating, I shall always see and know something that he, from his place outside and over against me, cannot see himself: parts of his body that are inaccessible to his own gaze (his head, his face and its expressions), the world behind his back, and a whole series of objects and relations, which in any of our mutual relations are accessible to me but not to him. As we gaze at each other, two different worlds are reflected in the pupils of our eyes.[13]

You may, for example, see things behind my back, such as a painting (if we are in a museum) or passing clouds (if we are outdoors), that are hidden from my view, while I may see things that your position denies to your vision, such as a different painting on the other wall or a storm brewing behind your head. This difference determines that, although we may be in the same event, that event is different for us both.[14] If we stand alongside one another, facing in the same direction, the difference will be minimal. But, to the degree that we stand far apart or face in opposite directions, the difference will be great and, for that very reason, the "excess [or surplus] of seeing"[15] that each of us can offer the other will be all the more interesting.

Bakhtin explores the implications of this surplus of seeing in terms of both interpersonal and intercultural relationships.[16] His early essays focus on the former. If my relationship with another individual is to be "rendered meaningful ethically, cognitively, or aesthetically," Bakhtin writes, it requires what he calls "live entering (*vzhivanie*)," a simultaneous exercise of empathy (entering into the other's world) and "outsidedness" (viewing the other from the perspective of my own world).[17] As Gary Saul Morson and Caryl Emerson put it, first paraphrasing and then citing Bakhtin directly, "In *vzhivanie*, one enters another's place *while still maintaining one's own place*, one's own 'outsidedness,' with respect to the other. 'I actively live into (*vzhivain*) an individuality, and consequently do not, for a single moment, lose myself completely or lose my singular place outside the other individuality.'"[18]

---

[13] Mikhail Bakhtin, *Art and Answerability*, eds. Michael Holquist and Vadim Liapunov, trans. Vadim Liapunov (Austin, TX: University of Texas Press, 1990), pp. 22-3.

[14] Clark and Holquist, p. 70.

[15] Bakhtin, *Art and Answerability*, p. 23.

[16] Morson and Emerson, pp. 52-6.

[17] Bakhtin, *Art and Answerability*, pp. 25-6.

[18] Morson and Emerson, p. 11.

A Russian friend tells me that *vzhivain* is used in novels of espionage to describe the activity of spies who must, at one and the same time, enter wholly into the target culture, understanding and observing even the smallest conventions of language, commerce, and etiquette, so as to be indistinguishable from the natives, while at the same time fully retaining their identity and their capacity to observe as citizens of their own country.[19] Bakhtin's own, most startling illustration of *vzhivanie* is the Christian doctrine of the Incarnation, according to which God became fully human without, for a moment, surrendering his divinity. "One way to imagine Christ," according to Morson and Emerson's paraphrase of Bakhtin, "is to see the incarnation as an act of *vzhivanie*. According to this analogy, Christ did not empathize with people; rather he became one of them while still maintaining his divine outsidedness."[20] "Christ's descent," Bakhtin wrote, is "the great symbol of activity" that conforms to the pattern of *vzhivanie*.[21] Both illustrations point to the fact that, in *vzhivanie*, "empathy" and "outsidedness" do not alternate but, as Bakhtin puts it, simultaneously "interpenetrate each other."[22]

Just as I can understand the other better through a "live entering" into his or her world, so I can be understood by the other. But, Bakhtin adds, it is also the other who enables me to understand myself. For he or she is able to see me as I cannot see myself. By way of simple physical illustration, Bakhtin notes that only another can see me from behind, or view the expression of joy or sorrow on my face without the distorting self-consciousness of a mirror. What is true of my outward appearance is also true, Bakhtin suggests, of my inner being. The other's place outside me both limits what she can know of my inner world and affords her a perspective that I do not have. But, as I learn to see myself "through the eyes of another," as well as through my own, I am granted a more complete perception of myself than I could obtain alone. In a significant measure, "the self," to paraphrase Bakhtin, "is an act of grace, a gift of the other."[23]

In a later essay, Bakhtin applied the same principle to cross-cultural relationships. His immediate concern was that literary scholars should try to understand the total cultural context in which works from past

---

[19] I am indebted to Yuri Urbanovich for this insight.

[20] Gary Saul Morson and Caryl Emerson (eds.), *Rethinking Bakhtin* (Evanston, IL: Northwestern University Press, 1989), p. 11.

[21] I am indebted to Gary Saul Morson for providing me with a translation of this sentence over the telephone, 18 April 1991. I prefer Morson's translation to that of Mikhail Bakhtin, *Toward a Philosophy of the Act*, trans. Vadim Liapunov, ed. Vadim Liapunov and Michael Holquist (Austin, TX: University of Texas Press, 1993) p. 16: "A great symbol of self-activity the descending of Christ."

[22] Bakhtin, *Toward a Philosophy of the Act*, p. 15.

[23] Clark and Holquist, p. 68.

epochs were written. But the closing paragraphs of the essay admit a broader application. "There exists," he wrote,

> a very strong, but one-sided and thus untrustworthy, idea that in order to understand a foreign culture, one must enter into it, forgetting one's own, and view the world through the eyes of this foreign culture.... Of course, a certain entry as a living being into a foreign culture, the possibility of seeing the world through its eyes, is a necessary part of the process of understanding it; but if this were the only aspect of this understanding, it would merely be duplication and would not entail anything new or enriching. *Creative understanding* does not renounce itself, its own place in time, its own culture; and it forgets nothing. In order to understand, it is immensely important for the person who understands to be *located outside* the object of his or her creative understanding — in time, in space, in culture.[24]

It is not, then, simply a matter of furthering my understanding of the other culture by this simultaneous empathy and outsidedness. It is also the case, Bakhtin claims, that a culture, like an individual or a work of art, can yield its "meaning" to an outsider in a way that it cannot to itself or, in the case of a work of art, to its author. Earlier in the essay, he had applied this principle to the works of Shakespeare and of the Greeks, arguing that subsequent epochs have genuinely found "new significance" embedded in ancient texts, which neither the authors themselves nor their contemporaries "could consciously perceive and evaluate in the context of the culture of their epoch."[25] A twentieth-century production of *Oedipus Rex*, for example, may choose to incorporate or to ignore Freud's reading of the Oedipal myth, but a post-Freudian audience will certainly bring questions to the play that its original audience did not, and these questions will cause the text to resonate in ways that it could not have done to Sophocles.

At the close of his essay, Bakhtin asserts once more the importance of outsidedness in creative understanding and, therefore, in fostering mutually enriching cross-cultural dialogue:

> It is only in the eyes of *another* culture that foreign culture reveals itself fully and profoundly (but not maximally fully, because there will be cultures that see and understand even more). A meaning only reveals its depth once it has encountered and come into contact with another, foreign meaning: they engage in a kind of dia-

---

[24] Mikhail Bakhtin, *Speech Genres and Other Late Essays*, eds. Caryl Emerson and Michael Holquist, trans. Vern W. McGee (Austin, TX: University of Texas Press, 1986), pp. 6-7.

[25] Ibid., p. 4.

logue, which surmounts the closedness and one-sidedness of these particular meanings, these cultures. We raise new questions for a foreign culture, ones that it did not raise itself; we seek answers to our own questions in it; and the foreign culture responds to us by revealing to us new aspects and new semantic depths. Without *one's own* questions one cannot creatively understand anything other or foreign.... Such a dialogic encounter of two cultures does not result in merging or mixing. Each retains its own unity and *open* totality, but they are mutually enriched.[26]

Significance for Public Discourse

Bakhtin's ideas may be profitably brought to bear not only on the question of relationships between cultures that are chronologically or geographically distant from one another but also on the matter of civic discourse in a geographically unified society, such as our own, that seems nonetheless to be irrevocably fragmented into multiple ethnic and ideological subcultures. What we may learn from Bakhtin in this respect may be summarized, with deliberate simplicity, in a number of provisional conclusions:[27]

1. There are multiple points of view, within an individual, a couple, a family, a neighborhood, a town, a country, and the world. Some of these points of view may be grouped together and called "cultures," although it must be remembered that no living culture is truly closed, and that cultures have porous boundaries. That there are many points of view is both a fact of life and a political blessing, since multiple perspectives protect against monological thinking and totalitarian government.

2. I can see things that you can't see. You can see things that I can't see.

3. Were we to meet, you would soon know things about me that I don't know and I would know things about you that you don't know. Indeed, as you have read the preceding pages, you will have already formed a view of me to which I cannot gain access without your help.

4. You can help me know myself better. I can help you know yourself better. Dialogue is an aid to self-knowledge.

5. In order to listen to your point of view, I do not have to abandon mine. If I did, I would be subject to your limitations rather than my own, and I would have gained no "surplus of seeing."

6. In order to study another culture or set of values, I do not have to relinquish my own. To put it more fully, in order to examine the customs,

---

[26] Ibid., p. 7.

[27] These conclusions are adapted from Max Harris, "A Surplus of Seeing: Bakhtin and the Question of Multiculturalism," Stone Memorial Lecture, Beloit College, WI, 15 Feb. 1995.

literature, rituals, religion, music, and traditional values of another group, I do not have to abandon the art, ethics, and beliefs of my own group. If I engage in what Bakhtin calls *vzhivanie* (live entering), I can be true to my own culture while still learning to see what the world looks like from the point of view of your culture.

7. No human culture is inherently impenetrable by members of another culture. Understanding may be hard, but it is not impossible.

8. As I study another culture, I can see things in that culture that members of the culture themselves cannot see, and I can learn things about myself and my own culture that I could not learn without studying that other culture. As members of another culture study my culture, they see things in my culture that I cannot see without their aid, and they learn things about themselves and about their culture that they could not see without studying my culture.

9. The truth lies not in any particular point of view but in the dialogue between points of view.

10. To be afraid of multiculturalism, insofar as it advocates the study of many cultures, is to be afraid of self-knowledge.

11. To advocate multiculturalism, insofar as it promotes the isolation of cultures one from another, is to be afraid of self-knowledge.

Role of the Humanities

And this, finally, is where the humanities come in. For the humanities enable all of us who are necessarily limited to a single span of "threescore years and ten" to enter past epochs without leaving our own. History, whether it be the story of nations, literature, art, religion, or philosophy, is the narrative of others (of those who tell the tale and of those whose tale is told) who have seen things that we have not and who therefore offer us, in Bakhtin's term, a surplus of seeing. To the degree that we are able to enter imaginatively into the several worlds of the historian and of his or her subjects, while still retaining the perspective of our own time, we enter into dialogue with other points of view, learning more about ourselves and our time and, if we read well, gaining insight into past epochs that was not granted to those who then lived.

Moreover, although world travel is now much easier than it used to be, we are still more or less geographically confined. For many, fear of the unknown limits travel to well-beaten paths lined with recognizable amenities and, whatever resources and opportunities may come our way to travel far in our own time, even the most adventurous can still only be in one place at a time. But the humanities allow us, as we read, as we watch television documentaries, as we listen to and engage with visiting speakers, and as we wander through museum exhibits, to journey into distant territories without leaving the familiar setting of our own place. And, as we make the effort to do so creatively, learning for a little while to see both from our own perspective and through the eyes of others who are positioned very differently from ourselves (both the travelers who report to us and our distant neighbors of whom they bear us tidings), we abandon the monological frame of mind and enter into dialogue with others in the human community now living who offer us the benefits (and wonders) of a surplus of seeing.

We can say, then, that the humanities nurture (but can never guarantee) a frame of mind given to attentiveness and listening but not to the surrender of identity; that they incline the student (of whatever age) to an appreciation and evaluation of difference rather than to its suppression or, on the other hand, its unqualified acceptance; and that, at their best, they foster engaged and civil dialogue rather than the simultaneous shouting of dueling monologues. As such, we can argue, their place in the fabric of a society afraid for its future and prone, in its fear, to block its ears and shout louder, should be enlarged.

But it is, of course, always possible so to filter the perspectives of others through that of a narrator who sees things almost exactly as we do or through a personal or group prejudice that equates difference and error that we thereby lose the opportunity of a significant surplus of seeing. It is important, therefore, that we not only read outside our time and place but that we also read outside our ideology. If we have been persuaded by Bakhtin, we will do so both with the confidence of one who knows that to listen sympathetically to another's point of view is not to surrender one's own and with the humility of one who knows, too, that his or her own point of view is necessarily limited. The humanities cannot command such a splendid mix of confidence and humility, but they can encourage it, for the very habit of engaging over time with the rich variety of perspectives offered us by such disciplines as history, literature, cultural anthropology, and comparative ethics, will tend to reassure us that we do not cease to be ourselves as we read the works of others and, yet, that we know ourselves (and our virtues and vices and those of the time and place and group to which we belong) better as we learn to see ourselves with others' eyes. We know ourselves (and others) better but never, as Bakhtin would remind us, completely, for there are always others from whose perspective we have yet to see and whom we have yet to see from ours. The humanities encourage an ongoing dialogue rather than the silence that follows a final word.

James F. Veninga

The Humanities
and the Civic Imagination

It is often claimed that the humanities in America are in trouble. Critics point to the fragmentation of academic disciplines, the overspecialization of scholars, the priority placed on research over teaching at many universities, an abundance of esoteric scholarship, and an apparent slippage in societal support. While these criticisms need to be taken seriously, this paper seeks to demonstrate that there are some creative dimensions in the humanities today that hold great promise for the disciplines of the humanities and, more importantly, for American society. These dimensions include the public humanities — scholarship and programs that respond to public needs and interests. This essay focuses on the relationship between the humanities and critical challenges facing the American people.

This public dimension to the humanities has emerged at a critical time in the life of the nation. Challenges and problems continue to grow in severity — the erosion of public confidence in basic institutions of American society, frequent political deadlock in federal and state legislative bodies, rampaging crime, inadequate public schools, ethnic and cultural fragmentation, abused and neglected children, and urban deterioration. Indeed, these challenges and problems, now brought into sharper focus as preoccupation with Cold War realities gives way to clearer perceptions of where we as a nation have been and where we are, have resulted in a dramatic flight into private spheres. For the privileged and the well-off, the private sphere is often dominated by professional goals and materialistic pursuits. For the poor and the oppressed, the private sphere all too often is dominated by life on the edge, a life enveloped in poverty, fear, loneliness, and despair.

Deeper and more humane visions of our society, of how we are connected one to another, are needed to counter the loss of public space and the expansion of private space. The privileged seem to have lost a notion of a civic republic; the poor and dispossessed seem out of touch with the ideals behind the dramatic social movements of the past. For both, disconnection and rootlessness take hold.

In his book *The Radical Renewal: The Politics of Ideas in Modern America*, Norman Birnbaum points out the critical need in American society for the rehabilitation of public life and the reconstitution of citizenship.[1] Birnbaum joins an increasing number of concerned writers who recognize that old ways of thinking will not solve new kinds of problems. How can the struggle for survival give way to a nation made whole, a democracy of citizens committed to each other and to commonly shared goals and values? Without a sense of common ground, of an enlarged vision that transcends cultural, social, and political divisions, it is likely that the problems we now face will only grow in severity.

It is the thesis of this essay that the humanities have the capacity to help foster a communal vision that can revitalize American public life and that the humanities in their contemporary public dimension offer some remarkable avenues for the exercise of this capacity.

The Humanities and Civic Imagination

For this vision to emerge, the nation needs a rebirth of civic imagination. "Imagination," writes legal scholar and poet Charles Black, "is the bridge between human beings, not just once for all, not just now and then, but all the time, all day every day."[2] The *civic* imagination, I would add, allows us to grasp the social and political structures and forms that can be used to invigorate our public life, bringing citizens together to deal with societal challenges and problems. The civic imagination arms us with ideals and values that counter the weight and sharpness of that which would pull us apart. It is the civic imagination that allows us to create images of how we want to be, how we want to get along with others, how we want to organize our civic life, what we want to value collectively, how we want to use our resources. The civic imagination pro-

---

[1]   Norman Birnbaum, *The Radical Renewal: The Politics of Ideas in Modern America* (New York: Pantheon Books, 1988).

[2]   Charles L. Black, Jr., *The Humane Imagination* (Woodbridge, CT: Ox Bow Press, 1986).

motes connections among citizens and with those organizations and institutions so essential to democratic culture.

Nothing could be more important to American society and to the humanities than for more scholars to acknowledge that the cultivation of the civic imagination has become an important public priority. America needs a "community of thought" to help nourish the civic imagination and to serve as midwife to the ideals and values that can strengthen society.[3] A community of thought is a precondition to finding common ground, discovering shared values, and forging public policy that represents the will and thought of the people. "What images of human possibility," asked philosopher Charles Frankel, "will American society put before its members?"[4]

Despite challenges and problems in the humanities, there are plenty of reasons to hope that this task of cultivating the civic imagination will be taken seriously by more scholars.

There are small comforts from history: the inspiring societal visions offered by Renaissance and Enlightenment humanists, for example, or, closer to our time, the intellectual shapers of various nineteenth- and twentieth-century social movements, such as the abolitionist, suffragist, and civil rights movements, which remind us of the possible connections between humanistic ideas and social change.

And there are comforts from our own times. The core disciplines of the humanities continue to be taught and studied in many schools, colleges, and universities. While the humanities may have been marginalized in recent years in some institutions, they remain vibrant and appreciated disciplines in many others. This is an important point, because the teaching of the humanities in elementary, secondary, and postsecondary settings is central to the development of a community of thought and to the civic imagination. All other efforts are dependent on this foundation.

Some contemporary models of the humanities engaged provide additional hope, such as the compelling visions of culture offered recently by feminist scholars, the documentation of local history, the application of the humanities to particular public issues, such as issues related to the environment, and the clarification and interpretation of issues of life and death

---

[3] Birnbaum maintains that a community of thought is not necessarily identical with a community of scholars. "The universities," he writes, "can hardly be regarded as the sole or privileged repositories of thought. In the most creative periods of American intellectual life, they were sometimes silent, sometimes connected to creative currents outside themselves" (p. 193). The community of thought most certainly includes university scholars, but it also includes independent scholars, public intellectuals, and educated and imaginative citizens in general.

[4] Charles Frankel, "Why the Humanities?" in *The Humanist as Citizen*, eds. John Agresto and Peter Riesenberg (Chapel Hill: National Humanities Center, 1981).

offered by a small but growing number of scholars working in medical environments — models that are often relevant to challenges before us.

Important models of the humanities engaged in a more comprehensive and public fashion are offered by the state humanities councils, funded by the Congress through the National Endowment for the Humanities (NEH). Working under a congressional mandate, state councils have encouraged and sponsored projects that bring together scholars and the public. Each year, more than 3,000 projects are sponsored by councils operating in all 50 states, the territories, and the District of Columbia. Aside from these discreet projects, many councils have launched initiatives to heighten public awareness of the importance of the humanities to democratic culture. Undoubtedly, the state humanities program represents this nation's greatest experiment in a sustained effort to enrich American society and culture through the public humanities.

At the beginning of the state humanities program in the early 1970s, all councils had as their federally mandated focus the sponsorship of public programs in which the humanities would clarify and interpret pressing public issues and concerns. This emphasis declined through the 1980s, giving way in many states to programs of more general cultural interest. This latter trend, first encouraged by the Congress itself when reauthorizing the NEH in 1976, was endorsed enthusiastically by NEH Chairs Bill Bennett and Lynne Cheney, who expressed skepticism about the usefulness of the humanities in addressing political, social, and economic issues. The humanities have much to contribute to the betterment of society, they argued, but primarily through the education of individual minds through the study of — and here they were fond of citing Matthew Arnold — the best that has been thought and said.

Those who believe that the humanities have much to contribute to the cultivation of the civic imagination and to the transformation of American society are pleased that the early state council effort to engage the humanities with important public issues is now being revitalized by Sheldon Hackney, the current NEH chair. Hackney has made the expansion of public audiences for the humanities a top priority, and he has called on state councils and other organizations and institutions to deepen and expand through the humanities national conversation on critical issues facing the American people, especially issues related to ethnic and cultural pluralism and American identity.[5] For Hackney, the humanities provide important resources for public dialogue, and it is time, once

---

[5] Transcript of Hackney's address to the National Press Club, November 10, 1993. See also press coverage of this initiative in *The Chronicle of Higher Education* (December 15, 1993) and *The New York Times* (January 16, 1994).

again, to put these resources to work in the public arena.

In the 25-year record of the state humanities councils, we find some important models of engagement enhancing the civic imagination that can guide future efforts.

State Councils and Public Service Scholarship

In thinking about the work of state humanities councils, it is useful to note that the legal structure of the councils provides the framework for such engagement. State councils are required by federal law to ensure that there is equal representation of academic and public sectors on their governing boards, so that all policy and funding decisions may be informed by public as well as scholarly interests.

In terms of practice, the state humanities program promotes what my colleague James Quay and I have called "public service scholarship." We have pointed out that the terms "scholarship" and "public humanities" all too often stand in opposition, with scholarship thought of as "private" or "academic" humanities and the public humanities as the simple dissemination of humanistic learning to receptive but essentially passive out-of-school adults.[6] It may be more useful to consider scholarship and the public humanities not as two distinct spheres but as parts of a single process. As such, the public realm can help initiate, direct, and shape humanistic scholarship.

However, the important role the state humanities councils have in the dissemination of the humanities should not be minimized. Indeed, in the last major planning document that the Texas Council for the Humanities (TCH) submitted to NEH, it drew from an inspiring passage in Henry David Thoreau's *Walden* to underscore its continuing commitment to provide communities throughout the state with programs that express this important but more limited understanding of the public humanities.[7] In this passage, Thoreau indicted his town, Concord, for its gross neglect of the intellectual needs of its citizens. Thoreau complained about how little Concord did to enhance its own culture: "We have a comparatively decent system of common schools, schools for infants only; but excepting the half-starved Lyceum in the winter, and latterly the puny beginning of a library suggested by the State, no school for ourselves." He stated, "It is time that we ... did not leave off our education when we begin to be

---

6   Jim Quay and James F. Veninga, "Making Connections: The Humanities, Culture, and Community," in the report of the *National Task Force on Scholarship and the Public Humanities*, American Council of Learned Societies, Occasional Paper No. 11, 1990.

7   Proposal of the Texas Council for the Humanities to the National Endowment for the Humanities, April 1, 1992.

men and women." Indeed, he argued, "It is time that villages were universities" and citizens "the fellows of those universities."

Thoreau offered readers his vision of a New World democracy composed of educated citizens. He contrasted the life of the European noblemen "of cultivated taste" who surround themselves with art, science, and books with the intellectually Spartan existence of Concord. His plea was "to act collectively" to use the resources of the town to create an "uncommon school" that provides learning for all the citizens of the town. Instead of having a society composed of a few well-learned noblemen surrounded by the dull-witted, ignorant masses, Thoreau envisioned — and pleaded for — a society where the common man became the enlightened citizen through access to lifelong learning opportunities.

Thoreau wanted to unlock the treasure-house of learning and wisdom. "Let the reports of all the learned societies come to us," he said, "and we will see if they know anything." After all, "shall the world be confined to one Paris or one Oxford forever?" He also asked: "Can we not hire some Abelard to lecture to us?" Here, indeed, is one model for the public humanities, scholars who speak to public audiences about their area of learning — their discipline, or perhaps their latest book or article.

Such activity is related to another endeavor, that of humanists writing for a broad public audience. While scholars are often criticized for writing only for a small group of peers, with publication in a professional journal the highest goal, there is a growing number of professional humanists, inside and outside the university, who consistently and with considerable success write for large public audiences.[8] And a few scholars have reached even larger audiences through television documentaries and other media programs.[9]

Thoreau and his public humanist descendants provide a valuable model of the public humanities, but it would be a mistake to let this model stand as the all-encompassing model promulgated by state humanities councils. As noted above, the term "public service scholarship" implies something more. If the Thoreau model were all we had — if this were the only model of the public humanities — we might see this work as an extension of teaching. By using the phrase "public service scholarship," an added dimension is implied, a dimension that stresses collaboration between the scholar and the public and that promotes a form of research and learning in which the public is contributing to and helping

---

[8] For example, Daniel Boorstein, Paul Kennedy, Jonathan Kozel, Patricia Limerick, Robert Coles, among many others.

[9] For example, scholars who worked with Ken Burns in the production of the PBS series, *The Civil War*.

to shape the inquiry undertaken, as well as benefiting from it.

With deference to Thoreau and his model of the public humanities, I wish to argue that it is this more provocative understanding of the public humanities that needs to be understood and promoted, for it is this model that may hold the greatest capacity for the development of civic imagination.

Although the interested public might perhaps be fascinated by anything that Abelard's humanities descendants may have to say, it is far more likely that the public would prefer that these scholars tackle interests and issues that are of genuine concern to them, issues of fundamental importance to their very own city, town, and neighborhood, rather than any topic of these scholars' choosing. Further, they don't want these scholars just to ride in, display their humanistic pearls, and ride out. Rather, these scholars need to be good listeners, for the public wants to work with them in thinking through these concerns and issues. These citizens want to share their ideas with these scholars. And then they want these humanists to go about their scholarly endeavors, to analyze these issues and concerns, to conduct original research if that is appropriate, to collaborate with other scholars and resource persons whose fields and expertise might have something to offer, to find fresh and alternative ways of viewing these matters, and to test initial ideas not just with academic colleagues, but with them as well. And these citizens would like to work with these scholars in finding the best possible formats whereby others could learn of this work and help shape the next stage of this project which might involve endeavors to reach beyond their own immediate community.

If the state councils serve as a bridge between the academy and the community, as is often said, this larger concept of the public humanities means that there is traffic — people and ideas — in both directions. It is easy enough to understand the movement of the scholar into the community. It is much more difficult to understand the movement of the public into the academy. The very thought of this public involvement tends to conjure up the worst fears of many academics, with images of new structures created by state legislatures or regents or trustees that provide expanded opportunities for meddling in internal university affairs quickly coming to mind. We should not let such fears divert us from finding and claiming appropriate ways whereby the public can interact with the scholarly community, ways whereby public issues can be placed on the agenda of higher education.

In commenting on the significance of the 1965 legislation establishing the National Endowment for the Humanities, Charles Frankel wrote that "nothing has happened of greater importance in the history of American humanistic scholarship than the invitation of the government to scholars to think in a more public fashion and to think and teach with the presence of their fellow citizens in mind."[10] Undoubtedly a true statement, but a fuller reading of the legislation leads to the conclusion that another kind of invitation was also extended, one that invited the public to reclaim the humanities as important resources for individuals and communities. What the federal government has done, in this sense, is to encourage the public to gain ownership of the humanities, to put the humanities to work on behalf of the public, to invite scholars to work side by side with them in addressing important public issues.

Public Humanities in Texas

How then has the public, through the work of state councils, responded to this invitation? And how have scholars responded to this expanded, more democratic, understanding of ownership? By looking at the work of one council, the Texas Council for the Humanities, we may be able to find some tentative answers.

One of the first things that needs to be said is that regional and local influences have undoubtedly weighed heavily in how these invitations have been received in different parts of the country. I suspect that the cultural, intellectual, and political diversity of the country have influenced deeply the nature and shape of public humanities endeavors undertaken by the councils. Thoreau's New England, Jefferson's Virginia, and Sam Houston's Texas all provide strikingly diverse heritages for the public humanities.

Unlike Massachusetts or Virginia, Texas doesn't seem to provide an abundance of fertile soil for the cultivation of the civic imagination through public service scholarship. A state with a complex political, cultural, and economic history, it lacks a significant intellectual tradition. Texas is a society that has traditionally claimed the frontier ethic of its Anglo-Texan origins. Deep in the Texas psyche — at least its majority part — is a preference for action over contemplation, autonomy over community, and opportunism over longer-range thinking. Unlike Virginia or Massachusetts, the model of the person of letters is not much a part of the state's heritage. True to Richard Hofstadter's landmark study on American anti-intellectualism, Texans have traditionally admired intelligence, which has practical aims, but intellect, which "examines, ponders, wonders, theorizes, criticizes, imagines," has been suspect.[11]

---

[10] Charles Frankel, "Why the Humanities?"

[11] Richard Hofstadter, *Anti-intellectualism in American Life* (New York: Alfred Knopf, 1970).

As a result, the state humanities council in Texas has tilled some difficult soil, sowing public humanities seeds in an environment not very conducive to public deliberation. We wish this very special invitation from the federal government were taken more seriously, not only in neighborhoods and communities across the state but in the board rooms of corporations and in the halls of the Texas Legislature as well. Yet there is a record here worth looking at; indeed, a record that inspires. I limit my exploration to one of the long-standing concerns of the TCH, that having to do with the relationship between majority and minority cultures in Texas.

From the inception of the state humanities program in Texas in 1973, Texas' extraordinary ethnicity has been a matter of great interest and concern. Black and Hispanic members of the board of directors — public as well as academic — took the lead early on in making the case that the humanities had much to offer in broadening Texans' understanding of the state's diverse cultures, and that the state council could play a significant role in stimulating new scholarship and making that scholarship available to the public as an important step toward equal participation by all groups in the civic, cultural, and economic life of the state and nation.

Mexican-American studies in Texas as a field by and large preceded African-American studies and, to this day, the body of scholarship dealing with Texas Mexican-American history and culture exceeds that of Texas African-American history and culture. While it would be possible to document the state council's role in expanding public understanding of African-American history and culture, for the purposes of this essay, it is probably more fruitful to look at TCH's work focusing on Mexican-American history and culture.[12]

Historian David Montejano points out that in the history of Texas "Mexican-Anglo relations have traversed a difficult path, from the hatred and suspicion engendered by war to a form of reconciliation" present by the mid-1980s.[13] According to Montejano, "the Texas Mexican community still lags far behind on all mainstream indicators in the areas of education, health, income, and political influence," yet there are a number of signs that indicate that an intense clash of cultures has abated and that "a mea-

---

[12] However, it would be just as fruitful to examine the role played by the Texas Council for the Humanities in its response to growing public interest in the history and culture of women, locally, regionally, nationally. Like Mexican-American studies, early research, public programming, and publication in the field of women's studies in Texas began outside the university — in the community — and only slowly and over considerable time emerged as a disciplinary field inside the university.

[13] David Montejano, *Anglos and Mexicans in the Making of Texas, 1836-1986* (Austin: The University of Texas Press, 1987).

sure of integration for the Mexican-American" has been achieved. In the Mexican-American community, Montejano points to knowledge of English as well as Spanish, intermarriage, the development of a middle class, and the emergence of Mexican-Americans as political actors in the state. In the wider community, one can certainly point to broader recognition of Mexican-American history and culture and the potential benefits of a pluralistic society. Progress has occurred and, as Montejano points out, this would not have happened without the political mobilization of the Mexican-American community in the 1960s and 1970s, a period in which the Texas population of Mexican descent grew from 17 to 25.5 percent.

By the time TCH made its first grant awards, Chicano activism was in full swing. The political party Raza Unida presented a candidate for governor in 1972 who received nearly a quarter of a million votes. Mexican-American studies, as an emerging interdisciplinary field in the humanities, received its impetus not so much from the academy, which in many places showed little interest, if not outright resistance, but from the community. That is, the Mexican-American community demanded that the history and culture of Mexican-Americans be studied, written, published, taught, and disseminated, for without a public history, full participation in society was impossible. There were stories to be told. For an emerging number of Chicanos who had pursued graduate studies in the humanities, new opportunities arose for working with the public to document Mexican-American history and culture, thus providing the scholarly and intellectual foundation for a broadly based social and cultural movement as well as a more comprehensive understanding of the American Southwest.

This engagement of scholars with the community on matters of concern to the Mexican-American population can be found in the earliest projects supported by the TCH. The council worked with the Intercultural Development Research Association of San Antonio in sponsoring a series of public conferences in six communities that explored moral values underlying the system then in place to finance public education, and moral values of alternative systems, a project that coincided with the birth of a profound 20-year legal struggle to ensure a more equitable funding system that would not discriminate against financially poor school districts that tend to have heavy minority populations. In south Texas, Colonias Del Valle, Inc., of San Juan, located near the border, was awarded funds for a series of meetings over several months in which scholars and the public met to discuss the history and status of the colonias and to ascertain the historical and cultural reasons why these unincorporated communities lacked basic municipal services, including water. The major organizer of this project, a community activist who believed that the humanities had something to offer in understanding the political, cultural, and ethical dimensions of this problem, was later elected to the Texas House of Representatives. The Alice Public Library, located in south Texas, sought to respond to the needs of its community by sponsoring with the TCH a workshop on special consumer problems that occur in bilingual/bicultural communities. Anglo and Hispanic scholars in linguistics, ethnic studies, business history, and ethics, participated. Scholars from Trinity University, the University of Texas at Austin, the University of Texas at San Antonio, Pan American University (now the University of Texas–Pan American), and Collegia de Mexico (Mexico City) worked with attorneys, government officials, social workers, and civil rights activists to sponsor a major public conference, "Immigration and the Mexican National," a two-day event that drew an audience of 500. Mexican-American scholars at Corpus Christi State University (now Texas A&M University–Corpus Christi) responded to the community's interest in Chicano literature by organizing a major conference that drew 26,000 people for 51 separate activities that took place over eight days. An anthology of Chicano literature was published as a result of the project.[14]

Case Study: University of Houston Symposium

One of the more important early efforts to promote dialogue and advance public service scholarship was a public symposium sponsored by the new Mexican-American Studies Program at the University of Houston and the TCH.[15] The organizers of this 1979 project, and the group that set the agenda for the symposium and the published papers that followed, included five Mexican-American scholars from the university as well as a Mexican-American United States Attorney, the executive director of the Association for the Advancement of Mexican-Americans, and the deputy director of the Mayor's Office of Community Development, among several others.

Organizers established five objectives for the project: (1) to promote interest in and a greater knowledge of Mexican heritage in Texas; (2) to

---

[14] Some 15 years after this was published, the scholar who served as project director told this writer that no source other than the TCH responded favorably to requests for publication support and that to his knowledge the Texas Council for the Humanities was the only funding source available in Texas at that time for the dissemination of this and other new scholarships in Mexican-American studies.

[15] Texas Council for the Humanities Grant M79-526, awarded in March 1979, in the amount of $12,790.

provide an opportunity for a group of humanities scholars to present the results of their research to the public and to receive public response to that scholarship; (3) to encourage Chicano scholars, in a special way, by providing them with a public forum; (4) to stimulate a dialogue between Mexican-Americans and Anglos regarding the present and future aspirations of the people of Mexican heritage in Texas; and (5) to foster greater understanding of problems faced by Mexican-Americans and to suggest recommendations for more responsive public policy. The last objective caught the eye of the U.S. Commissioner of Immigration and Naturalization, Leonel J. Castillo, who encouraged the TCH to support the project.

The major symposium presentations, published later as conference proceedings, included an analysis of Chicano demographic trends and their significance, 1950-1970; Chicano labor history in the last half of the nineteenth century; an analysis of the political origin of the term "Chicano" and its usage; the experience of Mexicanos along the Texas-Mexican border during the period of the Mexican Revolution; trends in Chicano literature; Chicano culture as seen through music and dance; an analysis of the educational status of the Mexican-American; and Chicano political strategies.[16] Other scholars responded to these presentations, and most of these responses are published in the proceedings as well.

In reviewing this body of work, one is struck by the participants' engagement with critical issues facing the Mexican-American population of Texas. In the preface to the proceedings, the editors note that "Mexican heritage, a basic component of Texas culture, has not always been considered an asset in Texas … public discussion is necessary in order to examine negative attitudes, and their causes, toward Texans of Mexican descent." The editors then state:

> This symposium, cosponsored by the Mexican American Studies Program at the University of Houston Central Campus and the Texas [Council] for the Humanities, initiated what is hoped will be a continuing discussion leading toward better understanding of Mexican heritage and Texas culture. The Symposium stimulated the beginning of a dialogue between the Mexican American community and the Anglo American community regarding the present and future aspirations of the people of Mexican heritage in Texas. We hope this written record of the Symposium will foster greater understanding of problems faced by the Mexican American people of Texas, and will suggest recommendations for more responsive public policy.

[16] Margarita B. Melville and Hilda Castillo Phariss, eds., *Reflections on the Mexican Experience in Texas* (University of Houston: Mexican American Studies, Monograph No. 1, 1979).

These scholars perceived their work as serious engagement with issues of contemporary public life. Examples of such engagement can be found in the published papers. One scholar, after a thorough presentation of demographic facts, observed that every available statistic indicates that, although progress is being made, "the Chicanos have a long road to travel before they achieve full participation in the mainstream of America." A commentator responded by pointing out that "unless educators begin to plan now for the influx of Mexican-American students and their cultural and academic needs, the educational situation of Mexican-Americans in Texas is going to get much worse before it gets better."

After providing a brilliant analysis of Chicano labor history in south Texas in the last half of the nineteenth century, another scholar observed that

> for those who have dominated the writing of Texas history, Chicanos do not merit a place in the chronicle of the state. Anglo historians cannot fathom a changing, evolving, and effervescent Tejano population taking the initiative in an effort to alleviate adversity. Yet ... the South Texas Tejano community between 1848–1900 held its own before ambitious Anglo businessmen, cattlemen, and farmers bent on reducing them to powerlessness. In truth, Mexicans took their understanding of the white economic system and used it to wrest a living despite antagonistic circumstances.

In responding to this paper and the conclusions drawn, a noted scholar stated that "the author ... fills a void in Texas history that never should have existed." And another scholar said that

> this is an exciting time ... to watch historians, most of whom are young Chicanos, broaden our understanding of the past to include a people who had been shoved off of the stage of history by writers whose sole interest was in the Anglo-American players. [These] historians ... are moving the minority players back onto the stage, one by one, and we will all be the richer for being exposed to the full cast of characters who shaped the political, economic and social history of the state, the region, and the nation.

Through this research, one inescapably is pulled into a broad cultural project. The research points to the obvious: the prevalence of racism in our society; the negative consequences of stereotyping; the need to document cultures that have been ignored by majority scholars; the need to legitimatize stories that were lost; the need to document contributions of Mexican-Americans to Texas history and culture; the need to address social wrongs; the need to ensure equality of opportunity; the need to organize politically; and so forth. Unabashedly, the original proposal that brought TCH funding and cosponsorship noted that public policy implications would flow from the research undertaken, a concern that was seen in a positive light by the TCH board of directors.[17]

But the symposium itself was not a total success. The program was held on the campus of the University of Houston, which limited public attendance, and too many of the presentations involved the reading of papers, rather than presenting shorter summaries that work better in public settings. But, reflecting on the project as a whole 16 years later, I draw the conclusion that it was a significant event in authenticating new scholarship on the Mexican experience in Texas, in fostering dialogue between Mexican-American and non-Mexican-American scholars, in expanding public involvement in and understanding of the inter-relationship of majority and minority cultures, and in stimulating more research and projects that would grapple with the pluralistic heritage of Texas. Through this public service scholarship, an important contribution was made to our civic imagination.

Allied Efforts

There have been more projects — well over 100 during the past 15 years. Here are a few examples of continuing engagement. The Mexican-American Chamber of Commerce and the San Antonio City Council asked the San Antonio Museum Association for more programming on Hispanic culture. With TCH funding, the result was a 1981 30-minute multimedia presentation, *Mil Colores*, which, after a brief historical outline, documents the influence of Hispanics on San Antonio and discusses some key issues such as bilingual education and the development of Mexican-American political organizations. As noted by a local newspaper, the key to the success of this project was a small group of San Antonio-based Hispanic scholars.[18]

There have been efforts to document and expand the public understanding of the rich tradition of Hispanic theater. TCH worked with scholars to develop newspaper supplements disseminating new scholarship on the history of Mexican-Americans in Texas. It has supported research and production cost for a one-hour dramatic film on the life and music of singer Lydia Mendoza. It has funded radio programs interpret-

---

[17] While encouraging sponsors of such projects to examine options to particular public policy issues and even to recommend among these options, the Texas Council for the Humanities, consistent with federal guidelines, prohibits partisan politics or the direct influencing of legislation. It also has consistently supported the idea that all programs need to be open to multiple perspectives and viewpoints.

[18] *San Antonio Light*, September 1, 1981.

ing Mexican-American literature and research and public programs on the unique architecture found in Texas' border cities. It has supported research and programs on the image of the Mexican-American in American film and literature. It has financed research, lectures, readings, and discussions in five Texas towns on Mexican-American women in literature and the arts. It has sponsored research and a symposium allowing Mexican, Anglo-American, and Mexican-American scholars to offer fresh interpretations of the Texas revolution. A number of projects that have sought to document the connections between the history and culture of Mexico and the history and culture of Texas Mexican-Americans have been funded by TCH. It has supported many museum exhibitions that document and interpret Mexican-American history and culture, from the specific, such as the meaning of the religious and secular observance *Día de los Muertos* to the general, such as the relatively unknown cultures of ancient West Mexico. And the TCH has helped many communities across the state document their local history, working with citizens to uncover this history and place these stories in a broader social and cultural framework and often in the context of regional, national, and international history.

Advisory committees for these projects have included public as well as academic representation. Some of the sponsors have been universities (especially in more recent years), but others have been local community organizations and institutions, such as Casa de Amigos in Midland; La Pena, Inc. in Austin; Guadalupe Cultural Arts Center in San Antonio; Institute for Intercultural Studies and Research in San Antonio; Southwest Center for Educational Television; and Houston Hispanic Forum, to name a few.

TCH itself has also stimulated this scholarship of engagement in a number of special ways. The March/April 1984 issue of *The Texas Humanist* was devoted to an exploration of "The Borderlands: Grappling with a Dual Heritage," with original essays by a number of leading scholars and writers. In 1986, TCH launched "The Mexican Legacy of Texas" as its special emphasis topic for the year of the Texas Sesquicentennial. Funding from the NEH allowed TCH to combine its own work with work undertaken by grantees. Through a request for proposals, the TCH approved eleven grants for public programs dealing with various facets of this subject, with these programs held in Houston, Kingsville, Abilene, Edinburg, Harlingen, San Antonio, Austin, Brownsville, Dallas, Fort Worth, and College Station. TCH commissioned essays by leading Mexican-American scholars, with presentations drawn from these essays given in a number of public settings. Excerpts of papers given at the 1986 Texas lecture and Symposium on the Humanities were published in the Spring/Summer 1987 issue of *Texas Journal of Ideas, History and Culture,* the successor magazine to *The Texas Humanist.* One can also point to a new round of public service scholarship focusing on Mexican-American history and culture as a component of TCH's 1992 special emphasis on "Encounter of Two Worlds," to mark the Columbian Quincentenary. Conferences, exhibits, lectures, media programming all flowed from this initiative.

Much of this work has moved into the mainstream of humanistic scholarship, as seen for instance in the increasing number of titles of books published by university presses; for example, a collection of essays published under the title *Tejano Origins in Eighteenth-Century San Antonio* by the University of Texas Press.[19] These essays stem from a TCH-funded symposium and exhibit focusing on community development and identity in a Spanish Borderlands region. In their acknowledgments, the editors state that the book "is evidence of the enthusiasm displayed during the last several years by many people interested in better understanding the relevance of the history of Spain and Mexico in the regions that now constitute the United States Southwest." They also note that "it was the enthusiastic support from San Antonio's community organizations which made the symposium a great success."

The dissemination of this scholarship has led to greater public awareness of Mexican-American and Latino culture in general. For example, the Fall/Winter 1994 issue of *Texas Journal of Ideas, History and Culture,* devoted to a survey of Latino literature in the United States, offers a 16-page resource guide and selected bibliography for teachers, librarians, and general readers. Of the 256 works cited, none was published before 1967, and only a handful were published before 1980.

This new scholarship has reached very large audiences throughout the United States through film and television. I think of Hector Galan's work and the 1993 broadcast of "The Hunt for Pancho Villa" as part of *The American Experience* series on PBS. Working with a talented group of scholars, Galan drew on old black-and-white photos, rare archival film, and oral histories to shed new light on an extraordinary period in the history of Mexico and the U.S. Southwest, and offered fresh perspectives on Villa as an agent of historical change.

In this model of engagement, the Mexican-American community of Texas, and many others outside this community who were supportive of

---

[19]   Gerald E. Poyo and Gilberto M. Hinojosa, eds., *Tejano Origins in Eighteenth-Century San Antonio* (Austin: The University of Texas Press, 1991).

its efforts, asked something very special of the scholarly community — to document the history and culture of a people, to further prepare that people, and those from other cultures and traditions — including the dominant culture — for a cultural, political, and societal pluralism in which all groups stand on equal footing. In this intellectual and social project, a project still far from complete, the state humanities council appears on the scene as a catalyst, helping to bring the needs, interests, and insights of the public to the scholar and the growing knowledge and insight of the scholar to the public.

This model of the humanities engaged, which promotes dialogue among citizens of diverse backgrounds, what Cornel West calls "transracial communication," surely serves to cultivate the civic imagination, expanding public understanding of how peoples and cultures are bound together.[20] "The essence of the humanities," states the Commission on the Humanities in its 1980 report, "is a spirit or an attitude toward humanity. They show how the individual is autonomous and at the same time bound, in the ligatures of language and history, to humankind across time and throughout the world."[21] The humanities allow the individual to imagine the life of another, with the result that empathy is evoked. But bonding also occurs, as autonomy gives way to an enlarged sense of community. We cannot hope to build institutions and cultural structures that bring together the American people and that work to advance American society without an adequate and empathetic understanding of the histories, traditions, and experiences that bind us together. Nor can we deal with those forces that would pull us apart, leaving us to twist in the cold winds of ignorance and prejudice, without this understanding.

Reconstructing the Public Role of the Scholar

How shall we understand this model of scholarly engagement? It certainly offers a fresh and invigorating model that differs fundamentally from previous models of the scholarly profession which may still inspire but which now may be obsolete, models that have received considerable scrutiny in the last several years.

On the one hand, we have Allan Bloom, who grieves over the loss of the traditional intellectual scholar who in his view has become the victim of all that is wrong with the modern university.[22] The traditional scholar that Bloom wishes to resuscitate is one who stands above and outside

[20] "A Conversation with Cornel West," *Humanities*, March/April 1994, vol. 15, no. 2.

[21] *Humanities in American Life: Report of the Commission on the Humanities* (Berkeley: University of California Press, 1980).

[22] Allan Bloom, *The Closing of the American Mind* (New York: Simon and Schuster, 1987).

the clash of cultures, outside competing economic and political interests, and yet one who has a vision of the good life, knowledge of the best that has been thought and said, an ideal of what it means to be an educated person, and one who, in this view, serves as the bearer of an intellectual tradition that ought to shape the moral development of individuals.

On the other hand, we have Russell Jacoby, for whom the problem is the opposite in that the challenge for the contemporary scholar is not the intrusion of the public on the university but the shrinkage of the public sphere within the university.[23] The contemporary university scholar stands in contrast to the public intellectuals of the past, writers like Lewis Mumford, who knew how to write for a general, albeit well-educated, public audience on matters of public interest. These intellectuals, Jacoby argues, have vanished, giving way to the narrow, self-absorbed scholar whose work is read more and more by fewer and fewer people — mainly associates whose subspecialties match his or her own (on this point Jacoby and Bloom agree). Jacoby notes that "literature, history, and philosophy belong to the common stock of humanity; their importance resides partly in their accessibility to an educated reader."[24] Intellectuals have become isolated academics, and in the process they have lost not only the ability to communicate with large audiences, but the ability to interact on contemporary social problems as well. The university, Jacoby maintains, is now cut off from the society and culture in which it exists.

Jacoby might be right in his assessment of the decline of public intellectuals in the Mumford tradition. And Bloom certainly is correct in pointing out that the day is over when, as Carl Boggs comments in his book *Intellectuals and the Crisis of Modernity*, "traditional intellectual work could be carried out in a relatively self-contained, autonomous university setting, when the contemplative life could flourish without the bothersome intrusions of social conflict."[25]

What this model of engagement shows, I believe, is that there are many roles being played by today's scholars with which Bloom would surely disagree and with which Jacoby unfortunately seems ignorant. Boggs observes that while "Bloom and Jacoby each bemoan the passing of genuine intellectual activity in modern society, they have altogether different agendas in mind." Yet "if both embrace romanticized visions of an independent intelligentsia, they also agree that authentic rational

---

[23]   Russell Jacoby, *The Last Intellectuals* (New York: Basic Books, 1987).

[24]   Russell Jacoby, *Harper's Magazine*, September 1994, from "Journalists, Cynics and Cheerleaders," *Telos*, number 97.

[25]   Carl Boggs, *Intellectuals and the Crisis of Modernity* (Albany: State University of New York Press, 1993).

inquiry has been marginalized within the public sphere, if not abolished completely." Boggs correctly points out that contemporary experience contradicts this assessment. Since the 1960s we have seen the rise of "a highly visible critical intelligentsia in the United States," and this, coupled with "the growth of a radical culture and intellectual subculture … suggests that the thesis of intellectual decline needs to be fully reconsidered."

The model of engagement that I have offered demonstrates how some scholars are responding to critical public issues of our time. It demonstrates, as Boggs maintains, that "older modes of understanding the role of intellectuals are obsolete, demanding fundamental new theories and concepts." As noted earlier, thousands of scholars from public and private colleges and universities participate each year in public projects supported by the state humanities councils, and of these there are a significant number who are exploring models of engagement that depart radically from the traditional public humanities model.

In understanding this development, I offer four components of this model of public service scholarship as seen in the work of those Texas scholars focused on Mexican-American history and culture in public projects supported by TCH, elements that set this model off from the ones offered by Bloom and Jacoby.

First, these scholars seem to derive their intellectual interests and energy from the people with whom they have maintained or have established genuine conversation. They see themselves as inside, not above or outside, this community. The inspiration for their work comes as much from the people as it does from their own intellectual curiosity.

Second, these scholars see themselves as part of a community of scholars who are concerned with this particular history and culture — its past, present, and future — and they tend to be open to interdisciplinary and multidisciplinary collaboration.

Third, they believe that they are closing the gap between social and cultural life and politics. They recognize that their intellectual work can and should support a broad civic agenda, empowering citizens to exercise their rights and responsibilities as citizens.

Fourth, these scholars are carving out an expanded understanding of their profession, giving concrete expression to the idea of service, and offering alternative models for how the profession conducts its business and for the values that it holds.

This public service scholarship model gives hope that as the twentieth century closes we may see the reconstruction of the role of the scholar in American society. The key factor in this reconstruction will be the public, for the transformative power of the projects that express this model rests not in bringing scholars before the public, although that is surely a public good, but rather in bringing the interests, concerns, and ideas of the public to scholars. When that happens, when that connection is made, and when scholars respond with enthusiasm, those participating scholars inevitably will be about a magnificent task, that of working side by side with the public to enhance the civic imagination.

But this model of engagement remains overall a promise. This important work has only begun, and further development and refinement of the model is needed. Can the humanities community be motivated to connect with the public, to take on the cultivation of the civic imagination as a primary task? Where might these connections occur? And, if these connections are made, how might a rebirth of civic imagination lead to the rehabilitation of public life, the reconstruction of citizenship, and the transformation of society? How can we intellectually connect the humanities to primary public issues? How can we stimulate scholarship on issues and themes that weigh heavily on the public's mind? How and what will scholars learn from the public? And how can we develop a community of thinkers — citizens willing to use the humanities in public deliberation — on whose shoulders such a project ultimately rests? Where exactly might the points of engagement be? And, most importantly, what will scholars and the public learn together, should serious engagement occur?

There is no shortage of issues that are of deep interest to the public and that call out for scholarly engagement. I offer one example — the consequences of exploding crime and violence in American society, a matter of deep concern to communities across the country. Increasing crime has led to an ever-expanding prison population, with 1,012,851 persons incarcerated in state and federal prisons as of June 1994, a figure that does not include an additional 440,000 persons in local jails either awaiting trial or sentenced to short terms.[26] In less than a decade, the United States prison population has doubled.

Texas is first in the nation in the rate of incarceration. According to state officials, in a few years only China and Russia will have more prison beds than Texas.[27] Texas has under way the largest public works project undertaken by any state in the United States, a $1.3 billion effort to double its prison capacity, to a total of 145,000 inmates. And officials see no

---

[26] As reported by the Associated Press, *Austin American-Statesman*, October 28, 1994.

[27] Statistics on prison expansion in Texas are drawn from an article in the *Austin American-Statesman,* April 6, 1994.

end in sight; by the year 2000, Texas will need a total of 206,000 beds. The chairman of the Texas Board of Criminal Justice defends this extraordinary project, arguing that "we have no alternative, no other choice.... If there's any criticism, it's been that we're not building fast enough."

No other choice? What kind of investment in the state's future are the citizens of Texas making? Perhaps before embarking on this unprecedented and prison-building project, more preliminary questions should have been asked — questions that beg for extended public deliberation. Why the crime explosion? Why are Americans almost five times more likely to be the victim of a violent crime in the 1990s than in 1960? Why did juvenile crime in the United States increase 47 percent from 1988 to 1992? Why are we such a violent society? What are we as a society doing wrong? What are the root causes of violence and crime? What do the demographics of the prison population tell us? And what do the horrific illiteracy and school dropout rates tell us as well? What values shape our response to crime and to issues of punishment and rehabilitation? What might we learn from other societies? What are the characteristics of those democratic nations that have low crime rates? And what does it mean when the prison budget is second only to public education in a state budget, when a prison budget explodes from $91 million a year in 1980 to a projected $3 billion a year 20 years later, and when we seem prepared to allocate an estimated $40,000 a year to maintain a prisoner for the next 30 years but argue endlessly over whether spending $5,000 a year on each public school student may be too much? Have we really explored all the alternatives? Upon what basis — what moral and political foundation — do we proceed to build more and more prisons, expending vast sums of scarce public funds, when it seems abundantly clear that the penal system is broken, that incarceration for the purposes of deterrence, punishment, and/or rehabilitation no longer work? What values are operative in the public policy chosen? In public policies *not* chosen?

The Humanities and Communal Vision

As we look to the twenty-first century, the development of an educated and engaged citizenry has increasingly become a matter of personal and societal survival. If the humanities are to help cultivate the civic imagination, if this becomes a national project involving as many citizens as possible, then we know that more scholars in the humanities will need to allocate more time to interaction with the public and to critical issues facing society. These scholars will need to be good listeners, to hear with empathy the questions being asked by their fellow citizens. We need ongoing conversation between scholars and the public, not onetime programs. We need projects in communities across the nation that promote the kind of sustained dialogue and thinking that fosters the civic imagination and lifts scholars and their fellow citizens beyond the social, cultural, and political divisions of our time. We can hope that such projects will inspire people to rebuild a terribly weakened civic infrastructure. Scholars who participate in these projects have an opportunity to make an invaluable contribution to American democracy.

Within the university community itself, as public issues are taken more seriously, increasing energy will need to be focused on undergraduate teaching and especially on those courses that all undergraduates — regardless of majors and planned careers — should take, if we are to nourish intellectual leadership in the community. Undoubtedly, more attention will have to be paid to multidisciplinary approaches to inquiry and learning and to successful models for the stimulation of civic imagination, models of interaction and learning that might hold relevance for public programs. And, for this project to be successful over the long haul, graduate education in the humanities, the preparation of individuals for careers in the humanities, will need to focus increasingly on this project and on the relationship between scholarship and citizenship. In so doing, the humanities community, in replanting itself, may very well be preparing a very different kind of scholar for the twenty-first century.

Carl Boggs reminds us that "the intellectual realm has been viewed throughout history as a wellspring of creative innovation." In its financial as well as moral support of the humanities, especially through state and federal appropriations, the public should request the engagement of the scholarly community. We Americans need a vision of a revitalized Republic, an engaged citizenry willing to ask tough questions about American identity, about what it is that we as a people value, about how we want to be and how we want to live, individually and collectively. The humanities, which have their foundation in the community as well as the academy, have much to offer in fostering this vision.

Jean Bethke Elshtain

The Humanities and the Democracy of Everyday Life[1]

When I agreed to appear before this distinguished and important national humanities conference, I began to recall some of my own "war stories," my conscription, so to speak, into programs sponsored by state humanities councils. There was a meeting held under the auspices of the New Jersey council on individualism, citizenship and community, a conference well attended by scholars and citizens. Even more memorable was a statewide event sponsored by the Montana council, back in the bad old days of the Cold War, a conference focusing on nuclear weapons and international and domestic politics. Although none of the speakers was a "cold warrior," there was an interesting divergence of views about how best to make peace. Most of us talked about politics and strategic concerns, some about history, but one of our key panelists, an iconoclastic theologian, gave a presentation about saving lemurs. Yes, lemurs. It seems that his university is the site of the largest lemur colony in the world today, lemurs having been pretty much wiped out in their native habitat of Madagascar, or Malagasy. Loving these creatures, tending to them noninvasively, making peace in this small way was a good way, so he argued, to live out an alternative to grand dreams of military strategy and national glory. Well! Many people didn't get it, and some were even

[1] The paper was given as a keynote address at the 1995 National Humanities Conference sponsored by the Federation of State Humanities Councils.

a bit off-put — it seemed as if he had just blown off the entire topic — but I thought I knew what he was talking about, and I will return to the theme of "everydayness," making democracy and peace on the small scale, later in my presentation. But I wanted to begin by offering you my recognition of the energy and diversity of ideas that emerged at this particular meeting and the others of which I have been a part. I am grateful for these and other opportunities sponsored by the state humanities councils.

The Humanities and Democratic Possibility

I began to think about the humanities and democracy, particularly the democracy of everyday life, as I pondered my appearance before you. It is odd to be called on to draw this connection. To be sure, I gave myself the assignment. Why? Because I fear we are in danger of losing the link between the humanities and democracy. The word *humanities* derives from human, and human pertains to our common natures. There are many variants on the nature we call human, but no serious humanist can deny that there is something — perhaps more fragile than many previous eras assumed — that can properly be called human and properly be said to be held "in common." Democracy, too, is an enterprise that presupposes the possibility of commonalties. "We hold these truths to be self-evident: all men are created equal." As I point out in my book, *Democracy on Trial*, this self-evident, bold declaration by our classically educated framers is now a point of controversy, so much so that some are prepared to jettison this claim as just froth, window dressing to hide particular interests. My friends, let us not be so hasty. Forgive me, if you will, a few words drawn from *Democracy on Trial*, for I can think of no better way to place certain themes on the table than to offer a few extended passages.

Democracy, I argue, is not simply a set of procedures or a constitution, but an ethos, a spirit, a way of responding, and a way of conducting oneself. Not being simple, democracy does not afford us a straightforward answer to the question of what education in, and for, democracy might be. A delicate line separates the overpolitization of education from the awareness that education is never outside a world of which politics — how human beings govern and order a life in common — is a necessary feature. Education always reflects a society's views of what is excellent, worthy, and necessary. These reflections are not cast in cement, like so many foundation stones; rather, they are refracted and reshaped over time, as definitions, meanings, and purposes change to democratic contestations. In this sense education is political, but being political is different from being directly and blatantly politicized — being made to serve interests imposed by militant groups.

Consider the following example. A class takes up the Declaration of Independence, with its grand pronouncement that "all men are created equal." But when the Declaration of Independence was written, women (and many men) were disenfranchised, and slaves were not counted as full persons. How could this be, the students wonder? What meaning of equality did the Founders embrace? Were any of them uneasy about it? How did they square this shared meaning with what we perceive to be manifest inequalities? What was debated and what was not? What political and moral exigencies of that historic movement compelled what sort of comprises? Might things have gone differently? This classroom is an instance of reflective political education in and for a particular democracy — the American version — and its perennial dilemma of the one and the many.

But let me put a second and a third example, exaggerated in order to mark the differences between these latter instances and my first example as clearly as I can. In a second classroom, the teacher declares that the Founders were correct in every respect. To be sure, slavery was an unfortunate blemish, but it was corrected. As a democratic educator at the end of the twentieth century, she must reaffirm her students' devotion to the Founders and the Republic. After all, did they not distill the wisdom of the ages, good for all times and all places, in their handiwork? They were statesmen, above the fray, not politicians. Here, uncritical adulation triumphs.

The hagiographer's mirror image is offered by my third teacher, who declares that nothing good ever came from the hand of that abstract all-purpose villain the "dead, white European male." The words and deeds of such men, including the Founders, were nefarious. Nothing but racists and patriarchalists, those blatant oppressors hid behind fine-sounding words. All they created is tainted and hypocritical. All is foreclosed. All presumably has been exposed. Debate ends or is discouraged. To express a different point of view is to betray a false consciousness, venality, or white patriarchal privilege. Demonology triumphs.

These last two examples are instances of unreflective politicization. Each evades the dilemma of democratic equality rather than offering us points of critical reflection on that dilemma. This sort of education fails in its particular and important task of preparing us for a world of ambiguity and variety. It equips us only for resentment or malicious naiveté. There are two off-kilter positions, then. In one, the mesmerized worshipper of authority, who will brook no criticism of the Founders, denied herself the critical freedom that is hers as an educator and that should be imparted to her students. In the other, the agitated negator of all that has gone before preaches freedom from the dismal and spurious past and what she sees as an all-persuasive and menacing tradition that she would cast off, and she insists that her students see it that way, too. But a genuine education in and for democracy helps us engage in a debate with interlocuters long dead or protagonists who never lived save on the page; and, through that engagement, to elaborate alternative conceptions through which to apprehend our world and the way that world represents itself. "Perhaps," wrote the political philosopher, Michael Oakeshott,

> we may think of the components of culture as voices, each the expression of a distinct condition and understanding of the world and a distinct idiom of human self-understanding, and of the culture itself as these voices joined, as such voices could only be joined, in a conversation, an endless, unrehearsed intellectual adventure in which, in imagination, we enter into a variety of modes of understanding the world and ourselves and are not disconcerted by the differences or dismayed by the inconclusiveness of it all.

This openness to diverse voices helps to keep alive both our distinctiveness and the possibility of commonalties.

I think of my own education, and my democratic dreams, as these were nurtured in the rural Colorado village in which I grew up, the Timnath Public School, District No. 62, incorporating grades one through twelve in a single building. Our text for high school English class in this isolated little place was *Adventures in Reading*. I still have my copy — I bought it from the school because I loved so many of the stories and poems in it. The table of contents lists "Good Stories Old and New" with such bracing subsections as "Winning Against the Odds," "Meeting the Unusual," and "Facing Problems." We read "Lyrics from Many Lands" and "American Songs and Sketches." I looked at this text recently as I thought about democracy and education. By no means was it dominated by a single point of view. We read Mary O'Hara, Dorothy Canfield, Margaret Weymouth Jackson, Elsie Singmaster, Selma Lagerlöf, Rosemary Vincent Benét, Katheryn Forbes, Sarojini Naidu, Willa Cather, and Emily Dickinson, among others. We read the great abolitionist Frederick Douglass, and the black reformer Booker T. Washington. We read Leo Tolstoy, Pedro de Alarcón. We read translations of Native American warrior songs. This reading was undertaken on the assumption that life is diverse, filled with many wonders. Through *Adventures in Reading*, we could make the lives and thoughts of others our own in some way. I was taught, as the preface to the textbook said, that "reading is your passport to adventure and faraway places. In books the world lies before you, as paths radiating from great cities to distant lands, to scenes forever new, forever changing.... Reading knows no barrier, neither time nor space nor bounds of prejudice — it admits us all to the community of democratic experience." Clearly, I was a lucky child, a lucky *democratic* child, for I learned that, in Oakeshott's words, "learning is not merely acquiring information ... nor is it merely 'improving one's mind'; it is learning to recognize some specific invitations to encounter particular adventures in human self-understanding."

One sees here the close intertwining of humanities — of education as the emergence of habits of the heart — and democratic possibility. It would have flabbergasted Americans to think a democratic culture could be built on any other foundation, for we are a credal people: we are built on a proposition or a set of propositions. These propositions have to do with what is humanly possible and just possibly most human — the human person at his or her best, most judicious, fair, openhearted, and generous. One of the most appalling things about slavery, for example, was the way it ill dignified the human person — and those who have protested their treatment historically have talked about respect due them as much as anything else. Our greatest president, with admirable economy, expressed his view of democracy in one pithy sentence: "As I would not be a slave, so I would not be a master." Neither slave nor slavishness; neither master nor preemptory mastery, then. This is a reading of the human condition and of the possibility of democracy that stresses its very necessity, the way it lies at the heart of a core or cluster of human aspirations.

A Humanities Story: Hull House

I find, as I grow older, that I have moved to a storytelling mode, to a recognition that stories lie at the heart of the humanities — the human experience — and as well at the core of the democracy of everyday life. So I want to tell you one very big story, one we are in danger of losing. It is the story of one of our greatest public citizens, Jane Addams of Hull House.

One of the most extraordinary features of the Hull House, as Jane Addams describes it and as one encounters it through other accounts, was the role it played in the cultural and intellectual life of Chicago and beyond. One reads, with a tinge of envy, of evenings spent in debate and discussion; of University of Chicago professors journeying over to lecture in a 750-person capacity Bowen Hall at Hull House on a variety of topics, from those of an immediate concern to new scientific theories about the galaxy. Hull House was, among the many things that it was, a space for the exchange of ideas in a nonprofessional setting, one not bound by and hemmed in by the minutiae, the mind-numbing jargon and the trendy enthusiasms that too often beset the contemporary academy. Few such spaces, if any, remain. Oh, yes, we are a society overtaken by support groups and honeycombed with self-help societies, but these are not the same thing. If you glance on any given week at the list of nonfiction books the public is lapping up, you will be struck by the dominance of diet books, cookbooks, exercise books, confessional books, all focused on that American obsession — me, myself, and I, as my mother liked to say. Is there a general reading public any longer of folks engaged by civic matters, but from a stance of disinterestedness, in the best sense of that word? If there is such an audience, I fear it is dwindling. Jane Addams could assume such an audience. In part because of that, her life and thought is quite literally unthinkable if severed from the America that gave birth to her and that she, in turn, played a major role in creating and imagining. Thus any story of her work is necessarily a story of her country. This requires a task of interpretation. Much as Jane Addams saw the central mission of Hull House as one of interpreting the social classes to one another, I want to interpret Jane Addams to us today as an exemplary figure in a story of the humanities and the democracy of everyday life.

This was her challenge, in part. How does one convey compellingly quotidian concerns? How does one dramatize the ordinary and the everyday? Great stories are often about great conflicts, unto death in those Greek or Shakespearean tragedies much beloved by Miss Addams. The heroic die young more often than not. But what about being sentenced to life, to a long life, to inexorable dailiness? Where is the dignity in this, where the adventure? Jane Addams was insistent that there is a dignity in the everyday and in the provision made for tending to the bodies, bread for stomachs, cool hands on fevered brows. Harder by far to muster a defense of that, and not simply because it is women's work, hence historically devalued. The labor of the male peasant on the field, the grinding repetitiveness of assembly line factory production, are scarcely the stuff of riveting drama either.

One of the things Addams was up to was to try to dramatize the quotidian, to show the adventure and conflict in it, to display the heroism and despair, the little defeats and victories that are the stuff of a life. If tragedy as invented by our Greek forebears was a form of public discourse that aims to inculcate civic virtue and enhance the capacity of citizens to act with foresight and to judge with insight, then Addams would form daily life into a narrative that mirrored such stern stuff and invited us into similar forms of recognition. If you want drama, what about the bathos, the mingling of stark terror and human dignity, the fusion of the small with the great or, better said, the one vignette, a little story, that would never have appeared in the world as complex and terrifying and conflicted in its redemptive power as anything devised by Sophocles. The story is from Jane Addams' masterwork of American autobiography, *Twenty Years at Hull House*. I call it the story of "The Old German Woman Clinging to her Chest of Drawers," and it is one example of Addams' narrative skills and her evocative power.

> Some frightened women had bidden me come quickly to the house of an old German woman, whom two men from the county agent's office were attempting to remove to the County Infirmary. The poor old greater had thrown herself upon a small and battered chest of drawers and clung there, clutching it so firmly that it would have been impossible to remove her without also taking the piece of furniture. She did not weep nor moan nor indeed make any human sound but between her broken gasps for breath she squealed shrilly like a frightened animal caught in a trap. The little group of women and children gathered at her door stood aghast at this realization of the black dread which always clouds the lives of the very poor. The neighborhood women and I hastened to make all sorts of promises as to the support of the old woman, and the county officials, only too glad to be rid of their unhappy duty, left her to our ministration. This dread of the poor house, the result of centuries of deterrent "poor law" administration, seemed to me not without some justification one summer when I found myself per-petually distressed by the unnecessary idleness and forlornness of the old women at the Cook County Infirmary, many of whom I had known in the years when activity was still a necessity, and when they felt bustlingly important. To take away from an old woman whose life has been spent in household cares all the foolish little belongings accustomed, is to take away her last incentive to activ-ity, almost to life itself. To give an old woman only a chair and a bed, to leave her no cupboard in which her treasures may be stowed, not only that she may take them out when she desires occupation, but that her mind may dwell upon them in moments of reverie, is to reduce living almost beyond the limits of human endurance.

In this mini-drama, Addams grips with a story of old age and loss, reminds us that an entire life may be decocted to the pinpoint of a cup-board, a chest of drawers, in my own grandmother's case, her sewing chest and drawers, all the neatly wound balls of thread and rickrack and small containers of buttons sorted by size, color, and shape, the tiny pieces of cloth that might yet become a patch for a torn pant or a patch in a colorful quilt, these she went over again and again in her twilight years, reminding you that she had built the drawers herself, for she was a carpenter as well as a seamstress. I imagine her, when finally her wits had deserted her altogether, dreaming of thread in tiny rows and bold pieces of cloth and all those quilts she had lovingly made and given away over all the years. From such recognition, open to the lessons of pity, Addams calls us into shabby rooms in decrepit buildings on a mission of discovery where what is learned is both empathy and humility, where the tears shed join an ever-flowing underground stream that gives life its inexorable sadness and makes of some lives a tale of ill dignity and where there are limits to what those less bereft can do to "ameliorate" or to "mitigate" — two of Jane Addams' favorite terms. She was fond of recalling George Eliot, who tells us at the conclusion of *Middlemarch,* "the growing good of the world is partly dependent on unhistoric acts."

In many vital ways, Jane Addams' was a literary life, a story-shaped character. A partial list of references in *Twenty Years at Hull House*, not so much cited or displayed as flowing forth, having been absorbed, having become her second nature, include Ruskin, Carlye, DeQuincey, Browning, Plutarch, Irving's *Life of Washington*, Thomas Green, Gibbons' *Decline and Fall*, Emerson, Bronson, Alcott, Homer, Plato, Sombart, Maeterlinck, Darwin, Gray's *Anatomy, The Illiad*, Mazzini, H. G. Wells, Comte, Tolstoy, George Eliot, Hawthorne, Victor Hugo, John Locke, Pestalozzi, Beatrix Potter, Henry George, J. S. Mill, Schopenhauer, Tolstoy, Engels, Masurek [sic], Dewey, Goethe, Kier Hardie, G. B. Shaw, Sidney and Beatrice Webb, Carl Liebknecht, Luther, Graham Taylor, William Dean Howells, William James, *Antigone,* Wordsworth, Walt Whitman, Galsworthy, Harnack, Ibsen, Yeats, Dante, Bakunin, Spenser, Shakespeare, Gorki [sic], Herbert Spencer, St. Francis, on and on. These were part of the air she breathed; these molded the dreams she dreamt; from Cedarville, Illinois, and out into the wide world she made her own. Her mind was densely populated; her ken generous, her knowledge extensive, her recall keen, her devotion to mind unwavering. She embodies humanities and the democracy of everyday life.

Let me, in this final section, offer you words from two women, who as girls spent much of their time at Hull House. Their names are Marie Thalos and Ruby Jane Delicandro (as children, Marie Bagnola and Ruby Jane Gorglione). In their conversation with me Ruby starts off: "Miss Jane Addams was like a mother to us." Marie enjoined me to be certain to note that at Hull House "they never made us feel like paupers. They treated us on an equal basis. Everything was top drawer, the best." Trying to capture the complex flavor of the place, Ruby talks about how everything was "so naturally done. It was just a way of life. You didn't even know you were learning. Our Hull House was like a home, like a well-kept home. Be sure you put that in."

Ruby and Marie can scarcely conceal their pride and enthusiasm, nearly a half century later, at the world they entered when they walked into the doors of Hull House. Ruby became one of the star pupils of Edith deNancrede, leader of the Marionettes, one of the junior theater and dance groups at Hull House. She recalls her role in the production of "Merman's Bride." Marie notes that her mother helped to sew the costumes, and both Marie and Ruby describe a beautiful theater, gigantic, and "it had everything conceivable." They note the "huge gym," and the music, dance, and literature groups. They "belonged to everything. You had access to everything that was there." Several times over Marie tells me, "What Ruby and I are trying to say to you is that the children there were not delinquents. We loved our Italian neighborhood. It was a real neighborhood." For them, Hull House offered entré into a world that enlarged rather than supplanted their own. Ruby: "I was Puck in *Midsummer Night's Dream*." Marie: "We had musicians, cellists, piano players, violinists, concerts. We even went to classes with Martha Graham. Everything was the best." They both "grew up" at Hull House, they tell me, from preschool-age children to their teen years. Hull House was "a second home ... we lived there." They came and went and life was full. Their mothers were intimately involved in Hull House activities and felt supported in their own efforts with children. They rambled pleasantly about the "Punch and Judy Club" and a painting club in which a teacher gave them the names of flowers. As I listened, I felt reassured about my own sense that Addams was one of those rare people who integrate the views and lives without the banality and arrogance and mawkish sentimentality. Marie: "You know, Hull House was a wonderful place. It was all the best. We try to get this across to people in conversation but nowadays they don't seem to understand." Both Ruby and Marie tell me they don't even talk about their Hull House years anymore because "people look at us as if we were little criminals or something. You say settlement house and they think welfare and paupers." Marie goes on to talk about a painful childhood stutter. She had a "whole two pages to say" in her first play — "Puppet Princess" and she cried and she said she wouldn't be able to do it, but Miss deNancrede said, "Marie, yes, you're going to do it, and I did it, every night I did it. I did it."

Asked to summarize Hull House and Miss Jane Addams, the words tumble out.

They opened up a whole new world for us. She was a great lady. She emphasized responsibility: You can do it, she would say, you can do it. And we did it partly because we didn't want to disappoint her. If you wanted books the librarian would talk to you and find out what you were interested in. This is for Ruby or this is for Marie. They paid attention to you as an individual. Everything was personalized. You weren't just another kid. To me Hull House was like my second home. They wanted you to be the best you could be. You couldn't be anywhere that you felt more comfortable. You didn't even know you were learning, it was done in such a caring and loving way.

They describe playing and working together. They describe a sense of equality. "We never heard racist stuff. We heard some academics say Hull House was racist. This made us furious. Our schools were integrated, there were all kinds of people. We didn't even know this ugly word 'racist'. But you know Miss Jane Addams never said you're Spanish or you're Italian. We were children. She taught us to respect each other's traditions. She took any immigrant in. The world now is a bunch of terrible words and it's very hard to explain." Marie: "What we're trying to say is that Hull House introduced us to so many things, such as a rich environment. We've read stupid stories about how the neighbors were suspicious of Hull House, but we *were* the neighbors. Nobody I knew worried about taking children to Hull House." Ruby goes on to describe a campaign speech made in her behalf for president of one of the clubs and she recalls singing Mexican, French, Czech, German, and Italian chorales. Marie: "It was the center of our lives." Ruby: "Yes, the center."

It is hard not to be touched by this, even in a time grown as sharp-edged and mean-spirited as our own. Ruby and Marie's assessment, their wonderfully colorful rich memories, dovetail precisely with Walter Lippmann's eulogy for Jane Addams: "She had compassion without condescension, she had pity without retreat into vulgarity, she had infinite sympathy for common things without forgetfulness of those that are uncommon. That, I think, is why those who have known her say that she was not only good, but great. For this blend of sympathy with distinction, of common humanity with a noble style, is recognizable by those with eyes to see it as the occasional but authentic issue of the mystic promise of American democracy."

It occurs to me that when we most need the leaven such a one or such an ethos might provide, we are least likely to seek it out — perhaps because we no longer know what we are looking for, nor indeed where to search. That is the challenge faced by those of you concerned with the humanities and the democracy of everyday life.

The Power of Shared Experience

I close with a passage from one of my favorite writers, the great Willa Cather. The book is *My Antonia*, a book I have always loved in part because the character of Antonia Shimerda reminds me of my dearly beloved grandmother, Mary Frank Lind, an immigrant to these shores as a young ethnic German — a child of German descent whose family lived in Russia. Hers was a small people, a people with no state to call its own. She and my grandfather, William K. Lind, were people of little education, whose English was always shaky, although powerful and resilient enough to tell jokes — Grandpa — and morality tales — Grandma. And although the severities of the Depression years meant their two oldest daughters, my own mother, Helen, and my aunt, Mary, had to quit school after the eighth grade to do stoop labor in the sugar beet fields of northern Colorado, every single one of my grandparents' 20 grandchildren completed a college degree of some sort; every single one coming out of little schools in rural or small-town Colorado. This is an American story and it is by no means unique, and it is a story I hope future generations will be able to tell. We cannot tolerate the loss of our young people to violence, crime, drugs, premature childbearing, suicide, despair, and ignorance.

But the note I want to end on is a lyrical one, a reminder of that evanescent yet altogether powerful experience we share when we share a moment from a work of art, in this case theater. Paul Burden, Cather's protagonist, has attended a play with Lena Lingaard, one of the servant girls in *My Antonia*, who is on the rise as a dressmaker. Paul is by then a college student in Lincoln, Nebraska, having moved to the big city from the small town of Red Cloud. A touring theater company will perform "Camille." The actress is a bit old for Marguerite, but Paul and Lena are caught up in the drama the characters have created, come to life. The play episode of *My Antonia* ends with intimations of immortality, of something outside the self, of a common humanity that helps to make us who and what we are. These emanate from Cather's words, and all of you devoted to the humanities are charged — it is your sacred burden — to keep such moments alive for all our citizens.

> When we reached the door of the theater, the streets were shining with rain. I had prudently brought along Mrs. Harling's useful commencement present, and I took Lena home under its shelter.

After leaving her I walked slowly out into the country part of the town where I lived. The lilacs were all blooming in the yards, and the smell of them after the rain, of the new leaves and the blossoms together, blew into my face with a sort of bittersweetness. I tramped through the puddles and under the showy trees, mourning for Marguerite Gauthier, as if she had died only yesterday, sighing with the spirit of 1840, which had sighed so much, and which had reached me only that night, across long years and several languages, through the person of an infirm old actress. The idea is one that no circumstances can frustrate. Wherever and whenever that piece is put on, it is April.

I wish you many Aprils.

David Mathews

Afterword:
Inventing Public Scholarship

More than a decade ago, the Kettering Foundation began exploring the idea that the liberal arts were best understood as the civic arts; that the purpose of a liberal or humanistic education was to prepare people for public life. This publication tells you where that notion has taken us.

When I think about all the conversations leading up to this volume, I am reminded of the instigating ambition — to push beyond what had already been envisioned as the relationship of the humanities to the public — not because what had been said by Charles Frankel and his generation were wrong in insisting there was a relationship but because "the public and public life," having been a phantom for most of the twentieth century, are coming out of the shadows. Today, we are rediscovering the importance of public life. And it is becoming easier to understand as we learn more about the way a civil society (the society of public citizens) works. One thing is clear, the public is not an audience at a play or, for that matter, an audience for humanities scholars. It is a diverse but interrelated body of citizens who must claim responsibility for and act on their common problems through particular kinds of associations and practices.

The central question now is how scholars relate to public practices and public work. That question takes us well beyond what is usually meant by "public engagement." The challenge to humanities scholars is to align their practices with the practices of democratic public life. The old response — that the humanities "informed" the public — won't do. It takes no account of how a public informs itself, how citizens learn to act wisely and effectively.

This book takes us into a search for a better answer, which begins with Tom Bender's insight, that academic truth has some similarities to political truth. Peter Levine picks up that lead with a discussion of ways of knowing, contrasting technical reason, which has come to dominate much of academe, with a more public form of communicative reason. Max Harris locates this way of reasoning in public discourse and associates it with the humanities. Now, deep into issues of public epistemology, Alejandro Sanz offers a personal account of what happens when a scholar incorporates the practical knowledge of citizens into his research and teaching.

This kind of experience changes scholars — and it changes the meaning of scholarship. So much so that Jay Rosen invites academics to create a new field of intellectual work — one defined by its publicness. We might call it "public scholarship." That strikes me as an invitation, not to abandon the current definition of scholarship, but to add something to our understanding of what scholars do. If we are looking for something more, we can safely assume that we aren't equating public scholarship with what we already have — the social criticism of public intellectuals, with the public service and technical assistance provided by many academics. We aren't talking about the ways scholars treat the public in their work or even about what goes on in the public outreach programs of the humanities.

This isn't to say that public scholarship is wholly different from anything we have ever imagined. It may be that there are elements of what we are looking for scattered about, waiting to be put together in a new form, which would be more than the sum of the parts. As I reported in the last edition of Kettering's *Higher Education Exchange,* we already see several trends that, combined, could add a new way of understanding the work of scholars.

The first trend is an effort to rethink the relationship between the expert and the public, a relationship presumed to be between those who have knowledge and those who don't. Second, and closely related, is the current reexamination of what knowledge is and how it is produced. This reexamination has led to questions about one of the prevailing conventions, which is that the knower has to be (and can be) separated from what he or she is trying to know. Third, I sense a revival in the field of rhetoric and an emphasis on communication, particularly on the importance of a deliberative dialogue, which has to do with knowing and acting, seen as one phenomenon, not two. Any number of people are rediscovering the importance of what Pericles described as the talk we use to "teach ourselves first." I am not only referring to Jürgen Habermas but also to scholars like David Zarefsky and the modern rhetoricians who are rescuing Mikhail Bakhtin from academic obscurity.[1]

As I have already mentioned, public life is being reconceived as civil society by still another group of academics. Civil society offers a different set of lenses for looking at what makes a public choate, for getting at what Walter Lippmann missed. One of the striking features of a healthy civil society is how interconnected it is — not how homogeneous but how integrated. Because modern scholarship divides life into categories that correspond to various disciplines, there is reason to wonder whether the disciplines miss these connections. That thought could unsettle the foundation for the usual organization of higher education, unsettle it in a way that even interdisciplinary studies couldn't repair.

A powerful reason to look for a better understanding of scholarship may be the declining legitimacy, if not collapse, of the modern state, a state rooted in the scholarship of positivism and the assumptions of intellectuals turned expert. I have just read Václav Havel's address on the responsibility of intellectuals.[2] Havel lived in a state informed by a scientific expertise so infallible that even though his experiences said he wasn't well-off — if Those Who Knew Better said he was, he was not to believe his lying eyes. This led him to reject the claim that human society can be known in its entirety, and that scientific knowledge can generate surefire strategies for reform. That claim not only seemed arrogant — given a world held together by "billions of mysterious interconnections" — but flat wrong. Havel has become a champion of incremental improvement continuously modified by shared experiences. Intellectuals have some responsibility for those improvements. They aren't, in some objective way, detached from the world, and the rest of humanity.

So, who are the new public scholars being created by these trends and what do they do? They may be identified by how they go about producing knowledge, by how they stand in relation to the public, by the kinds of questions they raise and, most of all, by the richness of their concept of public life.

If the role of public scholars is defined by the tasks of society, making continuous improvements gradually, then those scholars have to be involved in the production of knowledge about the necessity for and

---

[1] David Zarefsky, in "The Postmodern Public," *Kettering Review* (fall of 1995), argues that deliberative public discourse is necessary for articulating the bonds that hold people together and the vision that moves them toward their goals. Max Harris, in "A Surplus of Seeing: Bakhtin, the Humanities, and Public Discourse" (Part Two of this volume), enriches the definition of public deliberation with Bakhtin's phrase "communication between simultaneous differences."

[2] Václav Havel's March 31, 1995, address at Victoria University in Wellington, New Zealand, reprinted in *New York Review of Books* 22 (June 22, 1995): 36–7.

direction of change.[3] Such knowledge is socially constructed to answer questions that no expert can, questions of what we *should* do or how we *should* act in a society that has to adapt to a mysterious universe, one that offers no certainty. In order to distinguish the content of this knowledge from others, I have played off of Michael Sandel's notion of knowing goods in common that we can't know alone, modifying it somewhat to include not just "goods" but many other things we can know when we are together and never alone. By "together" I don't mean just standing around, I mean engaged so intensely with one another that our experiences are joined and we are changed. This happens, as Sandel noted, when politics works as it should. I would add that this kind of knowledge doesn't preexist the effort to create it. It isn't like an Easter egg hunt, where the eggs are prepared before the search begins. This knowledge doesn't exist before you and I become a "we" or a public and begin our search. It can't because it is about who *we* are and what *we* are willing to do.

Public scholars may also be identified by the way they stand in relation to the public. They have to be participants in public life, though not standing on a platform to proclaim some special knowledge or just to criticize what goes on "below." Public scholars have to stand *with* other citizens. And that stance prompts the question of what do they do with their scholarship. What does that mean? When scholars stand with the public, are they just being citizens? What use is their scholarship?

Public scholars, as I imagine them, don't so much provide expertise or extract information from the public as they join with other citizens in the creation of knowledge, a point I have already made. Their scholarly training, which has made them proficient in producing knowledge, should allow them to contribute to producing public knowledge, knowledge of what we *should* do with the problems that invade our common lives. Here is what I mean by that. If the knowledge we need to change our situation — to progress — has a moral dimension beyond the reach of expertise, then expertise may be useful but it is not enough. If what we need to know doesn't preexist our coming together, then the evidence of things past, which scholars bring with them, is useful but not sufficient. And, if this knowledge has to be created through the interaction of many different people, then the skills developed as a solitary thinker are potentially beneficial, though not adequate. It is the *way* I

---

[3] I shouldn't go on an epistemological binge here because in a recent issue of the *Higher Education Exchange*, I argue that academe has certain ways of knowing, often associated with the humanities, that seem very much like the knowing that is directed toward identifying the common good and that comes from particular kinds of social/political interactions.

have learned to create knowledge as a scholar, to derive meaning, to make judgments, that I bring with me to a public setting. But I have to adapt that way of knowing to a process in which citizens engage one another as political equals, all with relevant experience about what needs to change.

Understanding where and how public scholars stand in the public sphere becomes a bit easier if we look at how scholars interact with those professionals who deal regularly with the citizenry. I have seen some I would call public scholars, play the role of a "paradigm shifter." Rather than providing information or a critique, they suggest other perspectives or a different language for understanding "the public," which is otherwise a term with very thin meaning and little power to inform professional behavior. I have heard public scholars ask questions like "What is implied in our statement?" or "What would happen if we changed our language this way?" For example, in the public journalism work, I have seen the powerful effects of asking, "How would we cover a story if we thought of people as citizens or 'political actors' rather than just readers?" Notice that I have intentionally said "we" rather than "you" in reporting the way these scholars phrased their questions because they placed themselves inside the profession they were addressing even as they look outside it. To be a public philosopher should be much like being a practicing public philosopher. To me, philosophers aren't people who know about philosophy; they are those who know how to pose the questions that can reveal our relationships to the world.

The questions public scholars raise will surely reflect conceptions of what a public is, or of what public life is that are different from the prevailing understanding. And concepts will inform their scholarship. They will be open to the possibility that a public is not a "phantom," that it exists through the dialogue it is in with itself and through the common work that grows out of that dialogue.

A scholar who had become public will have experiences that affect the meaning of their research and change the way they practice their disciplines. No one has explained these effects more directly and honestly than Alejandro Sanz, whom I mentioned earlier. His essay is an account of the soul-searching journey of a conventional economist doing research on rural communities who becomes convinced that intellectuals have to create a radically different way of producing knowledge *with* citizens rather than *for* them. This requires, he says, superseding the conventional (and, he might add, unnatural) separation of subject and object. Research becomes the creation of knowledge with those who will use it rather than experts producing knowledge to be "deposited in the unknowledgeable."

Sanz has carried his new ways of creating knowledge from the field into his classroom using the insight that what students experience becomes more important than what they are told. He argues that formal education is damaging political life. Universities, he says, can produce tyrants who, though experts on democratic theories, may undermine what they say by exercising power undemocratically in their relationships with students.

The effort to invent "public scholarship" goes on in the lives of people who are examining their own discipline or profession in order to find a new role in public life. Some humanities scholars are struggling with questions of their own identity and legitimacy. It is a very personal, often lonely, sometimes painful quest. Those who have contributed to this book have given all those on this journey, not a map, but perhaps a compass for charting their own course.

Ultimately, if there is to be a new, public dimension to scholarship, I think it will come from the way scholars position themselves in public life, from a different kind of public experience. I believe that when scholars stand as learners themselves, in the company of other citizens, who are also learning how they should act and live, they will see their work anew. That is what has happened to all of the scholars I know who have changed the way they entered public life. Public scholars should be continuously reflecting on what they are learning about their work and contributing those reflections to the learning of the communities or professional groups where they are located. What they have to say is not, "Here is what you should do (either from a moral, intellectual, or technical vantage point)." It is, "Here is what I am learning and here is how I am going about learning." That, I believe, is how a scholar best becomes involved in the production of public knowledge.

CASE STUDIES OF
THE HUMANITIES ENGAGED

Michael A. Gordon

Milwaukee, Wisconsin's Sherman Park

The Kettering Foundation's "Humanities and Public Engagement" initiative seeks to expand the traditional role of humanities scholars in community projects that are funded by state humanities councils. In public programs, humanities scholars typically help to disseminate knowledge through various forms of oral and visual presentations. The National Endowment for the Humanities has joined the Kettering Foundation in calling on scholars to build even stronger ties between academia and localities by collaborating with citizens on projects that seek to strengthen communities.[1]

Among other things, this initiative stems from growing interest in helping humanities scholars rediscover their important role as partners with civic groups in addressing pressing social problems. Some like James Veninga believe the Kettering initiative could spur state humanities councils and humanities scholars generally to address more fundamental concerns. On leave in 1995 from his duties as executive director of the Texas Council for the Humanities to move this initiative forward, Veninga believes humanities scholars must play central roles in addressing "the current crisis in American democracy."[2] He agrees with the historian

---

[1] See "Humanities Scholars Practice What They Teach," *Connections* (Kettering Foundation), 6 (Spring 1995), pp. 2-5. See also, James Veninga, "What Campus Walls? The Democratization of the Humanities," unpublished paper for the session, "The Engaged Campus: Organizing to Serve Society's Need," at the American Association of Higher Education 1995 National Conference on Higher Education, and Sheldon Hackney and David Mathews, "An Open Letter to Chairs of State Humanities Councils and Convenors of National Issues Forums," NEH and Kettering Foundation, 1994.

[2] James Veninga, "State Humanities Councils and the Current Crisis of Democracy," unpublished paper prepared for the National Humanities Conference, September 10, 1995, p. 1.

Robert Wiebe's claim in *Self Rule: A Cultural History of American Democracy* (University of Chicago Press, 1995) that during this century forces of "centralization and hierarchy" had contributed to the decline of democracy. In order to revitalize democracy in America, Wiebe argues that we must attack the primary constraints on it by doing what we can to foster "popular access to government and a responsive governing system." For Veninga, Wiebe's call has special relevance for the Kettering initiative and public humanities programs. "The key to revitalizing democracy," he argues, "is the dramatic expansion of public space and public dialogue. In the public sphere, as citizen concerns, issues, and interests are dealt with, the two great constraints placed on democracy, centralization and hierarchy, are consciously countered. The values, policies, and practices of public and private sectors are open for scrutiny."[3]

I fully share these concerns and the belief that humanities scholars can and should play key roles in revitalizing democracy. The humanities have always contributed to the kind of individual empowerment that is essential to democracy, and many public humanities projects have been conducted in that spirit. The value of learning how to develop and collaborate community *history* projects that foster individual empowerment and strengthen democracy has been the cornerstone of the University of Wisconsin-Milwaukee's Public History Program since I became the program's coordinator in 1987. This approach has been inspired by the splendid community work of such public historians as Linda Shopes, James Green, Jeremy Brecher,[4] and especially Michael Frisch. Frisch urges historians to reconceptualize the way they usually develop public programs. Instead of preparing programs in isolated academic settings and then presenting them to the public, Frisch argues that we must develop a *shared interpretive authority* in such projects. He claims that public historians "need better to respect, understand, invoke, and involve the very real authority their audiences bring to a museum exhibit, a popular history book, or a public program. Although grounded in culture and experience rather than academic expertise, this authority can become

---

[3] Ibid., pp. 3 (Wiebe) and 3-4.

[4] For examples of committed public history work, see Susan Porter Benson, Stephen Brier, and Roy Rosenzweig, eds., *Presenting the Past: Essays on History and the Public* (Philadelphia: Temple University Press, 1986); Elizabeth Fee, Linda Shopes, and Linda Zeidman, eds., *The Baltimore Book: New Views of Local History* (Philadelphia: Temple University Press, 1991); Jeremy Brecher, Jerry Lombardi, and Jan Stackhouse, eds., *Brass Valley: The Story of Working People's Lives and Struggles in an American Industrial Region* (Philadelphia: Temple University Press, 1982), and Jeremy Brecher and Tim Costello, eds., *Building Bridges: The Emerging Grass Roots Coalition of Labor and Community* (New York: Monthly Review Press, 1990).

central to an exhibit's capacity to provide a meaningful engagement with history — to what should be not only a distribution of knowledge from those who have it to those who do not, but a more profound sharing of knowledges, an implicit and sometimes explicit dialogue from very different vantages about the shape, meaning, and implications of history."[5]

The insights of Frisch and the others that have helped to shape my own public history projects also piqued my interest in the Kettering idea of reconceptualizing the role of humanities scholars in public programs generally. Thanks to a grant from the Wisconsin Humanities Council, I have had the opportunity to begin a project during the summer of 1996 that seeks to develop an approach commensurate with the Kettering initiative. Called "Listening In: Developing Public Programs with Sherman Park Residents in Milwaukee," the project represents the first installment of a three-year commitment to work with various Sherman Park organizations on developing public humanities programs that address local concerns. Although the project is not finished, even at this early stage it may be useful to summarize its approach and suggest its possible value and significance.

Sherman Park is a four-square-mile area with 44,000 residents located about three miles northwest of downtown Milwaukee. It lies within the Milwaukee city limits, extending east to west from Thirtieth to Sixtieth Streets, and north to south from Capitol Drive to North Avenue. Visual landmarks that help identify these boundaries include Washington Park on the south, the Capitol Court shopping center and postwar Parklawn public housing complex on the north, the Wauwatosa city limits and Lincoln Memorial Park cemetery on the west, and an industrial and rail corridor on the east, dominated by the A. O. Smith Company on the northeast, and by the Master Lock Company on the southeast. The other four major Sherman Park landmarks are Washington High School, the *park* called Sherman Park, the Mary Ryan Boys and Girls Center in the park, and St. Joseph's Hospital, the largest birthing hospital in Wisconsin. The area also is dotted with grade and middle schools, numerous churches and two orthodox synagogues, small parks, the stately older houses on Grant Boulevard, the nearby Parc Renaissance condominiums, and modest and also run-down single houses, duplexes, and middle-income houses and bungalows.

One hundred years ago, the area that is now the Sherman Park community was beginning the transition from farmland to a residential area,

---

[5]   Michael Frisch, *A Shared Authority: Essays on the Craft and Meaning of Oral and Public History* (Albany: State University of New York Press, 1990), xxii.

as the city's near-north-side skilled German workers and their children and grandchildren sought the slightly larger lots and other amenities that characterized middle-income life-styles in those years. In the 1930s and 1940s, they were joined by more Germans and by many Eastern European Jews, who built six of the city's eleven synagogues there. The two synagogues that remain, and a new Jewish school, testify to the continuing vitality of Sherman Park's Orthodox Jewish community.

Since the 1960s, African-Americans have followed the German model of expanding from the central city outward into Sherman Park. Many African-Americans migrated to the city during and just after World War II, but by 1950 Milwaukee's 21,000 African-Americans still comprised just 3 percent of the city's population. By 1967, the number of African-Americans had grown to 90,000, or 12 percent of Milwaukee's population. They were concentrated in just 5.5 percent of the city's land area, making Milwaukee one of the nation's most segregated cities. Even so, some African-American migrants to Milwaukee arrived early enough to find good jobs at A. O. Smith and other companies. But like African-Americans elsewhere, many others arrived too late to take advantage of such jobs. In the ten years after 1975, the city lost over 50,000 manufacturing jobs to corporate flight, corporate takeovers, or corporate collapse. Most of the well-paying, stabilizing, union, family jobs in what economists call the primary labor market at places like A. O. Smith had gone to males. They were replaced by secondary labor market jobs that often go to young women. These largely nonunion jobs pay low wages and provide little job or family security.

A brief profile of Sherman Park's 44,000 residents, based on the 1990 census and other data, reflects some of the changes that have resulted from Milwaukee's recent rise to prominence as a national leader in low-wage jobs, and as one of the most racially segregated and polarized cities in the nation. It also suggests some of the sources of division in Sherman Park. Indeed, it is often said that Sherman Park is desegregated but not integrated. Residents are divided by race, gender, and class. African-Americans comprise nearly 60 percent of Sherman Park's population, but most live between Thirtieth Street and Forty-third Street (which is Sherman Boulevard) in economically disadvantaged neighborhoods. Whites and African-Americans, most of them middle income, do equitably share the area from Sherman Boulevard to Sixtieth Street, but most do not attend the same places of worship or take part in common social functions — except for block parties and the annual blues festival called Shermanfest, which is sponsored by the Sherman Park Community Association (SPCA). Ten percent of Sherman Park residents age 18 and over are unemployed, and about one-quarter of all residents — over half of whom are under age 18 — live below the poverty level. In 1990, 42 percent of the 10,610 families in Sherman Park were headed by women, and one-third were headed by single mothers — figures that undoubtedly are much higher today. The majority of Sherman Park residents rent their housing. More than half pay over one-third of their income for rent.

The accelerated desegregation of Sherman Park in the 1960s created serious problems for African-American and white residents alike. Unethical real estate agents took advantage of African-Americans' need for housing, racial stereotypes, and white fright, and engaged in blockbusting and racial steering. In May 1970, the Milwaukee School Board changed the boundaries — and hence the social composition — of Washington High School but did not commit the necessary funds and personnel to ease the transition or address student needs. And city planners proposed constructing two new freeways through the area that would have fractured community life, fostered residential segregation, and separated businesses and schools from neighborhoods.

Concerned about these problems, seven married couples formed what eventually became the SPCA in the fall of 1970 and quickly established committees on housing, education, and freeways. It was this organization that gave the name "Sherman Park" to the area. From the beginning, the SPCA's goals in all of its activities have been to foster stable integrated neighborhoods, to keep housing stock in good repair, to promote economic development, to help ease the transition to integrated schools, and in general to act as an advocate for the needs and interests of Sherman Park residents.[6]

I have done two previous projects in Sherman Park. In 1991 and 1992, some of my public history graduate students and I began conducting oral history interviews with former founders of the SPCA. In 1995-1996, my public history students worked with the SPCA on a project funded by the Wisconsin Humanities Council called "Common Ground: Unity and Diversity in Sherman Park." Designed to help the SPCA observe its twenty-fifth anniversary, the project produced a new series of oral history interviews, a commemorative photography exhibit that tours Sherman Park, a booklet containing the pictures and the exhibit text, and a community anniversary forum called "Where Do We Go From Here?" Because of these projects — and because I live in Sherman Park — I have

---

[6]   For profiles, see Juliet Saltman, "Milwaukee: The Sherman Park Community Association," in her *A Fragile Movement: The Struggle for Neighborhood Stabilization* (New York: Greenwood Press, 1990), chapter 4, and Jonathan Schell, *History in Sherman Park: An American Family and the Reagan-Mondale Election* (New York: Knopf, 1987).

a number of connections throughout the community that have been useful in my "Listening In" project.

My plan was to spend a good deal of time listening to — and participating in — various discussions among Sherman Park residents and SPCA members about their concerns and needs, and then to work with the SPCA and other local groups to develop humanities projects and other kinds of programs and resources. I tried to do this in several ways. First, I attended numerous open meetings of Sherman Park church and civic organizations about community issues. One, for example, focused on a proposed new youth group home which some residents feared would affect nearby property values. Another concerned a drug store's application for a liquor license. A third considered neighborhood safety. These and other meetings explored a variety of issues that often arise in communities like Sherman Park.

A second way I tried to obtain a sense of local issues was by assembling seven small discussion groups of from four to six people for ninety-minute conversations. Composed of a good but not complete cross section of Sherman Park residents, these groups explored specific issues as well as the meaning of community generally. The conversations were unstructured, except that I initiated each with one or two general questions, sought clarification on points that were discussed, and in other ways probed deeply into issues throughout. One group was composed solely of SPCA staff members. All discussions and the community forum were transcribed.

Finally, I talked informally to probably another 40 or 50 people about Sherman Park in my daily walks around the neighborhood with my dog and children and on other occasions. Such discussions lasted from ten to thirty minutes and almost always were prompted by my simple opening question, "So, how do you like living in Sherman Park?" Many of these impromptu discussions were quite revealing and very helpful. Some of the people I talked with in these settings likely were more candid than they might have been in the small groups or the community forum and because of this I plan to conduct another round of oral history interviews in 1996-1997 to delve more deeply into the lives and concerns of local residents. The new interviews will add perspectives to the nearly 30 conversations that we previously conducted, which I listened to again during August 1996 as I thought about future stages of this project.

In my conversations, and in the meetings I attended, I have tried to do what I think all of us in the humanities should do in projects like this one. I have listened carefully to what others have said, but I also have tried to question, provoke, challenge, enlighten, and stimulate — in short, to be something of a constructive troublemaker. My goal in all this work is to produce some immediate concrete products and some long-term possibilities. The products include reports to the WHC, the SPCA, and other local groups that summarize what I have learned and suggest programs that address residents' concerns and some possible sources of funding for them. The long-term possibilities stem from my promise to donate up to 100 hours over the next two years to work on various projects that may develop from this initiative.

What did I learn from this work, and what suggestions will I make? The discussions and meetings generated dozens of specific issues about race relations, crime, safety, youth, housing, jobs, business, schools, playgrounds, and other typical neighborhood issues. But I believe that all such issues really concern the nature of community, individual and collective empowerment, and race. And all are interrelated. Indeed, discussions about the specific issues almost always led to perceptions of *how* the issues are related to the kind of community life that the participants believe already exists, or *should* exist, in Sherman Park. In other words, many of the people in the discussions and meetings associate the idea of "community" with Sherman Park. For them, "community" means both a geographical area in which they reside, as well as a notion of being involved in a common enterprise with others in this area to make the ideal of integrated community life work. So for these people, at least, Sherman Park is more than just a place to live. It is a source of identity, because living in Sherman Park expresses and reinforces certain values that give meaning to their lives. Some of them have moved to Sherman Park from wealthier neighborhoods expressly for this reason.

Yet a central problem abounds with this view of community that I think will provide many opportunities for public programs. People think of belonging to a community called Sherman Park, and yet they do not. When pressed in the discussions and the informal conversations, it is clear that for many people the notion of "community" actually has little to do with Sherman Park. For some, the primary source of identity comes from membership in the Orthodox Jewish "community," the Protestant and Catholic white or black (or integrated) churches, or specific neighborhoods. Social relationships are very much confined to such memberships. Middle-income people of different races, religions, and ethnicity have very few contacts with the great number of poor residents who live on the eastern one-third of Sherman Park. With that kind of separation — and segregation — it becomes clear that much work remains to be done to create the kind of community that indeed *is* based on a common sense of purpose amidst diversity that so many people say they seek in

Sherman Park. Such efforts could strengthen both the sense of community as a common enterprise as well as spark more participation in democratic processes.

I think it has been valuable to hear people talk about the different meanings of community as they discuss the more specific issues like safety and lack of trust that concern them — and they have said they also think this has been valuable. These discussions also have generated some preliminary ideas for public programs and other activities.

I already have taken some steps to form a group that can act as a new umbrella for some potentially valuable programs and projects in Sherman Park. I have drafted a proposal for a Sherman Park Arts and Humanities Council. The organization could sponsor, coordinate, and perhaps fund small local projects; disseminate information about activities and opportunities; and help organize such music groups as a chorus, a band, a jazz ensemble, and perhaps various quartets and quintets. It might also form a theater for children and adults to create and perform their own plays about life in Sherman Park, neighborhood history centers, a Sherman Park ethnic museum, a genealogy club, a Sherman Park oral and video history group, and perhaps an annual autobiographical essay contest patterned after the enormously popular annual national contests in Poland — among other things. The goal of the arts and humanities council and its activities would be to bring people together to do things they enjoy doing so that they could be involved in satisfying endeavors that might foster a sense of community identity and also help residents learn more about each other.

These are some suggestions for a new institution and some activities. What about public programming? At this writing, I have not fully fleshed out many ideas for discrete humanities projects, but here are some of those I have in mind. One might be called, "Who We Are." This would produce a statistical social profile of Sherman Park residents and also a series of programs in schools and churches, and perhaps a series of traveling exhibits produced by various subcommunities, about beliefs and values and cultural heritage. A second, based on extensive videotaped oral history interviews, would result in a videotaped history of Sherman Park to explore "Sherman Park: The Making of an Urban Community." A third is a historical play, again based on oral history interviews, to explore the issues that sparked the formation of the SPCA — a vehicle for exploring the early and continuing sources of unity and disunity, and the values SPCA founders associated with life in Sherman Park. A fourth idea for a humanities public program is based on the successful "Beyond Racism" project of the Milwaukee Interfaith Council. "Beyond Racism" facilitators conduct weekend retreats that, among other things, pair black and white participants for explorations into each other's experiences. My idea is to work through churches to develop oral history projects in which people interview people from different cultures and then discuss what they have learned in a series of small forums. A fifth idea focuses on the history of congregations in Sherman Park. My idea here is to conduct workshops in doing research on congregational history in order to see how changes in memberships have been linked to changes in Sherman Park over the years.

In these and other projects that may develop over the next several years from my "Listening In" work, my role as humanities collaborator will be to provide insights and suggestions as a local historian, and to help assemble resources from the humanities and other disciplines that are needed for meaningful public programs. Therefore, the ultimate significance of the "Listening In" project will not be known for some time. But in a more limited sense, the collaboration that is developing in Sherman Park as a result of this project between academic humanities and local residents already is generating the kind of working partnership and mutual trust that public humanities programs must have if they really seek to deepen the meaning of democracy right down to the neighborhood level. Developing a shared interpretive authority in all kinds of humanities programs — not just those involving history — is an important approach to involving the humanities in strengthening democracy. And extensive listening to local sentiment is the starting point for any such efforts.

Jo Taylor

Walthill, Nebraska

The information regarding The Humanities and Public Engagement Project, a collaborative effort of the Kettering Foundation, the National Endowment for the Humanities, and the Federation of State Humanities Councils, arrived at Wayne State College in the late summer of 1995. Since the college was expanding its relationship with Walthill, a nearby community, this project afforded a framework for that expansion. The central question posed by the project corresponds to ours, that is "How can scholars/institutions enhance the capacity of local communities to deal with tough public issues and strengthen the practice of democracy?" Because Wayne State College shares the Humanities and Public Engagement perspective that the "traditions of inquiry, analysis, reflection, conversation, and action are indispensable to the practice of democracy and social and cultural renewal," the college became a part of the national project and began to establish a series of conversations with the citizens of Walthill.

What follows is a delineation of the course of those conversations. I will provide some insight into the nature of the relationship between Wayne State College, the community of Walthill, and the Nebraska Humanities Council; cite some challenges related to engaging humanities scholars in civic discourse with members of the community; touch on the role humanities scholars play in strengthening civil society; and conclude with some brief remarks about such projects' potential for recasting the relationship between scholars/colleges/universities and the public.

Wayne State College, located in Wayne, Nebraska, is a regional four-year comprehensive college located in the northeast corner of Nebraska. As one of three publicly funded state colleges in Nebraska, its primary role and mission is to provide undergraduate education. Another facet of the college's role and mission is to serve the region. As Donald Mash, the president of Wayne State College puts it, "We're striving to serve as an effective regional center, a focal point, a catalyst in Northeast Nebraska, not only for the delivery of higher education, but also for the arts, cultural activities, and for assistance with community and economic development efforts." Members of the Wayne State College faculty and staff are well aware that the cultural and economic health of northeast Nebraska is essential to the region, the state and, ultimately, to Wayne State College. As a result, Wayne State College has established partnerships with several public and private two-year colleges, Chambers of Commerce, economic development groups, public schools, and communities.

Walthill, a village with a population of 747 (278 households) is located on the Omaha Reservation about 35 miles from Wayne State College. Over 36 percent of the total population is Native American, 31.5 percent of the population is under 18, and 80 percent of the total school population is Native American. The economy of the village and surrounding area depends largely on small farms and small shops/services; 140 of the 150 owner-occupied units are valued at less than $50,000. The community has a history of tolerance for diversity and a shared sense of community. But in the last few years, members of the community have become polarized in their views of school, governance, and economic issues.

The Nebraska Humanities Council (NHC) is an independent, non-profit organization affiliated with the National Endowment for the Humanities. The NHC cultivates an understanding of culture and history by funding quality educational programming. Typically, the Nebraska Humanities Council funds projects whereby scholars explore a variety of humanities topics including "India: A Search for Understanding," "Annual Traditional Native American Handgame," "International Conference on the Romanization of Athens," "Pre-Show Seminars for Shakespeare on the Green," "Riding the Rails: Children of the Great Depression," and the "Storytelling Festival of Nebraska." Whether the platform is large, such as Chautauqua, wherein scholars assume the persona of historical/literary figures and speak to audiences of 100 or more, or small, as in book discussion groups involving eight or ten individuals, scholars present information and provide insight into the region and the world. The members of the audience are always given an opportunity to interact with scholars — generally in a question/answer mode. Rarely do scholars and Nebraska citizens engage in a continuing dialogue that takes place over several months.

In contrast, in the partnership between Wayne State College and the Walthill community, the scholars have not overtly presented information on literature, history, culture, legal/ethical issues. Rather, for over a year the scholars have met with various members of the Walthill community, individually and collectively. In all of these meetings the scholars have listened far more than they have talked.

In the fall of 1995 two scholars, one Anglo, one Native American, one trained in humanities with expertise in Native American studies, one with expertise in education with emphasis in curriculum and reservation schools, began visiting Walthill. Prior to their visit, the director of the Nebraska Humanities Council, Jane Renner Hood, and I (the vice president for Academic Affairs at WSC), visited the meeting of the Board of the Picotte Center. The center, located in Walthill, is the restored clinic where Susan LaFlesche Picotte, the first female Native American in the United States to receive an M.D., practiced medicine. An ethnically diverse group restored the center, and the Nebraska Humanities Council provided funds to support the mounting of exhibits.

At the Picotte Center Board meeting we explained the work of the proposed collaborative effort to enhance the role of the humanities in public life, delineating the Nebraska Humanities Council and Wayne State Colleges' proposal to provide two scholars to conduct a series of conversations with members of the Walthill community to 1) determine what issues the community faced and 2) assist in finding ways to address the issues. We also said that in sponsoring the conversations Wayne State College had two long-term goals: 1) to enhance the capacity of Walthill to deal with tough public issues and 2) to form a long-term symbiotic relationship between Wayne State College and the Walthill Community.

Members of the Picotte Center Board, a group consisting of teachers, farmers, a small business owner, and a lawyer, responded very positively to the proposed project and provided the names of groups and individuals who should be a part of the conversation. The list of names included the county extension agent, local farmers and business owners, the staff of the Justice Center, members of the ministerial association, the village clerk and village board members, members of the Rodeo Club, and a consultant who provides business and legal advice to tribes.

In the fall of 1995, the scholars attended the annual Picotte Day Celebration as well as several Picotte Center Board Meetings and meetings of the village board; they visited with the Omaha tribe educational commissioner, teachers in the Walthill schools, farmers, businessmen, and members of the Walthill Community who were students at Wayne State College.

The issues which emerged from the conversations included:

1) School issues — of the 357 students in the school, 344 are Native American but, according to parents, the curriculum does not reflect their history, their culture, their lives. Parents have difficulty in communicat-

ing with school personnel; the high school dropout rate is high; parents and teachers agreed that K-12 students have not been held accountable for their education;

2) Economic and cultural issues — Walthill is something of a bedroom community — much of the population works out of town; businesses are not locally owned; there is no local newspaper. Several individuals and groups spoke of needing assistance in developing grant-writing skills, in developing a local Native American arboretum, and in developing a school improvement plan that includes teaching local history and culture.

In the spring 1996 term, ten or twelve field-experienced students, members of the Wayne State College education faculty, and the vice president for Academic Affairs met with school board members, visited the Walthill School several times to meet with the superintendent and principal, and met individually with several teachers.

As a result of the yearlong conversations between scholars and members of the Walthill Community, several positive initiatives are under way. The Walthill School and community have become participants in The School at the Center Project, a collaborative school improvement project that includes the University of Nebraska at Lincoln, Wayne State College, and several school districts in Nebraska. The premises of the project include 1) teachers and students must understand the relationship between the community's economic and cultural circumstances and be aware of their implications for school curriculum and reform; 2) local history and culture should be an integral part of the school curriculum; and 3) science and mathematics can be taught using local resources/examples.

In addition to collaborating in The School at the Center Project, the Walthill school and Wayne State College engaged in a number of other initiatives. Ten or twelve Wayne State College students in teacher training programs fulfilled their field experience requirement in Walthill. As a result of this *quid pro quo* arrangement, Walthill teachers gained some assistance in classrooms, and the students gained experience in a school setting with a diverse population. In another initiative, teachers at Walthill met with WSC faculty to discuss the opportunities and challenges of teaching at Walthill, focusing on such issues as the need to hear the community's voices with regard to curriculum and the advantages of changing curriculum to reflect the local community and culture, as well as ways to interest Walthill students in math and science.

In the fall 1996 term, a team of Walthill teachers and administrators and WSC faculty members worked with fourth graders on classroom projects; the students were invited to visit Wayne State College to attend children's plays and planetarium shows, tour broadcasting facilities, and visit with WSC faculty members. The goal of this project was to introduce students to the value of a college education.

In other related initiatives, Wayne State College offered to the Walthill Community the assistance of a WSC botanist in establishing a Native American arboretum, provided materials and advice to a Walthill teacher who established a wellness/fitness program at the school, and issued a special invitation to members of the Walthill community to attend a grant-writing workshop. Although the scholar's conversations with members of the Walthill community have had many positive outcomes, the project faces some challenges. Many of the Walthill teachers who talked with WSC faculty about the challenges and opportunities of teaching at Walthill took jobs elsewhere during the summer of 1996. Many of the members of the community who signed up for the wellness/fitness program at Walthill dropped out. Only two individuals from the Walthill community attended the WSC grant-writing workshop.

Another challenge is to sustain the conversation between humanities scholars and the members of the community. Humanities scholars are accustomed to a platform in which they are viewed as an objective deliverer of information/knowledge about the humanities. In continuing conversations with the public, scholars' expertise and perspectives are more likely to be challenged, and the scholars may be tempted to return to their traditional platforms. In traditional humanities projects, closure usually comes fairly quickly and, usually, to everyone's satisfaction. At the end of traditional humanities public presentations, members of the audience ask questions, scholars respond, and scholars and members of the community go home, their expectations for the evening fulfilled. In a continuing conversation, closure may be a long time coming and all parties may become discouraged.

Despite these challenges, the humanities have great potential for strengthening civil society. Humanities scholars engaged in a continuing conversation with rural community members, particularly those individuals whose communities are struggling economically, may remind the community that a strong economy constitutes only a portion of the "good life." A humanities-based continuing conversation reminds all participants that a strong sense of cultural heritage, an understanding and respect for diverse cultures and histories, and an analytical stance toward social/public issues are essential for civic discourse.

As Wayne State College continues the conversation with Walthill, we hope that this initiative will play a role in recasting the relationship between scholars/universities and the public. Today, the public's esteem for academia and the academic life is at a low point, with state legislators calling for accountability, parents asking why college costs so much and suggesting that faculty members teach what they want, not what students need. The public is calling for college/university faculty to be more responsive to student, community, and state needs. Continuing conversations among humanities faculty and the public may lead members of the public to reassess their view that colleges and the humanities are irrelevant to their daily lives. In turn, such conversations may lead faculty to rethink their disciplines, to reappraise and enlarge the nineteenth-century premise of "knowledge for its own sake," and to reaffirm/expand their service role. Continuing conversations with the public may lead scholars to move more quickly than before from a mode of lecturing to cover content to a mode of engaging students in conversations. In turn, students who have resisted the study of the humanities because they do not see the connection to the "real world" may begin to make the connection between humanities and the world. Continued conversations may lead faculty and students to a renewed sense that the literature, politics, and history they study come from the real world and that the disciplines come full circle when the fruits of scholarship return to and are integrated into that real world.

Edward S. Mihalkanin

Lockhart, San Marcos, and Wimberley, Texas

All theory, dear friend is gray — The Golden tree of life is green.

— Johann Wolfgang von Goethe, 1808

And politics ought to be adjusted, not to human reasonings, but to human nature; of which the reason is but a part, and by no means the greatest part.

— Edmund Burke, 1839

The prejudice which would either banish or make supreme any one department of knowledge or faculty of mind, betrays not only error of judgment, but a defect of that intellectual modesty which is inseparable from a pure devotion to truth. It assumes the office of criticizing a constitution of things which no human appointment has established, or can annul. It sets aside the ancient and just conception of truth as one though manifold.

— George Boole, 1854

The Civitas Project, a grant project operating in 1995-1996 and funded by the Texas Council for the Humanities (TCH) and Southwest Texas State University (SWT), was a phase of TCH's and SWT's Civic Responsibility and Higher Education initiative. This initiative arose from SWT President Jerome Supple's desire for his university to explore the civic and moral side of the public university in a secular society and from meetings of representatives of the Federation of State Humanities Councils, the Kettering Foundation, the National Endowment for the Humanities, and several state humanities councils.

President Supple assembled a task force in 1993 to lead in the exploration and elucidation of a set of values which possibly could be at the center of our university's life. In December 1993, March 1994, and in May 1994, the above named representatives met to explore ways in which the role of the humanities in American civic life could be enhanced. A consensus emerged at these meetings in support of a newer model of public engagement for the humanities that would use humanities resources to deal with grassroots concerns motivating many communities. This new engagement model views the role of humanities scholars as building long-term partnerships with local communities and that the local communities' generation of concerns and issues would drive the creation of future humanities public programs.[1]

Marion Tangum, associate vice president for Academic Affairs, headed a public symposium on "Civic Responsibility and Higher Education" on February 4, 1995. The symposium, supported by a TCH grant, attracted almost 200 interested citizens including leaders in business, education, government, and religion. The assembly examined the role the public university should have in educating its students to be citizens, in cultivating the character of its students, and asked if the university should promulgate such a role. While this first phase of the initiative discussed how civic responsibility is related to classroom instruction, the next phase explored the relationship between civic responsibility and the role of the university in the broader community.

Hence, the Civitas Project was designed to investigate what long-term responsibilities the public university might have to the broader community beyond classroom instruction and research and economic development work. I was brought into the project in June 1995 after its project director, Timothy Burns, assistant professor of political philosophy at SWT, had to bow out of the project due to receiving a postdoctoral fellowship.

The goals of the project were fourfold. First, the project was to discuss what the citizens of Lockhart, San Marcos, and Wimberley were most concerned about and to explore what these citizens thought could be done in partnership with SWT to resolve the issues concerning them. Second, the project was to investigate what these citizens thought could be done in partnership with SWT to help foster a fuller civic life in their communities. Third and fourth, it was hoped that the project could

---

[1]   The summary of the meetings and the new engagement model were taken from "Humanities and Public Engagement Project," Federation of State Humanities Councils, Kettering Foundation, and National Endowment for the Humanities, 1994.

encourage university faculty to become involved in these communities and to use their expertise to help citizens address the issues of concern to them, thereby forging a closer and ongoing relationship between SWT and these communities.

The communities thus engaged during the last academic year are geographically close but quite distinct in other respects. San Marcos has approximately 30,000 people and is the home of SWT. Pro-growth forces are in conflict with local environmentalists who are concerned with protecting the Edwards Aquifer from pollution and overuse and with many other native-born San Marcos residents who do not want to see their town continue to grow. [The Edwards Aquifer is an underground water table, which is the source for the springs which, in turn, are home to a few unique and endangered species.] There are tensions between the town and the university because most retirees and working people do not want students to disrupt their neighborhoods. The tensions are exacerbated for many reasons. Many people distrust higher education. Retirees are against tax increases to improve city schools. Ethnic tensions exist between and among the Hispanic, Anglo, and black populations.

Lockhart has around 9,000 residents and is the county seat of Caldwell County. The community is dependent on agriculture and government — city, county, and the school district. Most citizens are low and middle income and reflect the same ethnic split — Hispanic, Anglo, and black — as does San Marcos. Some people are trying to increase tourism by restoring and preserving historic buildings while others view this as misguided.

Wimberley is a nonincorporated and growing community of 10,000 in a valley that includes within it the incorporated town of Woodcreek. Wimberley has experienced increasing growth which has strained relations between newcomers and old-timers. People here have a strong civic sense without having a "civic." For many, Wimberley's growth is unwelcome since it is bringing with it a host of problems. Lacking a corporate charter, Wimberley cannot deal with its own destiny: it has no building codes, no city sewage codes, and no zoning ordinances. The old-timers resist growth and, in their minds, that is why they oppose incorporation. Others, concerned that the natural beauty of their community is being eroded inevitably, support incorporation as the best means to protect their community from unregulated growth.

To achieve the goals of the project I organized public meetings in the three communities. These meetings worked the best in Wimberley, reasonably well in Lockhart, and badly in San Marcos. The Wimberley meetings were successful due to the fact that they were organized under the theme of "incorporation" and were publicized as such. I made incorporation the theme of these town meetings because in talking to people in the community I discovered that people were concerned about population growth, land use, the continued identity of the community and environmental issues such as maintaining the natural beauty of the community, water quality, sewage systems, and construction. These issues all dealt with the ability of the residents to regulate what was going on in the community. All of these issues could be discussed in terms of options the community had, especially incorporation.

The Wimberley town meetings were also successful because a town meeting group was formed by volunteers who were willing to help organize and publicize the meetings.

The Lockhart meetings went well because of the support of many elected and appointed leaders of the town, such as Mayor Louis Cisneros, City Manager Joe Mitchie, City Councilwoman Marcia Proctor, and Secretary of the Lockhart Chamber of Commerce Beth Shirley. And yet attendance at the meetings in Lockhart was not as good as it might have been. Most importantly, Lockhart was badly divided a few years ago over a bond issue for a new public library building. Old friends stopped talking to each other. This public policy division reinforced ethnic divisions between Hispanic and Anglo and "politicized" the Chamber of Commerce in many people's minds.

The San Marcos public meetings were very poorly attended. After speaking to many community groups (this was done also in Lockhart to compensate for the unevenly attended meetings), I concluded that the major reason for low attendance at the public meetings was the distrust many had of SWT. To compensate for the low attendance, I spoke to many civic groups in Lockhart and San Marcos such as the Pan–American Golf Association, the Chamber of Commerce, city council, the Kiwanis, the League of Women Voters, and the Downtown Association. During the spring semester of 1996 I was also able to speak to members of the River Foundation, the Hospitality Association, World of Wisdom (a senior citizen group), Greater San Marcos Senior Citizens Association, and the San Marcos Police Officers Association. I also walked some neighborhoods such as Victory Gardens and Blanco Gardens. Permit me to relate what I discovered about the concerns of the three communities.

The people of Lockhart are uneasy about the future of their community. They are anticipating substantial growth in the near future and many do not think any of their local governments have made plans for it. Specifically, the citizens were concerned about a lack of medical facilities in the town, an emerging gang problem, lack of communication, and a lack of educational facilities.

For San Marcos, the meetings I had with people appeared to provide them with a venting opportunity, specifically an opportunity to complain about the university. Many people in San Marcos doubted that SWT wants to be a good citizen. People brought up many examples: the university's football stadium forced the town to spend hundreds of thousands of dollars for new drainage; the university doesn't pay for sewage plants that it necessitates, nor does it buy electricity from the local power plant; the university asked the state's attorney general to allow SWT to remove Aquarena Springs (a recently purchased amusement park) from the tax rolls; the university does too little to improve public schools in the city; and the university had failed to respond to calls from the League of Women Voters (LWV) to cosponsor a candidates debate.

The town meetings in Wimberley provided the project with a clear view of citizen concerns and, in turn, the project was able to provide information to the citizens. Due to the technical nature of many of the issues of concern to the residents, Jim Reed, of Reed Planning Investments, a certified city planner, was brought in to do a study of different issues concerning incorporation such as roads, police and fire protection, sewers, zoning, and taxes.

The top concerns expressed on sample ballots distributed by the project were rising taxes if Wimberley did incorporate and uncontrolled and unwanted growth if Wimberley did not incorporate. The next two issues of importance were the threat to the quality of life if Wimberley did not incorporate and the distrust of a new layer of government if it did. Other concerns expressed were lack of zoning authority, pollution, lack of local control, lack of police protection, the need for planning, annexation of Wimberley by another city, increased traffic, concerns about services such as roads, lighting, and fire protection, and a worry that incorporation would lead to a decline in volunteerism.

The straw poll ballots were counted by a group of volunteers. The totals were 271 against incorporation, 258 for, and 3 abstentions. Overall, the people of Wimberley, no matter what side of the issue they were on, were motivated by their concern for the well-being of Wimberley, and came down on the issue the way they did because they thought that was the best way to protect what they loved about Wimberley. Clearly, there is room for more deliberation on this issue.

The project developed initiatives in light of our conversations with the members of the respective communities. For Lockhart we concentrated on the concerns over gangs, medical facilities, and communication problems. Velma Menchaca, Department of Curriculum and Instruction,

SWT, hosted a workshop on gangs in Lockhart on May 14, 1996, on behalf of the project. Judy Renick of Community Mediation Service and Reyes Ramos of the University of Texas - San Antonio participated in the workshop. The participants presented information on gangs and then held a question-and-answer session with the public in attendance. Ms. Renick spoke about her experiences working with gangs and provided the audience with information on how to spot a son or daughter who was involved with a gang — looking for colors and types of clothing, how caps were worn, particular bandannas, and gang symbolism expressed in graffiti and hand signals. Dr. Ramos spoke about his research on gangs in San Antonio, especially on the issues of drug trafficking, women gang members, and adult (20-28-year-old) members of gangs. The audience then peppered the presenters with questions, with dialogue resulting. All the people who participated thought the evening was worthwhile.

A second initiative for the project in Lockhart is the development, distribution, and tabulation of a community health care survey. I organized a meeting of Wayne Sorenson, chair, department of health administration, SWT; Phillip Cook, city manager, City of Lockhart; and myself. Dr. Sorenson provided us with cost and time estimates and a commitment to provide a health care administration intern to oversee the health survey.

Chad A. Wasicek, who was selected to be the intern for the survey, interviewed the doctors in Lockhart, reviewed Lockhart demographic data, and planned publicity for the survey with the local newspaper. The survey instrument was distributed in October 1996. An analysis of the survey was completed in December 1996.

The last project initiative for Lockhart concerns communications problems in the city and youth/education issues. Lockhart has one paper which comes out once a week. I am making a commitment to work with the Lockhart High School and the Department of Mass Communication at SWT to develop five-day-a-week news programs written, produced, and directed by high school students to cover issues and events in Lockhart. I hope this can be launched by the 1997 autumn semester.

I was distressed by the hostility expressed toward SWT by the citizens of San Marcos. I made a fundamental personal commitment to try to improve the town-government relationship and do what I could to make the university more receptive to the concerns of the community. I am also currently working with Margaret Lindsey, of the San Marcos High School, and Phil Neighbors, president of the San Marcos Chamber of Commerce, on developing a school-to-work hospitality program for the high school students of our community. This program is designed to provide the high school students with both the academic and workplace skills they will need for careers in the hospitality industry.

The Civitas Project, the department of political science, SWT, and the San Marcos Area League of Women Voters cosponsored a candidates' debate on October 17, 1996, at the Teaching Theater of the Alkek Library on the SWT campus. We did this in response to a request from the Vice President for Academic Affairs, Robert D. Gratz. The debate featured candidates for Hays County clerk commissioner, constable, district clerk, sheriff, justice of the peace, and Texas House of Representatives, District 46. Newspapers in Hays County acted very cooperatively to publicize debate information. The debate was very well attended and the candidates and the audience thought the evening was a success.

After the close of the public meetings in Wimberley, the project, faced with a divided community, decided to recommend that an incorporation vote should not occur any time soon. We didn't want to recommend that a vote should occur to create a legally recognized political community if that vote could destroy an already existing civic community. The project did institute a small voter registration drive in Wimberley in the spring of 1996, but the more I think about it, the more I realize that holding the public incorporation meetings helped reinvigorate the civic life of Wimberley and helped its citizens identify and deal with important community issues.

The group created to help publicize the public meetings in the autumn of 1995 is still meeting regularly to discuss issues of concern to people in Wimberley. The group meets twice a month now and its members are in regular contact with their fellow citizens. At least in this regard, the project was a success in Wimberley.

I would like to turn to a few short suggestions that might help any future public scholar engaged in this kind of community work.

Three communities were too many for one public scholar. The scholar is entering three communities, two of which at least will be new to him/her, and also carrying the baggage of a university affiliation. It is simply impossible to establish the relationship in three communities necessary to ensure success of a project of this nature. Usually, the knowledge necessary for the success of a project like this comes from an association with a community longer than one semester. This inherent problem can be at least partially ameliorated by reducing the community load.

Second, it would be useful to begin the grant in the spring rather than the autumn semester. Some of the suggestions made to the project couldn't be done for the spring semester because there was just the short Christmas break between the semesters. The summer could be used profitably and without haste to set up the follow-through for the fall. An artificial calendar should not inhibit the flexibility of the process.

Third, some people doubted the commitment of the university to this project because it was staffed by an untenured assistant professor. It was a great experience for me to work on this project and I would recommend it to any academician. Yet, the relative low status of faculty vis a vis administrators is known, at least in central Texas, and it undermined the trust necessary for the project to be successful. It may be useful for two people to be involved — one from administration and one from the faculty.

Overall, what I found in the three communities reflected what Jean Bethke Elshtain calls the "culture of mistrust" — a deep cynicism and a massive distrust of government. Cynicism is no longer a disposition; it is acquiring the status of an ideology. People in the communities don't trust schoolboards, city government, county government, state government, or the national government. They are unsure that anything could be done about what they identify as their powerlessness.

What I heard, too, were complaints that the university, when it acted as a corporate body, acted with little consideration for the welfare of the town it was located in. That is, the university seemingly didn't know and, further, seemingly didn't care, how its decisions would affect the community. That, at least, is the public's perception.

If any university is committed to having its professors reach out to the broader community on behalf of the university, it must realize that its corporate actions can have a great effect on that community. University decisions on parking, land acquisitions, construction, and enrollment have a powerful effect on the surrounding community. In any city, if the university sees itself as separate from the broader community, no amount of public work by any number of professors can legitimately convince people of the university's concern for their welfare.

Yet, people are still active in these communities and express a need for what Pope John Paul II called "solidarity" — a determination to "commit oneself to the common good, that is to say, to the good of all and of each individual because we are all really responsible for all." They are deeply committed to what they would call "the common good" and are able, like John Leo's radio callers, "to conduct a very serious, informed debate with great civility." And what is striking is that their sense of the common good is rooted in their communities' specific history and locality. Their statements echoed Wendell Berry's, who observed that "our culture must be our response to our place, our culture and our place are images of each other and inseparable from each other and so neither can be better than the other."

Also, the people who participated in these meetings cared deeply about their communities. In their hopes for making their communities a better place, they reflect the sentiments expressed by Daniel Kemmis that "the strengthening of political culture, the reclaiming of a vital and effective and vital sense of what it is to be public, must take place and must be studied in the context of very specific places and of the people who struggle to live well in such places."

I found that the project was successful in presenting the spectacle of an academician *listening to* what citizens had to say about the problems facing their lives without lecturing them about instant solutions to their problems. As William M. Sullivan observed:"The great pressing problems which are beginning to define the new century are not matters to be handled by applying a 'technical fix' ... they require a more direct engagement with the moral and social dimensions of nearly all aspects of rational life."

Sullivan's call for "active partnership and shared responsibility" between the "public intellectual" and the community are what the citizens of the communities I visited wanted. They didn't want to be told by an expert what they were doing wrong; rather, they wanted a conversation with a university teacher about the problems facing them all as citizens.

Steven G. Kellman is correct when he says that taxpayers, any taxpayers, "will no longer abide the pretense of studious aloofness." They realize that "neutrality ... in the sense of independence from any system of values ... in the pursuit of knowledge was always an illusion." The citizens I listened to did not want an academic technician lecturing them on what to do. They wanted me to take part as a fellow citizen in "the deliberative process" which would lead to a strengthening of their civic culture, a culture appearing to dissolve as a rope of sand and yet a culture which remains, as Lincoln observed, "the last best hope on earth."

Works Cited

Boole, George. *An Investigation of the Laws of Thoughts* (London, 1854).

Burke, Edmund. "Observations on a Late Publication, Entitled *The Present State of the Nation*," in *The Works of Edmund Burke*, I (Boston, 1839).

Elshtain, Jean Bethke. *Democracy on Trial* (New York: Basic Books, 1994).

Federation of State Humanities Councils, Kettering Foundation, and National Endowment for the Humanities, "Humanities and Public Engagement Project," 1994.

Goethe, Johann Wolfgang von. *Faust. Part I*, translated by R. Jarrell (New York: Farrar, Strauss, and Giroux, 1976).

Kellman, Steven G. "An Evaluation of 'Civic Responsibility in Higher Education: An Exploratory Symposium,'" 1995.

Kemmis, Daniel. *Community and the Politics of Place*, (Norman: University of Oklahoma Press, 1992).

Leo, John. "The unmaking of civic culture," *U.S. News & World Report*, February 13, 1995, p. 24.

Pope John Paul II. *Sollicitudo Rei Socialis* (Boston: St. Paul Books and Media, 1987).

Sullivan, William M. "The Public Intellectual as Transgressor? Addressing the Disconnection Between Expert and Civic Culture," paper presented at the American Association of Higher Education Annual Conference, March 20, 1995.

Contributors

Thomas Bender, a recent chair of the New York Council for the Humanities, is University Professor of the Humanities and professor of History at New York University. The essay in this volume was published as Chapter 8 in *Intellect and Public Life: Essays on the Social History of Academic Intellectuals in the United States* (The Johns Hopkins University Press, 1993). Additional books by Thomas Bender include: *New York Intellect* (1988), *Toward an Urban Vision* (1982), and *Community and Social Change in America* (1978).

Jean Bethke Elshtain is Laura Spelman Rockefeller Professor of Ethics at the University of Chicago. She has written and edited many books on modern social and political thought, including *Public Man, Private Woman: Women in Social & Political Thought* (Princeton University Press, 1993), *Women & War* (University of Chicago Press, 1995) and, most recently, *Democracy on Trial* (BasicBooks, 1994).

Michael A. Gordon is associate professor of History and coordinator of the public history program at the University of Wisconsin-Milwaukee. His publications include *The Orange Riots: Irish Political Violence in New York City, 1870 and 1871* (Cornell University Press, 1993) and essays on labor, oral, and public history. He has received numerous grants from the humanities councils in Indiana and Wisconsin for projects involving newspapers, radio, and theatre.

Max Harris is the executive director of the Wisconsin Humanities Council at the University of Wisconsin-Madison. He is the author of two books, *Theatre and Incarnation* (1990) and *The Dialogical Theatre* (1993), and of numerous articles on Spanish and Latin American folk theatre, religion and culture, the civic role of the humanities, and the psychology of ethnic conflict. He is currently working on a manuscript entitled "Reading the Mask: Folk Dramatizations of Conquest in Spain and Mexico."

Peter Levine received his doctorate in philosophy from Oxford in 1992. He is now a research scholar at the Institute for Philosophy and Public Policy at the University of Maryland and the deputy director of the National Commission on Civic Renewal. His books include *Nietzsche and the Modern Crisis of the Humanities* (SUNY Press, 1995), *Something to Hide* (St. Martin's Press, 1996), and *Living Without Philosophy: On Narrative, Rhetoric, and Morality* (forthcoming from SUNY Press in 1998), from which the essay published here is drawn. He is currently completing a manuscript entitled, "The New Progressive Era: Toward a Fair and Deliberative Democracy."

David Mathews, Secretary of Health, Education, and Welfare in the Ford administration and a former president of The University of Alabama, is president of the Charles F. Kettering Foundation. Mathews taught American social and political history for many years. His books include *Politics for People: Finding a Responsible Public Voice* (University of Illinois Press, 1994) and *Is There a Public for Public Schools?* (Kettering Foundation Press, 1996).

Noëlle McAfee is the associate editor of the *Kettering Review* as well as a research fellow with the University of Texas Center for Deliberative Polling and a doctoral candidate in the department of philosophy of the University of Texas at Austin. She will defend her dissertation on subjectivity and citizenship in the works of Jürgen Habermas and Julia Kristeva in the fall of 1997.

Edward S. Mihalkanin is assistant professor of political science at Southwest Texas State University (SWT), San Marcos, Texas, where he teaches international relations and courses on politics in film and literature. He has published in these fields, most recently on "The Role of the U.S. Ambassador" with Warren Keith Neisler in David W. Dent, ed., *U.S.-Latin American Policymaking: A Reference Handbook* (1995). He directed the experimental Civitas Project, a collaborative effort of SWT and the Texas Council for the Humanities.

Jay Rosen is associate professor of journalism at New York University and director of the Project on Public Life and the Press, funded by the Knight Foundation. He also writes frequently on politics and the press.

Tomas N. Santos is professor of English and director of an interdisciplinary humanities program at the University of Northern Colorado. He also co-teaches an honors seminar, Public Engagement and the Social Good. Santos is a past member of the board of directors of the Colorado Endowment for the Humanities. In the fall of 1994, Santos spent a semester sabbatical at the Kettering Foundation where he researched and wrote about the conceptual links between the humanities and public politics. Santos' short stories have been published in *The Ohio Review*, *The Amerasia Journal*, and *The North American Review*.

Alexjandro Sanz de Santamaria is professor of economics at the University of the Andes, Bogotá, Colombia.

William Sullivan is professor of philosophy at La Salle University and coauthor, with Robert N. Bellah, Richard Madsen, Ann Swidler, and Steven M. Tipton, of *Habits of the Heart: Individualism and Commitment in American Life* (1985) and *The Good Society* (1991). The paper published in this volume was given as a panel presentation on "The Case for the Public Intellectual" at the 1995 National Conference on Higher Education.

Jo Taylor is vice president for Academic Affairs and professor of English at Wayne State College in Wayne, Nebraska. In recent years, Taylor has presented papers on contemporary writers such as Margaret Drabble and Rita Dove. She recently served on a panel of editors for the ASHE-ERIC report, *The Department Chair, New Roles, Responsibilities*, and *Challenges*. She is a past chair of the Nebraska Humanities Council and currently serves on the board of the Nebraska Humanities Foundation.

James F. Veninga is president and director of The Institute for the Humanities at Salado, Texas, and the former executive director of the Texas Council for the Humanities (TCH). He is editor or coeditor of a number of books, including *The Biographer's Gift* (1982), *Vietnam in Remission* (1985), and *Preparing for Texas in the 21st Century* (1990). In 1995, he directed the Humanities and Public Engagement Project. An earlier version of the essay in this volume was presented at the William Bennett Bean Symposium on the Humanities, sponsored by the Institute for the Medical Humanities at The University of Texas Medical Branch at Galveston, April 1994.

Jamil S. Zainaldin is president of the Federation of State Humanities Councils, where for the past ten years he has worked with councils in enhancing public involvement in, and support for, the humanities. He is especially interested in public policy and the humanities. He serves as an adjunct professor of History at Georgetown University. The essay in this volume was originally commissioned by the American Association for Higher Education for its second National Meeting on Faculty Roles and Rewards, held in New Orleans in January 1994. An excerpted version of the essay appeared in *Metropolitan Universities*, Summer 1994.